MW00585518

by John Neal and Barbara Marrett

Offshore Cruising Handbook

Mahina Tiare: Pacific Passages

Log of the Mahina

by John Neal

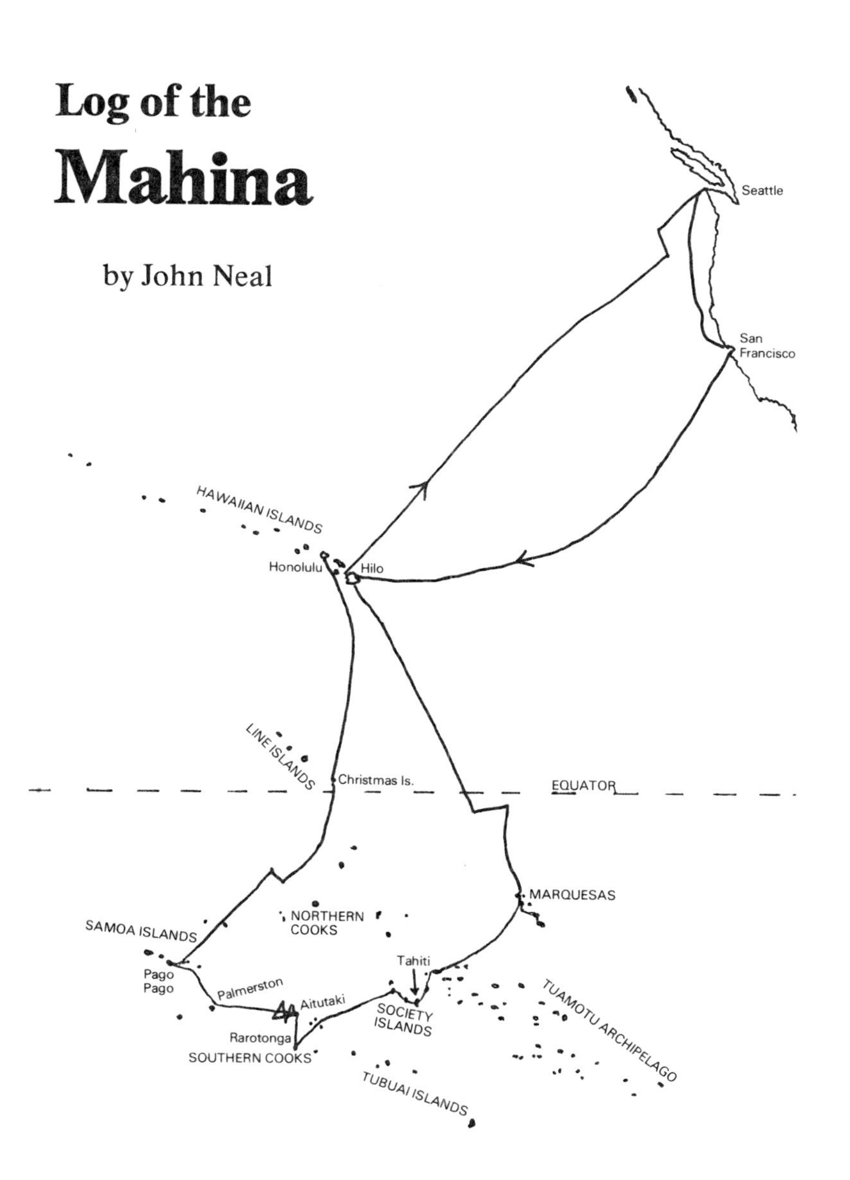

Acknowledgments

A special thanks to Ann Wightman who believed in this book before it happened and helped many hours with typing and revisions. I have also greatly appreciated Tom Kincaid's help in editing and planning. I would like to thank Archie and Margaret Williams for permission to use some of the material which appeared originally in *Castoff.*

All photos by John Neal except:
R. P. Wightman page 4
Diane Dring page 22
Kurt Scheel page 276
Jan Grant page 181
Bruce Cummins page 222
Ernie Weller pages 140, 154, 214

Copyright © 1995 John Neal, revised edition
All rights reserved. No part of this book may be reproduced or transmitted in any form or by any means, electronic or mechanical, including photocopying, recording or by any information storage and retrieval system, without permission in writing from the Author.

Library of Congress Catalog Card Number 76-150419

Pacific International Publishing
P.O. Box 101
Friday Harbor, WA 98250
(206) 378-5242

Printed in the United States of America

Log of the Mahina

For Nana, with love.

Chapter 1

Beginnings

This is the story of a 14,000 mile cruise around the Pacific in a 27' sailboat. The parts of it about passages are excerpts from the ship's log and the time spent on the islands is from my diary. It is all true, a few names are changed because I've forgotten them over the past two years. When I left, I had no idea of writing a book, I was just planning to sail to Hawaii for a little vacation. But one thing led to another, and that's how it happened. In the two months since I've gotten back, I've been asked a number of times, "What made you decide to do it?" I'm not really sure; I was in a job that was frustrating and didn't seem to be improving and had been going to night school trying to finish off a degree in Psychology that appeared to be another dead-end. It just seemed time to try something new. I had greatly enjoyed a two-week backpacking vacation in Hawaii, and decided that might be a nice place to sail to, so I bought *Mahina,* quit my job, and got a part-time job helping to build a 45' sailboat to learn more about boats and help my suffering budget. I repaired *Mahina's* frozen engine, replaced all standing and running rigging, and generally rebuilt her. In July of 1974, I felt I had *Mahina* ready to go to sea. I had taken a celestial navigation course (but hadn't done the homework) and had a grand total of about nine months sailing experience in Puget Sound in my previous 20' sloop, but had never done any offshore sailing. I had no special goals in mind, and wasn't out to set any records. The trip and this book just developed, and I'm offering them to you at this stage, because in a very real sense my relationship with *Mahina* is still an unfinished story.

On the morning of 7/14 I woke up early. I had many things to do if I was actually going to leave for Hawaii that afternoon as I had told my friends and family. I had already delayed the departure date once because the boat hadn't been ready, and if I delayed leaving again, I don't think anyone would have believed I was really going.

That morning before I would be ready to leave, I still had to install a kerosene tank for the heater, fill the fuel and water tanks, finish packing the first aid kit and stowing the groceries I had bought the day before, and tune the new rigging.

It was well after noon before I had these jobs done, and as I was getting ready for *Mahina's* christening I remembered I still had a dock box full of tools, paint brushes, half-empty paint cans, and miscellaneous junk. I gave away all I could, throwing away the rest.

After the christening, we opened a huge bottle of champagne for a little going away party with the friends on the dock that had come by to see what all the excitement was about.

By 1630, I decided that if we were going to get away that day, we had better get moving. Despite the fact that I had spent many hours working on the engine, it refused to start, so we cast off the dock lines and left the slip under sail. Unfortunately for us, it was a sunny Sunday afternoon, and the traffic in Shilshole Bay Marina made sailing out pretty exciting. In a few minutes, however, we were clear of the breakwater and on our way.

With me was DJ, a friend I had met on a recent trip to Hawaii. My girlfriend had planned to go with me, but had changed her mind at the last minute. I had made arrangements with DJ on less than a week's notice.

We beat toward Port Ludlow in a nice ten knot breeze. The wind held until we were past Foulweather Bluff and then died completely. After spending almost an hour taking apart and cleaning the carburetor and fuel line, the engine finally decided to run. At 0115 we were finally anchored at Port Ludlow and really slept well that night.

The next morning the engine wouldn't start and the anchor was fouled, but we managed to sail out with no trouble. By afternoon the light drizzle had stopped and we had a nice beat to Port Townsend. We sailed into Point Hudson Marina with just barely enough speed to make the turn into the breakwater; then, after we cleared the end of the breakwater, we caught some wind and shot into the first slip with a thud.

Tuesday morning I went to an auto parts store and bought some rubber fuel line. After it was installed, bypassing the fuel filter, the engine started right away. However, the baling wire that held on the condenser loosened up, causing a short circuit. We left Point Hudson with the engine barely functioning.

Off Point Wilson, we got caught in a tide rip; the knotmeter registered nine knots. It seemed we were flying, but actually we were doing about four knots. That afternoon I watched the engine while it was running, and I spotted the sparking condenser. I took the largest hose clamp I had and put it around the condenser and distributor, and that solved the problem.

The rest of the afternoon was a pleasant sail to Port Angeles where we willed up the gas tanks and bought some kerosene.

At 0130 we were awakened by a loud CRUNCH that nearly knocked us out of our bunks. A local trawler had run into us while trying to back into the next slip.

Wednesday was spent motorsailing to Neah Bay in light rain and fog. That night we ate out at the only restaurant in town. It was terrible!

Chapter 2

Neah Bay-San Francisco

7/18 1215 Log 584 miles We were quite happy to leave Neah Bay and really be on our way. We powered out to the No. 1 buoy off Cape Flattery and then shut off the engine. Pretty soon a nice breeze came up. It feels good to be sailing where there is lots of room. Joshua (the RVG self-steering vane) is working well.

2215 Beautiful sunset. As it got darker, we could see strobe lights flashing all around us telling us where the fishing boats were. I stood on the bow for two hours, fascinated by the phosphorescence in the water. It was so peaceful to feel the boat sailing along at four and a half knots, taking care of herself.

7/19 0915 A small pod of porpoises swam by. They were so graceful. The wind increased steadily, and I kept pulling down and changing sails until we are now doing five and a half knots under storm jib alone. I put up the new storm trysail; that seemed to steady our rolling.

1200 I think that we are in a U.S. Navy firing area. There is a ship which keeps steaming back and forth, firing its guns. We could see a flash and a puff of smoke, then we'd hear a boom and a CATHWUNK! as the shells hit the water. One shell landed so close we could feel the impact. We're sailing out of here as fast as we can!

2200 This afternoon we passed close to a couple of large, rusty Russian trawlers. It is hard to sleep when off watch because of the motion. A couple of waves tried to find their way into the cockpit.

7/20 0135 Course 190°. Speed four and a half knots. Storm jib and trysail. Seas rough.

0700 Just sighted a schooner off the starboard bow. It crossed in front of us under reduced sail. We ran the engine to charge the battery, but after fifteen minutes, I was tired of listening to it and shut it off again.

0845 Finally got the vane on again. I didn't want to use it when it was really rough because I was afraid it might gybe the boat. It steers within 10° — not bad considering that we have a fifteen foot following sea that keeps trying to join us in the cockpit.

1015 DR position puts us about fifty-five miles west of Ocean Shores. I picked up Astoria's weather station on VHF. They said there were only small craft warnings up. Oh! DJ is catching up on sleep. He looked exhausted as he came off watch. He doesn't have the feel of the boat yet and spends his four hour watches with his eyes glued to the compass and hand to the tiller. He also can't sleep when there is any noise around him.

1130 Joshua working well. Nice to have some time to catch up on the log and write a few letters. Spotted a fishing boat with a steadying sail up.

1710 Wind easing off. Storm sails down. No. 1 jib and triple-reefed main up.

7/21 Spent the entire day chasing light airs. Powered for four hours. Battery charged right up. Sailed

Russian trawler

across the bow of a huge, rusty Russian fish processing ship. They were moving slow, and slowed more to let us pass. Many people in white aprons came on deck and waved and took pictures. The men on the bridge motioned for us to pull alongside, but we just waved and sailed off. It would certainly have been most interesting to go aboard, but . . . I can see five other Russian fishing boats within about five square miles.

1430 Very light air. DJ scrubbed the decks and I worked on navigating and shooting the sun until my eyes hurt. Sure wish I had done my homework when I was taking a navigation class.

7/22 Day passed quickly. Beautiful sunset. I am really getting into the routine of sailing now. It took a few days to get used to sleeping only four hours at a time, but it's okay now.

7/23 0800 Seas and wind increasing again. We are surfing down huge waves under trysail alone at up to eight and a half knots. Everything is fine as long as we keep the stern square to the waves. But once in a while one comes off the stern quarter at the same time as another hits us squarely on the stern and we broach, filling the cockpit with water. The seas are mountainous and far apart. On the crests we can see for miles, but in the troughs, we have to look up to see the crest of the next wave. There are long streaks of wind-blown foam on the surface and it hurts to look into the wind. Conditions Force 8. It's hard to sleep even tied into the bunk with a canvas leeboard.

1030 We had to slow the boat down because I was afraid that we might pitchpole when the bow plowed into the bottom of the troughs at eight knots; so I looped every extra line on board off the stern: 200 feet of half inch nylon anchor line, 80 feet of half inch nylon anchor line, 100 feet of three-eighths inch polypropelene, 150 feet of three-eighths inch dacron, and 60 feet of five-eighths inch spare dacron jib sheets. This slowed us from eight knots to six.

1130 We hove to. Too much strain on the boat and on us. It seems that this might become an endurance contest between us and the sea. DJ has not been able to get much sleep and is exhausted. We both need some rest.

7/24 0630 We have been hove to under trysail for nineteen hours. The winds are still over fifty knots. The tiller is tied off so that we are presenting our stern quarter to the waves. Seas have increased during the night, some breaking over the boat, hitting the trysail and filling the cockpit. My wool Navy pants have been wet for three days but are always warm. The kerosene cabin heater is going night and day, keeping things dry below. The dodger hasn't collapsed; I never thought it would hold up in this stuff! (My hand-held anemometer goes to fifty knots — it wasn't until a week later, in San Francisco, that I got it unstuck and back to zero.) We took Avondayle (the inflatable dinghy) out of her bag and kept her in the back of the cockpit with the CO_2 bottle and emergency provisions inside here. We are wearing float coats and harnesses when on deck. The hardest part is just waiting. If we could just be making a little headway on our course it would help. A freighter just passed close by, signalling with a light. I wish I had taken the time to learn code so I could have answered them. Wind increasing with the dawn. Foam everywhere.

0645 A fishing boat went by very slowly, towing a disabled trawler alongside. They were having a very rough time of it; each time a wave hit them on the bow, their hulls would lift way up out of the water, and then crash back down.

1340 Wind eased. Running under trysail at five knots. Seas are still large — leftovers. At least they aren't filling the cockpit any more. I was getting tired of being wet twenty-four hours a day. Storm jib raised. Tacked down wind. Wind and seas on the stern quarter. A port shroud was very loose and from the cockpit it looked like it had pulled out. Actually, it had just worked loose during the night. I must get around to putting pins in the turnbuckles so they don't turn by themselves.

7/25 0800 Sunny morning and everything looks better. Back to main and lapper.

1800 Just sighted Cape Sebastian. It was right where it should have been according to my navigating.

DJ fixed a fantastic spaghetti dinner, complete with wine and garlic bread.

7/26 Another nice day — winds light and variable. Powered four and a half hours. We are on our last five gallons of fuel.

7/27 0200 Beautiful spooky night. Very dense mist and fog. I could hear a ship's horn off the starboard beam. A number of little twittering birds are flying around *Mahina*. All I can hear is the water gurgling by the boat, the birds twittering, and occasionally the fog horn. I think night watch is one of my favorites — but then, so are all the other watches. When I get sleepy, I go on the foredeck and do exercises. I feel more in shape now than I have in a long time, but I do miss walking and running and riding my bike. It'll be fun to read a newspaper and find out what's been going on in the world, or, even better, get a new sailing magazine. I think I have the ones on board memorized by now. I sure do like it out here. The days go by so quickly. There's lots of time and space out here—no city stuff to complicate things. But I do miss the trees and flowers and the smells that go along with them. We will be two weeks out of Shilshole Bay tomorrow. Time sure goes by fast out here. It took me about four days to really get into this. It seemed strange and lonely at first, but I sure like it now. I haven't talked with anyone but DJ in the past week, and I'm afraid he's getting pretty tired of all my babbling.

2120 No wind, just fog all day. Motored some — heard horns but didn't see any ships today. A porpoise or whale surfaced beside us. It is hard to visualize that we have traveled over 800 miles since leaving Shilshole.

7/28 0200 No wind. Tired of listening to the engine. Just sat and rolled, going nowhere.

0500 Changed course to 105°. Headed for Point Delgada and Shelter Cove to see if we can buy some gas at the resort there — we're almost out.

0715 A pod of six porpoises is chasing the boat — diving in and out like an underwater ballet and having a great time. Very graceful. You know, we haven't gotten any rain to speak of in the past two weeks. That's amazing, especially since we passed Oregon on our way here!

1600 Have been powering all day toward where I thought Shelter Cove was. A freighter just came by on a course that would tend to make me think that it just came out of San Francisco Harbor. Its engines are throwing off a lot of smoke; it looks like it just started up and its engines aren't yet warmed up fully. I wonder if my DR position could be off this far (100 miles).

2000 DR position is close to Point Arena; however, Farallon Island beacon off San Fancisco Bay entrance is much stronger.

2050 Bearing from Point Reyes light confirms my guess that we are a lot closer than DR position indicates.

2300 Fix from Fanny Shoal and Farallon Island light puts us very close.

7/29 0230 Passed Farallon Island. The light is brilliant and it is hard to tell how close we are to the island. A fleet of about thirty fishing boats are anchored in the lee of the island.

0550 Passed pilot buoy and can see the lights of the Presidio ahead.

0630 Fog rolls in and we can't see anything. Feeling our way from one buoy to the next and trying to avoid the ships that come barreling down this channel every few minutes. Good steady wind pushing us along at five to six knots. Good thing there's wind because there are just a couple of drops of fuel left in the tank.

0730 Log 1,408 miles Under the Golden Gate Bridge. It is rush hour up above us and the cars are bumper to bumper. I honked the horn until the can ran out of air.

After tying up in front of the Golden Gate Yacht Club, I went inside and talked to an old man who was cleaning up the bar from the night before. He said we were welcome to stay there for a day, but after that we would have to move because they were going to have a race. He asked if I belonged to a yacht club, and, surprisingly, he didn't throw us out when I said "no, just a cruising club." He was very nice about letting us use the shower in his apartment upstairs. I think he could tell that it had been over nine days since I had a shower.

After the shower, I met a marine biologist from Roche Harbor who was skippering the fanciest charter boat I have ever seen. He gave me a ride to Balinas, a neat little town on the coast, when he went to visit friends there.

The next five days went by very fast. I wore out one pair of shoes completely exploring the city, visiting the maritime museums, and looking at boats.

I had informed DJ that his services were no longer needed; he left for Southern California right away. Then I called all of my sailing friends in Seattle trying to find crew, because I didn't really want to singlehand to Hawaii; but everyone was busy.

On Thursday I went to a ship's chandlery store by Fisherman's Wharf to get some last minute hardware and marine supplies. I met a girl named Diane who was working there and I got to talking with her. It turned out that she had lived in Seattle only a few months earlier and had worked delivering boats up and down the West Coast. Of course I immediately asked her if she would sail to Hawaii with me. After thinking about it for a couple of minutes she said "yes" and walked over to tell her boss that she was sailing to Hawaii. This didn't come as a very great shock to him as this was the third time she had left to go to sea.

She stopped by in the morning to see the boat, and after she got off work that afternoon we went grocery shopping. We didn't have enough money to pay for all the groceries, so we ended up putting some of them back.

The next morning Diane tied up all the loose ends where she worked while I got the boat cleaned and ready to go. We sailed the measured mile off Treasure Island to check the log, then took the cable car to Chinatown for dinner. We had to walk back to the marina after dinner since all the cable cars had quit for the night, so it was 0130 when we finally arrived back at the boat.

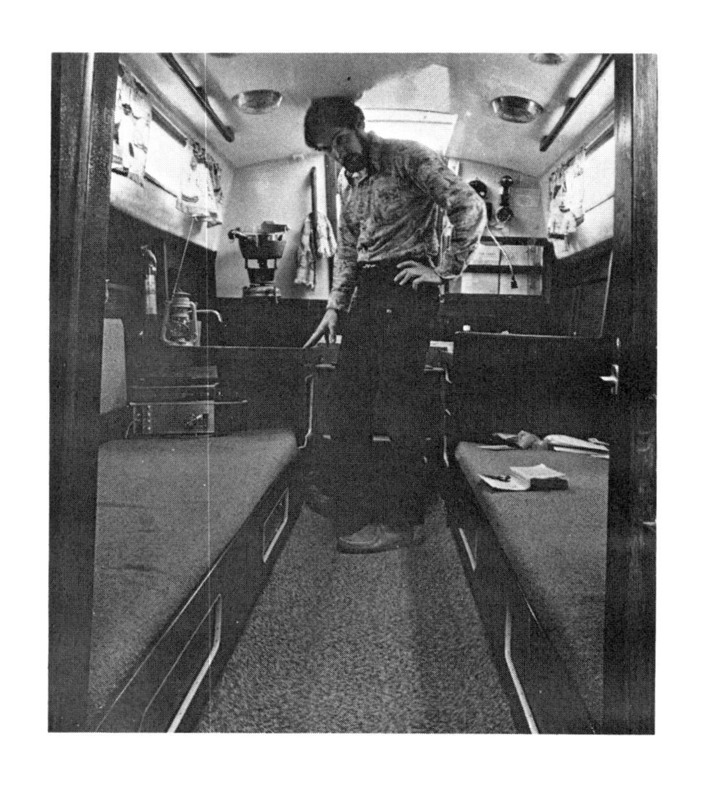

Chapter 3

The Broad Pacific

Golden Gate Bridge

8/4 0600 Log 1,420 miles We didn't hear the alarm go off at 0430 (I had wanted to catch the ebb tide leaving the bay), but we just passed under the Golden Gate Bridge and now we're on our way.

1600 We motored in very light air for five and a half hours, then drifted along at two to three knots under main and genoa. The day passed quickly.

2030 For dinner we had cantaloupe, cheese, and raisin bread.

8/5 0110 Freighter sighted off the starboard bow. Hard to hear it in the fog.

0500 Diane went to sleep like a log as soon as she went below. I'm having trouble keeping the old eyes open. It's almost ready to get light.

0900 A delicious omelette for breakfast. I finally got so tired of looking at a dirty stove that I cleaned it. The sun came out in the afternoon and we both got good naps. Glad to be out of the fog.

1900 The vane started slipping and wouldn't hold a steady course. Instead of steering by hand for the rest of the night and then fixing it in the morning, I made the mistake of trying to repair the vane in the middle of the night. I took the head of the vane off and tried to get to the clutch from the inside. When I did, I found out that the only thing wrong was the screw that held the clutch handle bracket on was loose, and the handle had slipped up so the clutch wasn't fully engaging. That was quick and easy to fix; but getting the vane back together while hanging over the stern pulpit, holding a flashlight in my teeth, was very difficult. The bolt that holds the sail and head of the vane dropped down in the shaft of the vane — about four feet down! Since the only way to get it out would have been to take the vane off the transom and turn it upside down, I tried replacing it with just a regular bolt (the one I dropped had a ball-bearing head). After dropping two more bolts down the shaft, I managed to get the head on, with the bolt sticking through, and get a nut on it. I tied dental floss to the bolt and pulled it through the head that way. Finally, after four and a half hours of frustrating work in the dark, the vane was back together and worked perfectly.

8/6 0800 Freighter passed off our stern. First ship sighted in two days. I hated to, but I threw out last night's soup. I still feel sick after only a half bowl of it twelve hours ago. Too much dill salt and MSG, I guess. So much for fancy seasonings.

0830 Diane sleeping — she looked pretty tired. Hope the sun comes out soon.

0900 YAHOO!!! First hundred mile day from 0900 yesterday to 0900 today — 100.83 miles, to be exact.

1800 Worked out today's fix — it was 25 miles off our DR position. I was beginning to be concerned about my navigational abilities again.

8/7 0800 Diane: Good morning and YAHOO!! From 0830 yesterday to 0800 today we have covered 125.36 miles according to the log. The sun's up, John's up, and an Albatross flew by and waved good morning.

1200 Sunny. This is the first time in a long time that I have been sailing without a shirt on. Feels great. Diane is trying to catch a nap in a rolling cockpit.

8/8 0000 Steady six and a quarter knots. A bit uncomfortable, and too much strain on the boat and vane.

0030 Main reefed and lapper up instead of genoa. This puts us down to a much more comfortable four and three quarters knots.

0730 Wind still increasing — traded lapper for storm jib. Vane steering great. Diane had a good five hours' sleep. Discovered a rip in the top batten pocket. It seems that the problem of the last voyage is reversed: DJ couldn't sleep, and Diane sleeps too much.

0930 Diane: Sun's shining. Finished whipping the splices on the man overboard pole and tried spray painting the food cans so they don't rust. John gets to sleep now.

1030 Diane: Nice quiet day. Doing five to six knots.

1800 We listened to Nixon's resignation speech via VOA shortwave. I feel very removed from that world — like that sort of thing was in its sphere, and I in mine. Diane said "bullshit" but said she didn't mean it.

1830 Filled gas tank from jerry jug. We have ten out of fifteen gallons left. Not bad. Ran engine five minutes—sounded good, and battery checks out okay.

2020 Reef shaken out of main. Lapper on pole instead of storm jib. Poking along at four and three quarters knots. I'll wait and see if wind is going to stay down before I hoist the genoa.

8/9 0100 Diane: I'm awake and watching. Incredible bad breath after garlic dressing on last night's salad. Another semi-overcast night. Joshua still going strong.

1050 Diane: I'm up and John's up, but the sun slept in again. Scrambled eggs and refried beans for breakfast.

1215 Engine started right up to charge the batteries. It sure sounded loud after not hearing anything but the wind and the boat for the past week. We should be crossing the LA - Honolulu great circle shipping route tonight. Maybe we'll see some traffic.

1500 Diane: I had a nice sort of bath in the cockpit. Ate the last box of Cracker Jacks. A **good** prize this time!

1830 Good filling dinner of mashed potatoes (Diane) and interesting gravy (John). The gravy started out with a can of mushroom soup and tuna fish and got alfalfa sprouts (which I grew in a jar) and diced onions added to it. Really good.

2030 End of whisker pole where it attaches to the mast broke and was crunching around. I lashed it to the mast with three sail ties. Hope it holds.

2045 I can see a squall on the horizon to the north. There are fair-sized swells with a lot of fetch between them. It just started sprinkling. This is the first time since the Oregon coast that it's rained. And today is our first day in the trades. It was cloudy-grey and overcast all day, but warm. (72°).

2200 Ship sighted dead ahead. We are approximately where the weather ship *Gallahad* is supposed to be, according to the chart.

8/10 0030 Diane: After messing around for a half hour trying to run wing and wing and make pudding and find the flashlight and catch up with the ship, we gave up on it all. We couldn't see running lights — only white lights fore and aft. Was it *Gallahad*? Anyway, it disappeared. Maybe it was *Gallahad*'s ghost. The pudding was good. The night is overcast and not terribly warm.

0315 Diane: A lonely night. Sails banging. My eyes hurt. The little breeze that comes up occasionally is cold. John woke up and said something unintelligible and went back to sleep.

0700 Sun reflecting off interesting cloud formation.

This is the third morning that it has been like this — clear at night with lots of stars and a moon, then cloudy at sunrise. Some nasty-looking black clouds are headed this way. And now we are supposedly 200 miles into the southwest trades. Bah!! Someone made a mistake on the August pilot chart.

0730 SAILBOAT SIGHTED ON THE HORIZON!!! Jib down, power on full throttle. Maybe I can get a check of our position. Am coming up with fixes that put us at any one of three positions. Don't ask how!

0930 GLASS BALL EPISODE NO. 1 Diane: Oh — it was so exciting! John sighted it and I ran up and hung off the bow pulpit, but it was slippery. John caught it off the port side. It had two tiny crabs on it, and many gooseneck barnacles. We took pictures and washed it. We are slowly closing on the sailboat ahead of us.

1225 Caught up with the *Pau Hana.* She was a Columbia 43 Mark III registered in Lahaina, but out of Santa Barbara. They said they were going to do charter work in Hawaii and asked us if we'd like a cold beer. We took pictures of them and they of us. I got a position from them that greatly helped my navigating. They said, "Have a nice sail — we'll see you in Hilo," and then they were off and on their way. They moved along quite a bit faster than us in the light air.

1600 Top batten pocket has ripped some more. The two lower battens are broken. Next time the wind dies I'll have to fix the pocket.

8/11 0120 Becalmed. Bang-squeak-slap-bang!

0650 Finally moving along rather consistently at four knots after a night of light (almost nonexistent) variable wind. Sky is just starting to lighten up. Diane stood a five hour watch. Bless her soul—I really needed the extra hour of sleep.

1140 Picking up beautiful FM classical station from San Diego. Breakfast was whole wheat and honey pancakes with sliced almonds on top and cold apple juice. Sails flopping again.

1430 We may not be going anywhere, but we sure are getting a lot of work done on *Mahina*. Optimus Sea-Swing stove de-sooted and polished, ice box cleaned out (it sure needed it!), ventilators recaulked, and clothes straightened up in the forepeak. Bright and overcast. Water is a beautiful deep purple.

2200 Smooth sailing and no sails banging. Doing three knots. Looking down from the companionway, I see Diane asleep on the settee. She looks so peaceful. I have a tummy-ache; ate too much macaroni and cheese for dinner.

8/12 0200 Slap-slap-slam-thunk-squeak-BANG. Where did the wind go? I am having a great time doing a stitchery picture by chartlight that I started a long time ago.

0330 Diane: Yawn! John watched six hours and is still sewing his little heart out. (Dear man.)

0700 Diane: Still the same old nothing, only it's light now. It wasn't very cold and things didn't get as damp as usual last night. My eyes won't stay open or focussed. There is nothing to be seen here except sky and water. But, amazingly, I don't feel far away, or all alone, or frightened in any way of anything. I was worried about my reactions, because I have been known to be impatient when I haven't seen land for a few days. Here it will be weeks — and if this first week was an indication, I'll be fine.

0815 Very dull day, quite overcast. Diane jammed tape deck; I pulled three feet of chewed up tape out of it. Diane tried fishing with the tackle out of the life raft provisions, but caught nothing. Commentary on vegetables . . .

Diane: Special care must be taken when dealing with fresh vegetables on an ocean cruise. Check daily for rot

— or they will — and boy do they stink!
John: You really have to stay on top of these little things.

1930 What a nice day after all! We swam in the ocean for the first time. I got two-thirds of the bottom scrubbed using a mask and snorkel and brush. It sure needed it. It also needs another coat of paint as I have scrubbed much of the paint off. We blew up the Avon and rowed around taking pictures of *Mahina,* and I

ended up rowing like crazy to catch her because I had left the main up and a little wind came up. Not very bright, John! Since then, the wind has held well and we've maintained three knots. I just finished washing my hair in the bucket on the foredeck and now it's Diane's turn for a shivery shampoo.

2300 Quiet night. I made some good soup and Diane fixed some fantastic grilled cheese sandwiches.

8/13 0305 Gybed main. Broad reaching now. This fills the sails better than running.

0650 Actually doing four knots for the first time in two days! Haven't seen any ships since the *Pau Hana.*

1145 Great breakfast of whole wheat French toast with butter and honey and apple juice to drink. Collapsible whisker pole keeps collapsing.

2000 Diane: Wow, it's eight PM, but it looks like five PM outside. (I haven't set the clocks to zone time yet.) John and I worked out the last sight together. I think I have the hang of it already. Today I washed the ceiling and both stoves.

2050 Sighted jet stream! Yahoo!! We're not in the twilight zone after all.

2200 Diane: All's well, nice night. John just woke up and said, "Somewhere there's a small tube of aircraft cement that's missing." I promptly assured him that I would find it in the morning. This seemed to please him and he went back to sleep. Doing a good four knots. Stars all over the place.

8/14 0015 Sat on the bow watching *Mahina* sailing along and thought about life for one and a half hours.

0200 Lumpy swells from behind. Made butterscotch pudding. It doesn't taste as good as vanilla.

0900 Diane: Everything is lovely. John is sleeping well. What **did** he put in that pudding? Still running at three to three and a half knots. Caught up on the Miles Per Day Log that I have been keeping. A few slow days. Oh — there was a rainbow yesterday.

1800 Diane: John working hard on oiling the interior woodwork. Semi-sunshine. Time to do the dishes. Yuk!

1835 Diane: Heard screams on deck. Rushed out to

find that John had lost his Boat Zoap overboard. Rather-than undo all the things that are tied down (boom preventer and broken whisker pole) we'll let someone else have it. Sorry, John.

2010 Working out day's fix. Diane napping. She is so nice. Sure glad I met her. Listening to a cassette I made a long time ago of 1910 foxtrot music. Great!

8/15 0010 Cooking beans for a midnight snack. Diane still asleep. Doing five knots. Sea is quite calm for this good breeze.

0200 Change of watch. Wind becoming variable; hard to keep on course. A rainy, squally night.

0745 I think I just saw my first flying fish. It was close to the water and going real fast. Also a beautiful white bosun's bird just circled the boat twice and headed SE.

1130 Wind variable. Seas quite lumpy. Diane actually heated tea water on the Sea-Swing stove with-out making a lot of smoke and flames. I am grumpy.

1300 Diane got some laundry done. Cockpit looks like a cyclone full of wet clothes just hit it. Nice day — cloudy, but bright.

1800 Worked out today's fix: W 138° 06', N 24° 40'. For the first time my fix and DR positions are close. (Only five miles off.) I guess I finally learned how to navigate. About time!!! I estimate another ten to eleven days (if the wind holds) and we'll be there. Aside from that, the beans from last night are still making news. I guess I didn't squish all the air out of them before I cooked them. Let's have something different for dinner tonight! What about spaghetti and garlic bread? Sounds great.

2030 Dinner was fantastic. A peaceful evening—reading and laughing.

Recipe for FANTASTIC HIGH SEAS SPAGHETTI 1000 miles from land.

A bunch of noodles (Spinach noodles or whole wheat noodles add more flavor.)
A can of tomato sauce
A small can of chopped mushrooms
Two or three small onions chopped up
Some shredded cheese
A cup of imitation hamburger (To make this I bought a carton of soy protein granules—they look like chewed up cardboard—from the health food store. First, a cup of the granules gets soaked in warm water for a minute or two, then it gets fried with soy sauce and Worcestershire sauce and a little oil)
Add chopped onions to mixture in pan. After a couple of minutes, soy granules are done—they realy taste as good as hamburger, if not better.
Then add tomato sauce and pour over noodles. Serve with garlic toast and wine, if possible.

2350 Doing four and a half knots. Wind changing direction. A lot of stars. Diane will like that. I wonder what the name of that bright one is?

8/17 0215 Diane: Had some good vanilla pudding. John found a Kauai radio station on the AM band. This has been a most enjoyable trip thus far. The days are warm; we wear swimsuits or shorts. The nights are not too cold, although sweaters and socks are sometimes nice and comfortable. During the day there is a lot or a little to do. Today we read a lot; on calm days a lot of cleaning and checking and oiling goes on. But today we were traveling at about five knots — too fast and rocky to get a lot done. After I broke the whisker pole, John set the spinnaker pole and I rigged a downhaul on it. First on the list of repairs to do is to sew up the top batten pocket before the batten inches its way out and into the sea. Every day we plan to do it, but we get sailing so well that we don't want to slow down. The nights for the most part have been cloudy, but sometimes the clouds disappear and we can see the Milky Way and gazillions of stars. The dawn is usually grey and cloudy, with the sun showing its face around noon or a little later. Midday is usually warm and sunny, and then the clouds gather again to watch us eat dinner.

Our watch system is pretty simple. During the daylight hours we do what we want — with someone always on deck or in the cockpit. About 2100 hours I go to bed and John stands watch. He does what he can in the dark with the flashlight — reads, sews, writes letters, and catches up in the log. Towards the end of the watch he makes pudding or tea or hot chocolate, and sometimes rocks the boat doing push-ups and jumping jacks on the foredeck trying to stay awake. He is on watch for four hours — or as long as he is willing — then he wakes me up when it's my turn. We listen to the radio or talk for a while, then I go into the cockpit. I watch for four hours, too — sometimes a bit longer, sometimes not. On John's watch everything runs smoothly — even the squalls are smooth. The minute I step into the cockpit, I feel the very forces of nature turn against me. Without my touching a thing the wind dies, the sails flap and bang, and the ship veers crazily off course. The waves turn to strike us at an angle that makes standing impossible and sitting highly precarious. When I get things back to semi-order, I try to read, too. But the flashlight goes out, the pages flop in the wind, and I give up, having unintentionally memorized the first three lines in Chapter Five.

0600 Diane: Very nice night. Got off course, but am back on and haven't tacked again. Sang lots of songs, did exercises, drank orange juice and ate a pilot biscuit with peanut butter on it. Stars are really bright. Have seen four falling stars. John woke up and asked me if I needed my glasses and fell back to sleep.

0730 Dear Diane stood a six hour watch. I really needed the sleep. My eyes feel better. The vane is rattling in its brackets quite a bit. I think I might try to replace the neoprene pads in it if the wind dies. A squall with a lot of rain is approaching, but it may pass to starboard. Inky black clouds. Still doing better than a hundred miles a day.

1015 Squall passed over. Morning LOP within twelve miles of DR position. Saw three flying fish.

1420 Diane took down the pole and gybed the jib by herself. In good fashion, I might say!

8/18 0015 Having trouble staying awake. Doing the usual tricks. Wind is uneven but strong enough to keep us between five and eight knots.

0105 Joshua is clanking louder. I must give him some attention tomorrow. Also need to catch up on the log book when it gets light.

0130 Diane: Wind strong, but direction variable. Compass swings from 240° to 280°. My finger hurts and my watch is broken.

0400 Diane: Finished making cheesecake. Isn't instant stuff wonderful?

0535 Wind picking up. Running at seven to eight knots. (The last week of our trip we hit one squall after another. The most we counted in a 24 hour period was seventeen. I think the reason for so many squalls was that we were sailing pretty late in the season. They got to be very tiring as many of them had enough wind to make us either change headsails or drop headsails completely and just run under main until the squall passed.)

1220 Diane: I think I wound my watch and it's still working. However, I could have sworn I wound it last night. Oh, well. John got the log up to date. It's going to be a beautiful day. We're traveling at about five knots, and John says that we are within 500 miles of Hawaii. That's exciting!

1300 Diane: Did the hair-washing routine with the bucket—feel much cleaner. The battle of the batten has taken an amazing turn. Mysterious forces have pushed the batten back **into** the torn pocket. Wonders never cease!

1330 GLASS BALL EPISODE NO. 2 Diane: Well, there it was — the biggest glass ball in the whole Pacific. We flew into action! I threw a buoyant cushion over and down came the pole and off with the preventer and we made two tacks up wind and spotted the cushion — **and the ball!** But try as we would (five times, I think) leaning over the rail, we just couldn't get it aboard. It was just too big and heavy. In the fray I cut my hand and the jib sheet snap shackle lashed up and smacked me in the eye so hard it popped one of the lenses out of my glasses. John got hit in the eye with the main sheet and all in all we didn't go anywhere or do anything but cause a lot of trouble. **I** spotted it, though, and it's **mine!**

2200 Five hundredth squall of the day. I was exercising on the foredeck and Ka Voom!!! It hit. After rummaging around in the cockpit lockers to find the plexiglass dropboards, I fell inside and tried to light a lamp. But alas, the non-skid strip on the step that we use for a striker was wet, and strike as I might, the match wouldn't light. With the help of a lighter, I got a lamp lit. I then rummaged around in the hanging locker, trying to find my foul weather coat, and ended up putting it on backwards because I couldn't see. Then I tried to find my safety harness. It is usually kept in the bin above the port berth along with tools, tape, chimney for the heater, plugs for the air scoops, flares, smoke signals, a broken curtain rod, a few paperback books, a winch handle, and whatever else junk may have collected there. Anyway, after dropping about half of that stuff on Diane while trying to pull the harness out (she just mumbles when I drop things on her) and finally getting it on, I opened the hatch to find:

it had quit raining
the squalls had passed
and the stars were out.

8/19 The morning was just one squall after another. We could see them lined up on the horizon, waiting for their turn to zap us.

1100 Diane: Very cloudy. Got all three of the Hilo AM stations on the radio. I have to cook breakfast. Wonderful John did the dishes.

1330 Diane: Did the lunch dishes. Did some laundry and drug my feet in the water for a while. Felt good. We decided we should not have given up so easily on that last glass ball. John wised up and found he wasn't getting as much sleep as me. Wow, I fooled him for two weeks! Very overcast day. Sailing a little rough at four and a half to five knots. It's sure hard to function without my glasses! (Diane is legally blind without them.)

1630 Main dropped. Battens replaced. Top sail slide sewn back on. I dropped a large roll of sail twine overboard while fixing the slide. I got it back by winding it around the acetone can. Sure took a long time. Oiled roller reefing gear. It is getting stiff and very hard to manage. Checked engine oil, added oil to the shaft bearing.

1830 We had smoked pheasant (from a can) and real mashed potatoes for dinner. Pretty spiffy! Set the clocks back three hours to Hawaii time.

2130 Diane: Ship sighted off the port stern. John woke up but not excited. I turned on all the lights and yelled YAHOO!!!

2230 Another ship. This one came over close to look at us then went on.

8/20 0120 I've been on the foredeck for one and a half hours again, watching *Mahina* sailing along and thinking of things to come. Squalls all day long. ETA 8/24 0930.

1520 and 1640 Saw two jet streams. We're not the only ones around after all! The first was still climbing and I could see the body of the plane quite clearly.

1740 Great sailing. Did I mention the tomato soup and grilled cheese sandwiches we had for lunch? Delicious! That sourdough bread from San Francisco is still good after two and a half weeks — we didn't even have it in a plastic bag.

1940 Beautiful sunset — fair dinner (cheddar cheese soup with peas and corn added). Diane is making a ladder from half inch nylon rope by using fancy knots.

8/21 0115 Squall with rain just passed. Good wind — five to six knots under slightly reefed main and lapper. After a pot of black tea I am finally almost awake. I want to keep a close watch as we are within fifteen to twenty miles of the LA - Honolulu Rhumbline Route. It looks like we might make it in twenty days instead of the twenty-one that I had expected. Fantastic! This sure has been a great experience.

0530 Engine on to charge battery as lights are getting dim again. Not much wind.

1510 Diane: Very nice day — fewest clouds ever. Good breakfast of fried eggs and refried beans again. I made a beautiful rope ladder, but John's feet are too big for it, and since it is nylon, it stretches and swings all over the place. I fell asleep last night and John came out to find us hove to. But it was only for a couple of minutes. (Sure, Diane!)

1700 Massive waterfight on the foredeck with buckets. We really needed to get cleaned up anyway. It is over 80° in the cabin now. I am thankful for the dodger. Without it we would get fried out in the cockpit. Diane says she won the waterfight because she got the wettest.

8/22 and 23 were beautiful sunny days that we used

to get a lot of cleaning up done. We didn't write much in the log — too busy and excited about landfall.

8/24 0300 I see some real faint lights on the horizon that either look like low stars or fishing boats.

0430 They are not stars or boats — that's the island of Hawaii right where it was supposed to be, according to my navigation. I am trying to decide if the aero beacon off the starboard bow is the one at Hilo, or the one at Upola Point. They both have the same characteristics. I headed for the light, and later discovered it was Upola Point.

0500 Diane woke up and was mad that I didn't tell her the minute I saw the lights. I had wanted to surprise her and be close to land when she woke up.

0600 By taking a couple of bearings I discovered we are headed for the wrong place. We spent three hours beating (with the help of the engine) against the current and trade winds north up the coast of the Big Island.

1200 We rounded Pepeeke Point and shut off the engine and prepared to go on a screaming reach into Hilo Bay, but the wind died down. It didn't matter. We fixed two cans of hot chile with lots of hot sauce (even though it was 85°) and enjoyed the scenery.

1230 Guess who just sailed by? The *Pua Hana* — the boat we had met in the middle of the ocean. They said it only took them seventeen days. They were sailing from Hilo to Lahaina.

Chapter 4

Hawaii

1400 Log 3,273 miles Finally inside Hilo Bay. Asked someone where to tie up—they pointed to the commercial dock with a giant freighter alongside. We ended up anchoring in Radio Bay in front of some fancy hotels. A funny old man without any teeth rowed over and said hello. He said it took them 45 days from Ensenada in a catamaran that looked like it should have sunk a long time ago.

We blew up the dinghy and were soon ashore. The first thing we did was to go to the little store in the Orchid Isle Hotel and buy two icy cold cans of guava juice. Then we took turns calling our families and saying we made it safely. It didn't take us long to make the two mile walk into town, and after exploring interesting old shops for a while, we had dinner at a great Chinese restaurant.

The next day was Saturday. We rented a car and drove around the northwest end of the island. It was beautiful. There were waterfalls, great beaches and fascinating little old towns. Sunday we drove to where a lava flow covered over the road a couple of years ago. We also saw where orchids are grown and visited the Queen's Bath, a beautiful cold fresh water pool in the rock where Hawaiian queens used to bathe. It was surrounded by green jungle and was very beautiful.

For the next two and a half weeks we anchored at a different place nearly every night. Diane said she would stay only as long as her money lasted; she didn't want to be dependent on me. I tried to persuade her it didn't matter, but it did to her. After leaving Hilo, we anchored at Kawaihae and tried to find some friends of mine. We had fruit juice at a very fancy resort — Moana Kea — where it cost $120 a night to stay. It was then on to Hana, Maui, which was a beautiful, friendly little town. There, we hitchhiked to the Seven Sacred Pools and went swimming in pools of icy spring water. From Hana we sailed to Makena Beach on Maui, then White Manele Bay on Lanai. We found Lanai to be a beautiful island with friendly people. Next stop was Lahaina where we anchored out because of the overcrowded harbor. We had dinner at a great Mexican restaurant. From Lahaina we sailed to Kaunakakai on Molokai, then back to Manele Bay, then to Kahoolawe, and finally back to the Big Island where we worked out way around to Hilo.

On Thursday, September 12, I saw Diane off at the airport at Hilo. She later wrote and said she cried when the plane took off, and she wished she hadn't left. I really missed her.

While I was at the airport I picked up my typewriter and folding bike that I had had sent from Seattle. Back at the boat, things seemed awfully quiet and lonely with Diane gone.

I spent the next three weeks in Kealakakua Bay on the Big Island, at Lahaina, and at Manele Bay on Lanai. I met a friendly couple on Lanai named Van and Flower and stayed at their little cabin for a few days. It was nice to be off the boat and to explore the island.

While in Kailua, I met Dean and Kopi Carmine from San Francisco who had just spent six months in the Marquesas Islands. When they told me how friendly the people were and showed me pictures of the islands, I decided that it would be a much nicer place to spend the winter than in Hawaii. Hawaii was okay, but very crowded in places. It seemed that most of the people there were from Southern California, and the real Hawaiians were not always friendly. (And understandably so, I think.) So, I sailed to Lahaina and put up some cards saying I needed crew, and started getting *Mahina* ready.

After a week I had met an interesting folksinger named Cindy who was from California and who was crewing on a seventy foot motor-sailer. After listening to Dean and Kopi talk about the Marquesas, she was ready to go. I sailed on to Honolulu and hauled *Mahina* and painted her in one day (by myself). Cindy came a couple of days later, with Dean and Kopi.

The Hawaii Yacht Club gave us two weeks' guest privileges even though I don't belong to a yacht club. The people there were very kind; they even took us to the grocery store and helped us cart $140 worth of groceries back to the boat. After ten days of steady work, *Mahina* was in the best shape she has ever been in, ready for 2,300 miles to windward. We met quite a few people who laughed when we said we were headed for the Marquesas in the winter; they said they had tried, but had given up and ended up in Tahiti. Our last day in Hawaii, Tuesday, October 22, was a very busy one, and I enlisted help from various friends to get all the last-minute jobs done. At one time there were five of us either working on *Mahina* or running errands. Finally, at 1745, everything was stowed and the engine warmed up. Nine of us, including three Japanese friends from a sloop out of Shimitzu, went upstairs to the bar in the yacht club for a Bon Voyage toast. Yoshio insisted on writing with a marking pen on my back, "Bon Voyage from Japanese Yacht *Cherrybra III*." The sun was just starting to make a beautiful drop over the horizon, so we all hurried downstairs. After hugs and goodbyes, we pulled in the docklines and stern anchor. It was just getting dark when we cleared the channel and hoisted sail.

Chapter 5

Hawaii-Marquesas

10/22 1830 3,962 miles Left Honolulu. Beautiful sunset. Wind 25 plus knots; seas six to ten feet. Kaiwi Channel wasn't going to let us leave quietly. We were both a bit queasy and tired and not quite ready for the spray and beating into rough channel seas.

10/23 0900 Beautiful morning. A few trade wind clouds passing. Lanai is off the port beam about fifteen miles away. We are under storm jib and triple reefed main. This close-hauled sailing into the trades is sure going to take some getting used to! Cindy seems happy and doesn't mind the rough sailing. I think she'll be an excellent crew for this passage.

1800 Beautiful sunset, seas still confused. Had good vanilla pudding for dessert.

10/24 Light air all day since we were in the lee of the Island of Hawaii which has two 13,000 foot mountains to stop the wind from reaching us. Motored a little.

10/25 0130 Back to storm jib and reefed main. Ka

Lae (south cape of Hawaii) is famous for its viciousness. I was reading yesterday in a sailing magazine that three boats lost their masts here in last month's Around the State race. Do hope we can avoid that!

1530 This has been a very rough day. We are under storm jib and triple reefed main and are pounding along at four and a half knots.

10/26 Lots of wind and rough seas — more of yesterday.

10/27 0100 Wind eased just a little and I put the lapper up instead of the storm jib. Left the main triple reefed. The roller reefing gears are still very stiff and it takes 45 minutes to go from a full main to triple reefed. We point better when the jib is bigger than the main, and since this is going to be a battle to get as much easting as possible to make the Marquesas, we better start working for every degree possible.

2000 We are crashing through very large head seas at five and a half to six knots under storm jib and triple reefed main again. The mainsheet block is all the way to leeward on the traveler and the boom is vanged down hard so that the mainsail is as flat as a board. Sure looks good.

10/28, 29, 30, 31 Days were all the same. We were pounding into big head seas day and night. A typical log entry reads: Everything was getting slowed down (four and a half knots) for the first time in three days and then POW!!! SUPER SQUALL HITS! *Mahina* is tearing along at six to six and a half knots with rail under and us hanging on behind.

11/1 Wind eased a little today. Finally got the storm jib down and the No. 1 jib up. Taught Cindy how to do LOP's today. She learned really fast and didn't make any mistakes. I think it's a lot easier to learn navigation by doing it at sea than by learning in a class and then doing it later at sea.

11/2 This was a grey, wet, and rainy day. The wind — when it occasionally came — was right on the bow. YUK! Cindy is making good cookies. She is a fantastic cook. I ate them all just as soon as they were done.

1700 Took 45 minutes to unroll reefed main. Went on starboard tack making good 90°. We are getting much needed easting. Cindy fell out of her bunk when I tacked, and, thinking it was morning, she came stumbling to the companionway to ask me why I hadn't wakened her for her watch.

11/3 According to the pilot charts, we will be out of the doldrums and into the SE Trades within 180 miles. Yahoo! When we went for our daily swim (on a line behind *Mahina*), we found the water much colder than the day before. We didn't have much wind and could see the squalls lined up all the way back to the horizon waiting to dump their load of rain on us. A rather miserable day. Motored some. Had good dinner of macaroni and cheese.

11/4 1730 It's been a pleasant day; we took turns dragging on the line behind *Mahina* and trying to shampoo at the same time. Feels good to be clean. Cindy had a good nap and I tightened and checked the portside rigging. Everything looked good.

11/5 Wind has been edging around to the SE and the best course we could make was 180°, which would have put us somewhere in the Tuamotus; so we went on to port tack again. Course about 115°. This will get us east in a hurry — **if** it holds.

11/6 1230 Still on port tack. Made ninety miles of easting in past 24 hours. Great!

11/7 1310 Went back to starboard tack. Course 185°.

11/9 0000 Brisk breeze. Lots of stars—no moon yet. Had a great spaghetti dinner.

1730 Put leather pads in between Joshua and the

brackets that hold him to the transom. The neoprene pads that come with the RVG are forever wearing out. A friend in Lahaina had the same problem with his RVG and gave me some leather to try. It is thicker than the neoprene and I don't think it will wear out. Also scrubbed down the cockpit.

11/10 EQUATOR DAY

1230 Crossed the equator. Tried to fire a flare off to celebrate. I discovered a whole carton of six flares worth $16 was defective because the primers were set so far in that the firing pin on the flare pistol couldn't hit them.

11/11 1625 Today's fix puts us only 390 miles north of Eiao, the northernmost Marquesas Island.

11/12 1615 Getting closer. Holding a great course of 120°. Shot four LOP's. Want to be sure we are in the right place!

11/13 1350 Only 115 miles north of Eiao.

11/14 0400 Only 35.25 miles to go! Finally starting to get excited about it.

0900 Log 5,959 miles Smudge sighted on the horizon bearing 175° M. Exactly where it was supposed to be. I was pretty excited, but there wasn't anything to do that would make us sail any faster, so I took apart and repacked all the life raft provisions. We wondered what the Marquesas would be like. We had heard such good things about them from our friends Dean and Kopi in Hawaii.

1205 Lapper down, genoa up. Bow and stern anchors readied. We're getting closer!

1600 Very close. Can see green hills and the prison that the Pilot talks about on the hill.

Chapter 6

Marquesan Idyll

1640 Log 5,990 miles Anchor down in what we thought was Vai Tahu Bay on Eiao. The only American chart of Eiao is in 1:962,050 scale and not much help at all. It turned out that we were one bay east of Vai Tahu Bay, and what we thought was the abandoned prison that the Pilot talks about was really a French underground nuclear test site that had been abandoned two years earlier. A Marquesan schoolteacher later told us that the island was strictly off limits and that the French might throw us in jail if they found out we had gone exploring there. Anyway, after we got the anchor down and the Avon blown up, we rowed ashore. There was a tremendous surf running and we were lucky to land high and dry on some huge boulders. We started up the one and a half mile climb to the buildings on the cliff even though it was dusk. We noticed a large sign that said something like "Dangerous - Strictly Forbidden" in French.

At the top of the hill we found about thirty little

plywood houses and a couple of warehouses — all of which looked fairly new and were empty. Cindy said the place gave her the hebbie-jeebies in the dark, so we started back down the trail toward the beach. It was pitch black when we finally got through the pounding surf and out to *Mahina.* I didn't sleep at all because there was a very large swell coming into the bay and I didn't like the looks of the rock walls that surrounded us on three sides.

11/15 By 0515 the anchors were up and we were under way. It was 73 miles to Taiohae, the port of entry for the Marquesas. We really would have to do some sailing to get there before dark.

0800 Cindy woke up from a nap and we had a great pancake breakfast.

1630 Cleared Atupa Atua and set a course of 180° for Cape Martin.

1845 Cleared Cape Martin and set course of 240° for Taiohae Bay. It was getting quite dark, but I felt we were too close to give up and heave to for the night. Besides, the Pilot says there is a lighthouse in the bay. Porpoises are swimming back and forth in front of the bow, leaving phosphorescent streamers behind them! A beautiful welcome!

1930 Green lights and scattered white lights sighted off the starboard beam. We turned into Taiohae Bay. The porpoises left us.

2000 The red and green lights that we were heading for turned out to be the running lights of a French ship that was leaving the bay as we were entering. I turned on our running lights (I had them off so I could see better), and the French destroyer gave us a long blast on its horn and shouted some things in French at us over the loudhailer.

2030 6,064 miles Anchor down. We had arrived! It didn't take us long to get Avondayle blown up and find our way ashore. We walked down the only street until we came to Becfin's Restaurant-Tavern (the only thing open in Taiohae on a Sunday night) and went inside. There were some guys singing and drinking Hinano beer who asked us to join them. All the lights in town went off when we were halfway back to the dinghy — the generator was shut down for the night.

Taiohae Bay

The next morning, we checked in with the gendarme and moved *Mahina* to the south side of the bay where five other cruising boats were anchored. We soon got to know everyone, then we collected our mail from Maurice's store.

The next two weeks went by very fast. All the yachties (fourteen of us) had a great time hiking, swimming, playing volleyball, and having feasts on the beach together. It was a lot of fun! Just before everyone left for different points, we all got on Bill and Carol's Islander 34 "*Offshore*" and sailed to Tai Oa Bay with Maxieme, a Marquesan friend, as pilot. At Tai Oa we met Daniel, a woodcarver, who was also Max's brother-in-law. Daniel's daughter Sophie led us on a rugged two and a half mile hike through the woods and over rivers to a spectacular 2,000 foot waterfall. We were all happy to go swimming in the icy fresh pool under the waterfall as Sophie had led a blistering pace and the temperature was in the nineties. We had a great picnic with lots of fresh-picked fruit and some cheese and, fortunately, an easier hike back to the boat.

Daniel at work, Tai Oa

The next morning three boats left in a race for Honolulu, another headed for Papeete, and Bill and Carol on *"Offshore"* headed for the Tuamotus. Four and a half days later *"Offshore"* struck Manihi at night and sank.

I stayed around Taiohae for a few days doing some hiking and helping Max dig sand to make cement for his house foundation. Cindy had sailed back to Honolulu on one of the boats and I was enjoying being alone, but wondering how I would manage *Mahina* singlehanding.

A few days later I was stopped by a French-Tahitian man who asked me if I was an American sailor. I told him that I was sailing *Mahina*, and he said, "You must sail me to Ua Pu tomorrow. I will pay you $100 American. Meet me in the tavern tonight at seven o'clock." With that, he roared off on the back of a Vespa driven by a huge Marquesan man. I had been feeling pretty weak after two weeks of dysentery from the bad water, but I thought for that kind of money I could sail fifteen miles no matter how I felt. That night he explained that he was a scientist from Papeete and that he had to see his wife who lived on Ua Pu.

It was 1530 by the time he was ready to leave the next day. I knew we weren't going to make it to Ua Pu before dark, but Jean-Pierre assured me that he knew the coast well. It **was** dark when we sighted the breakers and turned and ran south along the coast. I kept shining my flashlight towards shore hoping a fisherman in a dugout might come out and show us where to anchor, but no such luck. As we passed the village of Haakuti, some of the boys saw the light and all the boys in the village (eight of them) came down to the beach and started waving their flashlights. We anchored even though it was partially exposed and very rough, with a rock cliff not far behind us. As we headed in the Avon towards the boys, we saw that they were standing on a natural coral jetty over which the waves were occasionally breaking. The waves breaking on shore looked much worse, so we gave the coral a try. We rowed in close and crawled up eight feet to the top of the slimy, sharp coral jetty, pulling the Avon after us. Every minute or so a big wave would wash across the top of the rock and we all held on so we wouldn't get washed off.

We left Avondayle in a little cave in the coral and followed eight very excited boys up the path to the school tachers' house. Jean-Pierre immediately asked the two young and beautiful school teachers, who were friends of his wife, where he could get a horse. He explained to me that the people in the next valley didn't like him and that he must get through while it was still dark. So back down the hill we went. In the process of launching the Avon off the top of the coral in the pitch dark, I got smashed into a ledge when the dinghy suddenly dropped with the surge. After some very hard rowing, I managed to get us back to *Mahina.* My leg felt all numb, so I shined the light on it and found that it was smashed and cut in nine places, and the bottom of the dinghy had quite a pool of blood in it. I asked Jean-Pierre if he was sure he couldn't wait until morning to go ashore, but he said no. He got his bags out of *Mahina* and into the dinghy and we rowed back to the jetty. It went off somewhat better this time; nevertheless, I went back to *Mahina* exhausted. Then I tried to get the bleeding on my leg to stop. Jean-Pierre gave me 5,000 francs (about $40 US) for my efforts. It was hard earned!

The next morning, five of the boys skipped school and paddled out to *Mahina* at 0600, insisting that they would all show me the way to a better anchorage. Vaieo Bay was beautiful and protected. I anchored in fifty feet on a sandy bottom and spent the rest of the morning snorkeling and watching sharks while the boys speared fish. The water was the clearest I'd ever dove in and had

Max with octopus for dinner

many kinds of coral and animal life. In the afternoon, I hiked over the ridge and saw the village of Haakuti in the daylight. The beautiful schoolteachers asked me if I would marry either or both of them. Not a bad offer at all! Haakuti is a much poorer village than many; I met two men with leprosy there. After a couple of days there I went back to Taiohae to provision for my trip to the southern Marquesas.

11/16 Left Nuku Hiva at midnight. Arrived at Hana Menu on Hiva Oa at 1700.

No sooner had I dropped the bow anchor than Ozanne rowed out in a pram and gave me a hand setting a stern anchor. He said to set a second bow anchor in the morning as the winds blow 25 knots every day all day. He spoke very good English that he had learned from the yachts. After I had gotten things tidied up below, I rowed ashore and walked to Ozanne's hut with him. His two young friends that live with him had an excellent dinner of rice and beef hearts and liver waiting when I arrived. They had shot the animal that morning and the meat was really tasty. After dinner we sat around talking and drinking tea for a while, then I rowed back to *Mahina*. Ozanne asked me to stay in one of their huts, but I didn't want to leave *Mahina* alone.

I spent a week in Hana Menu, doing something different every day. Ozanne and his two friends were the only people living in the valley at that time. His wife had gone to Atuona, the nearest town, to have her fourth baby. She is only 24 and Ozanne is 25. Ozanne told me that only two hundred years ago there had been over 2,000 people living in the valley, but that the white man's diseases had wiped them all out. The last Hana Menuvian was Tuo, who died two years ago at 75.

One afternoon I walked back into the valley and saw hundreds of pai-pais (stone house foundations) and a number of burial houses still standing. Ozanne told me

Hana Menu Bay

Bull hide drying, Hana Menu

of a cave in the cliff where the skulls of chiefs were kept. Another afternoon we went many hours on horseback up on the plateau hunting beef. Ozanne finally found and shot a bull just at dusk. Within an hour they had all the meat stripped off the carcass and into gunny sacks on the backs of the horses and were headed back down the valley. The next day we took the beef to Ozanne's father's store in Atuona by outboard boat. The channel seas between Hiva Oa and Tahuata were rough as usual; so, to avoid the big rolling breakers, Ozanne stayed so close to the rocks that the spray from the boat washed some of the crabs off the rocks we passed. In Atuona we spent the night at Ozanne's father Lucien's store and went back to Hana Menu the next day. Another day we all sailed *Mahina* to Vai Tahu on Tahuata Island to get more gas for the speedboat.

One day we played many volleyball games and then went swimming and washed our clothes and things in the pool. It is the most beautiful pool I've ever seen — something so pretty that it looks like it must have been created for a movie set. There is a waterfall that comes tumbling down forty feet over rocks that are surrounded by giant ferns and giant green leaves into a rock-lined, sandy bottomed pool full of icy cold pure water.

After a week in Hana Menu, I sailed to Hapatoni Bay on Tahuata after hearing that the villagers there liked yachts and that there was a surplus of beautiful single girls. I had also heard that the anchorage was a bad one, but it was worse than I had expected. The bow anchor was in forty feet of water, the stern anchor in eight feet, and there was only twelve feet under the keel. The seas were breaking heavily on the coral less than two boat lengths to shoreward. The bottom was a jungle of giant coral heads about fifteen feet high that threatened to break the anchor chain.

I was met on the shore by a beautiful girl named

Rosalyn. She took me to some of her friends and we spent the afternoon singing and talking. The girls thought it bad that I had "no vahine" and was sailing alone, so they asked me if I would marry Rosalyn. That night I had dinner with a woodcarver and his family. I did okay on the poi-poi and mashed bananas, but when I came across a jaw with teeth in it in the pork I was eating, I suddenly lost my appetite.

Christmas was a few days later and quite unforgettable. After a fantastic dinner with Rosalyn and her family, I helped her father rig some Christmas lights he had gotten from the copra schooner to a small battery. The kids really loved the tiny lights that flashed on their tree. Then I walked over to the woodcarver's house where they were just finishing a huge outdoor feast. They insisted that I eat at least some cake and fish cooked in coconut milk. When everyone was done eating, we went inside and practiced Christmas carols for the services that night and Christmas day. Their singing was beautiful, with fine harmonizing. They had a Christmas Eve service at midnight which I didn't wake up for, but at 0700 Christmas morning they started ringing the church bell and kept ringing it until all forty-three people of the village were on their way down the path to church.

The church was an old wooden building put up just after WW II. The girls had surrounded the little nativity scene with palm branches and garlands of fresh hibiscus and candles. There was no priest, but one of the ladies led the chanting and the girls led the singing. Halfway through the service, one of the candles caught the palm branches on fire and there was quite a bit of excitement seeing whether or not the nativity scene would completely go up in flames. After the fire was out, there was more singing and then an offering was taken. When the man next to me saw that I didn't have anything to put in the basket, he gave me ten francs in a typical gesture of their kind generosity. They had another service at noon, and one at three, identical to the first. All 43 people went to each service.

The next day I hiked up into the mountains. There were pine trees to remind me a lot of hiking in the Cascades. The following day I sailed to the next bay, Vai Tahu, where I had promised to try and fix Ozanne's uncle's radio. After a windy night, I weighed anchor and sailed to Atuona on Hiva Oa. It is second in population (about 750) to Taiohae, and the people weren't as friendly as in the small villages; but I did meet some nice people there.

I left Atuona at 0600 on New Year's Eve morning and had a beautiful forty mile sail to Fatu Hiva, the southernmost island of the Marquesas. I anchored in Hana Vave Bay (Virgins Bay) just about an hour before sunset. The bay wasn't very wide and the Pilot says the holding ground is poor, so I put out two anchors. As soon as I got ashore I met some friendly people who told me in Marquesan that I was the first yacht there in over two months. It had been nearly a month since the last copra schooner had been to the island, so the people were pretty excited about having a visitor. One of the women asked me to come to her house. I did, and met her husband, a friendly man who had picked up a little English from the yachts. He told me that the next day all the village was going over to Omoa village for a big New Year's celebration. I found out that there weren't any roads, Vespas, cars, or other non-Marquesans on the island. The only transportation from the other islands was the monthly or semi-monthly copra schooners. There weren't any stores on the island.

After an excellent dinner of poisson cru (raw fish marinated in lime juice) and fish and breadfruit steamed in coconut milk, I walked back up the path toward the waterfall. The setting sun made strange shadows on the rugged, sharp pinnacles that made up the interior of the island.

The next morning, everyone in the village (about forty people) was dressed in his best clothes and drinking powerful red Algerian wine out of huge bottles. After much preparation, two pirogues were launched and headed for Omoa Bay. The pirogues were by far the most beautiful I've ever seen. One was lapstrake planking with a hollowed out log bottom, and the other was plywood and log. They both had bright paint jobs and brand-new Johnson 6 hp outboards and looked immaculate. Even though they were less than eighteen feet long, they managed to hold nearly thirty people and two dogs between the two of them.

An hour or so later, I brought *Mahina* into Omoa Bay with the help of a couple of local boys. The Pilot states that landing is dangerous, so I waited until it seemed like there was a slack time in the breakers and rowed like crazy. The two boys screamed when they saw the size of the wave coming up behind us, but it picked the dinghy up and set us down high and dry (and right side up) on the rocks.

By afternoon everyone in Omoa was pretty well smashed. I bought two interesting tapa murals made from bark of the breadfruit tree. I think I was taken on the first because I didn't want to offend the woman who made it by saying that I didn't think it was worth the price she was asking. A little way down the path another lady came out of a house carrying an armload of tapa. A little boy had run up and told her that I just bought some tapa, so she was ready for me. I offered her 800 francs instead of the 1500 she asked; she accepted and seemed happy about the deal.

I was getting anxious to see if any yachts had arrived in Taiohae because it had been one and a half months since I had seen another yacht — or anyone who spoke

English, for that matter; so the next morning I headed north to Tahuata. I anchored again at Hapatoni because I wanted to pick up some more carvings. The wind was blowing straight into the tiny exposed bay, so I decided not to spend the night anchored there. Just before I left, a boy who had insisted that I take a picture of him said, "Yock (yacht) in Vai Tahu with three vahunus and one vahinie." I got under way at once, excited to see another boat.

I was really surprised and happy to see an Australian ketch, the *Manana,* anchored right off the village. I had no sooner anchored than Chris, a young Australian crew member, rowed over and invited me for dinner. I soon met George Swinborne, a fascinating retired engineer who had completely built his sturdy forty foot ketch by himself. He even made all the stainless steel fittings and hardware himself. He had a nice girl friend named Gwen; his crew were a guy named Ted, an American, and Chris, who was from Melbourne. I had a wonderful hot water shower (first in three months!) before a superb dinner. Ted and Chris spent the night on *Mahina* and the next morning the three of us sailed *Mahina* to Hana Moe Noe to look for puka shells. In the course of the conversation, they mentioned that *Luana Kai* had just sailed in from Hawaii. This was pretty exciting news, as the skipper was a friend of mine from Hawaii, and there was a chance that my girlfriend from Hawaii whom I had planned to meet somewhere later on was aboard. Chris and Ted couldn't remember what the girl crew's name was, so I took off in a hurry so as not to miss the boat if Patty was on board.

The eighty-five mile sail took seventeen hours. Joshua wasn't working because his lower bearings were packed full of salt and I didn't know how to fix them. I was very tired when I arrived at Taiohae, having gotten only six hours of sleep in the past fifty-four hours. I was disappointed to find it was a girl named Julie and not Patty crewing on the *Luana Kai.* There were four boats besides *Mahina* in Taiohae Bay and I had a good time getting to know everyone.

After collecting mail and buying more food from Maurice, I sailed to Haka Maii on Ua Pu Island with a ketch named *Odyssey* from Aberdeen, Washington. We spent nearly two weeks in Haka Maii together. Gayle and Julie on the *Luana Kai* came over and joined us after a week. The bunch of us went hiking in the mountains, spearfishing, sailing, and tuna fishing together. The local schoolteacher, Etienne, was very friendly and had us all over to his house for a big feast for which we all cooked something. I cooked some whole-wheat muffins which no one but Etienne's two little boys would eat.

One day a copra schooner from Papeete anchored in the bay just behind us. We rowed out in our dinghies to buy food and look around, and I met the captain. He was a young Chinese-Tahitian and seemed really sharp. He had just come through the Tuamotus and told me it was rainy and cloudy and there was a rough swell running from the south. That was what I expected to hear since it was the rainy season, but navigating through the Tuamotus in cloudy weather could be a bit tricky. Since my three month visa was running out and had to be renewed in Papeete, I sailed back to Taiohae on January 21st.

1/24 0500 Woke up early and walked up to Maxime's house to pick up the third and fourth stalks of bananas we had carried down the mountain the day before. I hope the bananas will last until I get to the Tuamotus, where they will make excellent gifts as only coconuts and a few limes grow in the harsh environment of those atolls. I was surprised to find nearly everyone in the village up at such an early hour. Max insisted that I drink some terrible instant coffee with him before he went off to work planting coconut trees on the mountainside. I made two trips struggling down to the dinghy with the giant stalks of bananas. Then I walked across the street and said goodbye to to Maurice. After getting the bananas on board and getting *Mahina* ready to sail, I rowed over to the *Odyssey* and had a great breakfast of pineapple pancakes and tea. I then said goodbye to my friends on the four boats anchored close by. There was a good fresh breeze blowing so *Mahina* sailed to Taiohae Bay in good fashion at six knots.

Chapter 7

Marquesas-Tuamotus

0940 As soon as I cleared Nuku Hiva, the wind died. I got to work right away rigging the high, dacron lifelines I use when making passages and oiled the gooseneck and the latches on the spinnaker pole. The wind was very light all day. Two to three knots was the fastest we ever went.

2300 I was very tired after staying up late the night before getting ready, and it's been a long, windless day; so I dropped sail and lashed the tiller and went below to get some sleep.

1/25 0345 Woke up feeling much better and raised the sails. Doing two and a quarter knots. Better than nothing!

0420 First signs of the sun in the east horizon.

0930 Rigged a new flag halyard (the old one got blown away and my new French flag went with it) and put grommets in my new flag. The flag is really something. Julie on the *Luana Kai* sewed it up for me.

The red is an old cloth restaurant napkin that I got out of a rag barrel somewhere. The white is part of a flour sack donated by Ropa Wong, Taiohae's baker. The blue is a leg of my old blue jeans. A truly recycled flag! It was a little heavy and didn't fly quite the same as the fancy nylon one, but it had class!

1200 Ran the engine for a couple of hours and then it stopped all of a sudden. Plugged fuel line. Sure wish my fuel filter worked.

1415 Fuel line and carburetor back together and engine working great.

1430 WIND! Engine off. Sailing along at three and a half knots. Took three LOP's with my Ebco sextant and one with the Davis. Earlier, while checking the Ebco against Gayle's Plath on the *Luana Kai,* we discovered a cracked mirror holder and a fourteen degree error in mid-arc due to the plastic warping. I had asked around the different boats in Taiohae and found that everyone had had similar experiences with the plastic sextants and had either thrown them overboard or only used them for a spare. Unfortunately though, no one had a spare metal sextant, so I am quite worried about navigating through the Tuamotus with a broken sextant in the rainy season.

2345 No wind again. Sails down and to sleep. Ahhhhh . . .

1/26 0530 Wind. Sails up and doing three knots! Close-hauled, wind out of the west. Didn't expect that — for sure!

1400 Vane steering great. Finally there is enough wind to make it work and let me concentrate on navigating. Got a good fix from the moon and sun. Position is within a mile or two of the DR. Made a grilled cheese sandwich and had a good nap. Good steady wind all night.

1/27 0230 Vane steering is great! Lots of light with a nearly-full moon.

1200 Read John Steinbeck's "East of Eden" most of the morning. Had tuna salad with fresh cucumber and bean sprouts.

1400 Squall with **very** heavy rain.

1745 Still raining hard. Came inside and got out of foul weather gear. Nice to be out of that stuff. Sure glad Joshua's steering and not me! Listened to an opera on the nineteen meter band shortwave. I'm tired.

11/28 0300 Clouds breaking up some — finally. A little moon is getting through. Winds shifted back to north; broad reaching now at five knots.

0600 Reefed main more. Still raining lightly.

0700 Rain stopped and Joshua is steering great. Had a good breakfast of oatmeal with raisins and dried bananas.

0800 Just heard on WWV that tropical storm Carla is near Samoa and heading south. Hope she stays over there.

1200 Many squalls and much rain all morning. The wind is shifting 50° each time a squall comes.

1700 Nice evening — pretty sunset. Picked up the radio beacon on Hao, in the southern Tuamotus. It lines up on our beam, so I know that we are at least going in the right direction.

1/29 0230 and 0530 Shot MUL.

0800 Had good pancake breakfast and a shower in the cockpit during a passing rain squall.

1305 Good fix. It was fourteen miles off DR. I wonder if that is that mid-arc error? Fix puts us at S 12° 42'. W 146° 03', or only 160 miles from Rangiroa! ETA at Rangiroa 0200 1/31.

1430 Light air and big swells. Too much for Joshua. It will sure be nice to arrive somewhere! It has already taken five days and I only expected the entire trip to take four days.

1/30 0620 Beautiful morning — no squalls! Lots

of sun. Radio bearings on Tahiti and Rangiroa check with our DR position. Joshua steering well. Started taking sights at 0630 and had shot six sun and moon LOP's by 1650 using both sextants. I want to be very sure where I am in case it gets cloudy again and I can't get any more shots. I've heard too many stories in the last two months of boats being wrecked on the Tuamotus.

2130 According to my DR we have only twenty-one miles to go, so we had better slow down or else we'll go charging into Rangiroa at night. Genoa down. Still doing four knots under main alone.

2230 Rolling heavily; No. 1 jib up seems to steady us some.

2300 Radio beacon signal from Rangiroa suddenly lost power and direction. Tahiti beacon is coming in stronger.

2400 I heard a faint dull roar but didn't think about it. I decided to try taking a bearing in the cockpit. I was **very** surprised to see foaming surf and palm trees less than a hundred yards ahead. I quickly gybed the sails and headed along the coast at about 290°. I had reached Rangiroa thirteen miles earlier than my ETA. I later figured that I must have picked up a two knot current for the seven hours between by 1700 fix and landfall. I was very glad for the nearly full moon and few clouds as the atoll was very flat and the palm trees were all that could be seen above the crashing surf. I spent the rest of the night sailing up and down the coast waiting for daylight and trying to arrange it so that I would be right in front of one of the two passes at slack water, which was just about the same time as daylight. The Pilot states that the tide runs at over six knots, making passage impossible at any time other than slack water.

0530 I identified a small string of low islands that the chart showed to be seven miles east of Tiputa Pass. I had really hoped to go in Avataru Pass instead of Tiputa because it was four hundred yards wide, compared to Tiputa's 160 yards. The narrower the pass, the stronger the current. The Pilot states that Tiputa is subject to violent eddies.

Chapter 8

Tuamotu Archipelago

0645 7,024 miles Alongside Tiputa Pass. It doesn't look too bad. I sheeted the sails in hard and opened the throttle wide and went screaming through at seven knots. Once inside the lagoon the water was like glass, but the wind was still good as the island was no higher than five feet at its highest point. I shut off the engine and sailed slowly by the village of Tiputa. There were a few kids sitting on the stone wharf fishing, but other than that things looked deserted.

I decided to sail to Avataru where I had heard there was a research boat anchored. The sailing inside the lagoon was like nothing else! With the sun behind me and Polaroid sunglasses on, I could watch the water turn all shades of blue and green, and occasionally see a patch of coral under us. There was a sturdy looking forty foot ketch named the *Sea Quest* anchored in the pass at Avataru. The people on board looked quite surprised to see another yacht and yelled sleepy hellos. I backtracked

Landfall Rangiroa, Tuamotus

a little and anchored around the corner from the pass where I wouldn't be in such strong current. It felt good to be sitting still.

I put on mask and fins and jumped over into the water. It was the warmest and clearest water I had ever dove in. There were hundreds of fish of all sizes and shapes. They were totally fearless and it was a bit unnerving at first when they came bumping into me. After cooling off, I pumped up the Avon and rowed over to the *Sea Quest.* I learned that they were just completing a two and a half year research project on sharks of the Tuamotus. The next day I had a chance to dive with them in ninety feet of water outside the Pass. Even down that far, the current of the waves was so strong that it could throw you down on the sharp coral if you weren't careful.

I met Les, the friendly manager of the government freezer.

One of the first things he said was, "I think you had better have a freshwater shower. I'll show you where it is." I had four huge stalks of bananas from the Marquesas to trade, and the people were very happy to receive them. I soon had more lemons and breadfruits than I knew what to do with.

One day I took my bicycle ashore and put it together — for the first time since picking it up in Hawaii — and went exploring the atoll. There wasn't too far to go as the road was only five miles long. I stopped and took pictures of the *Kadana,* a beautiful forty foot Ferro-cement ketch from Vancouver, that had hit the reef at night six months earlier. The seas had washed her up so high that she was in just six inches of water. I stopped at Kia Ora Village, the only resort in eastern French Polynesia, and had a

cold pineapple drink with ice in it. The temperature was in the high nineties every day, so cold things are pretty special.

After being anchored at Avataru for a few days, I decided to try anchoring in front of Kia Ora Village. Before I had even arrived, Serge, the owner came roaring out in his Boston Whaler and showed me where to anchor. As soon as the anchor was down, he came alongside and insisted that I come ashore with him for a shower and lunch. He took me to his own hut and I had the first indoor shower I'd had in four months. It was cool and refreshing. Lunch was very French and quite fantastic. Lots of wine and different kinds of cheeses and eggs and ice cream.

I spent a couple of days anchored at Kia Ora and met some very interesting people from South America, France, Japan, and even an American couple. As my French visa was fast expiring and my food supply was nearly gone, I decided it was time to start thinking about sailing to Papeete; so I sailed back to Avataru and bought a few groceries. The day before I left, a folkboat sailed in crewed by two friendly guys whom I had briefly met in Taiohae. They had forgotten to get smallpox vaccinations before they left, so the Gendarme in Taiohae had run them out and insisted that they sail to Papeete. They were, but with a number of sidetrips along the way.

Rick was from Liverpool, and Dave from Aspen. We had a lot of fun diving together and sitting up half the night telling funny stories. The morning I left, Rick baked a fantastic coffeecake in the pressure cooker and we had a good last breakfast together. I had slack water figured just right, so at 1030 I sailed slowly out of Avataru Pass.

Chapter 9

Rangiroa-Tahiti

2/7 2300 Log 7,062 Trying desperately to stay awake. The wind is very light; I have averaged only two and a half knots since leaving Avataru. I can't go to sleep since the currents in between the Tuamotu atolls are sometimes strong and tricky. We are now between Tikehau and Rangiroa.

2/8 0320 Gave up on trying to stay awake. Took the genoa down, left the main up so we wouldn't roll too much, and went to sleep for an hour.

0530 Beautiful sunrise, and a little wind. Actually doing three knots.

0600 Makatea sighted. I have heard that the extensive phosphate mining operation have been abandoned, and I wonder about going ashore there.

1250 I was sailing close by the reef at Makatea when I heard someone whistling from one of the abandoned French houses up on the hill. With the binoculars I was just able to see three men waving at me to come ashore. I motioned for them to come down, and within a few minutes they had made their way down the 500 foot cliff and were in their canoes.

Four young men of about fifteen to twenty-five came aboard and were very excited to see a visitor. They couldn't speak English or Marquesan and my French was lacking at that time, but I got the message that there were only about 150 people living on the island now. None of them had been to Tahiti — ninety miles away — and there was no regular copra boat service. There had been over 1,700 people living on the island, but all except these 150 Makateans left the island when the last of the phosphate was mined. There were some very fancy French homes on the side of the cliff. The phosphate plant was immense. It consisted of an elevator to take trucks up and down the cliff, a huge refinery, and towers and loaders extending out over the water to fill up the ships.

There were three immense, ugly, rusty steel mooring buoys; but they were all within seventy feet of the reef, and I just didn't want to take a chance tying up to them, even though it would have been very interesting to go ashore. Anchoring was out of the question as it was over a hundred feet deep right up to the edge of the reef.

1445 Cleared Makatea and set a course of 200° for Tahiti.

2/9 0605 Tahiti sighted right where it was supposed to be.

1500 Sailed close by the Valley of Mahina to take pictures. It is very rugged and green and beautiful.

Chapter 10

Society Islands

I had no harbor chart of Papeete, only an old Navy chart of Tahiti and Moorea that was of little use, so I decided to follow the little sailboats that had been out racing as they went in. It turned out that they belonged to Yacht Club de Tahiti, and I ended up in Papawa Bay instead of in Papeete Harbor. The people at the yacht club were very friendly and helped me tie to their dock. They explained that I had come to the wrong place, but not to worry about that and come in and have a free drink. After talking and listening to the local racing sailors for a while, I got a ride into Papeete to see if there were any boats along the quay that I knew. One of the first things I heard was that Bill and Carol in the *Offshore* had hit Manihi at night and lost their boat on the reef. That was pretty sad news.

After hearing that, I decided to head back to the boat. Somehow, I managed to get hopelessly lost. Papeete isn't that big a town, but most of the lights are turned off at night and it looks like a different place. I finally stumbled into a Gendarmerie Nationale, or suburban police station. I tried to explain to the Gendarme that I was lost, but he didn't understand a word of English. I was hoping he wouldn't ask for my passport, as I hadn't cleared Customs and legally shouldn't have left the boat. Finally, with the help of a wall map, he drew a small map, and I found my way home to *Mahina*.

The next morning, I had a nice shower at the yacht club and was starting back to the boat when a beautiful French woman stopped me and asked me if I needed crew. After gulping a few times, I said, "Sure!"

Annick was from Paris and had spent nine years in Tahiti as a biochemist on the nuclear project. She wanted to sail to New Zealand for a vacation. She had money for food and had a lot of experience crewing on the local races. We arranged to have dinner in a couple of nights, and she left to go to work. That was almost too good to believe!

That morning I motored out of Papawa Bay and over to Papeete Harbor. Some helpful yachties rowed out and took a bow line ashore while I handled the stern anchor, and soon I was securely anchored with my bow to the quay. Officially entering Papeete turned out to be a full-day affair. After going to Customs, Immigration, Agriculture, and the Harbormaster, I had to go to the police station to apply for a visa extension. At each office I had to fill out miles and miles of forms that were full of ridiculous questions.

I had a lot of fun shopping at Alien's across the street from where the yachts tie up. Their selection of food was much better than in the Marquesas, and the girls that worked there were **very** friendly! They had French bread twice a day, excellent fresh vegetables, and even ice cream and milk.

Annick stopped by every couple of days, and one

night we went out to dinner at a strange, dark Chinese cafe. We made plans to sail to Moorea on Friday when she got off work to see how we'd get along together in such a small space.

During the week, I was able to get a message back to a friend in Seattle through a ham radio operator on another boat that my sextant had become warped and was useless. I asked him to try to find a used Navy sextant and send it airmail as there were no sextants to be had in Papeete.

On Wednesday, I met Shirley, a beautiful blond who had just flown in from California and planned to sail to Fiji on the boat tied up next to me. That night we decided to go "out on the town" and see what Papeete's nightlife was like. The first bar we came to was tiny and packed full of Tahitians singing and dancing and playing guitars. We were the only non-Tahitians there, but before we could find a place to sit down they had given us more bottles of Hinano beer than we could ever drink. They insisted that we dance with them and put flower leis around our necks. When we finally got back to *Mahina,* we were so exhausted that we fell asleep immediately. The next morning Shirley slept in while I was filling the tanks and the skipper of the boat that she was on (who was a Captain Bligh type) wanted to know where she was.

By the time a week had passed I was ready to head over to Moorea for a while where I wouldn't be running up a moorage bill while waiting for the new sextant to arrive. Annick came by early Saturday morning, and while I was warming up the engine she hoisted and repacked the spinnaker. She had been crewing on the quarter tonners at Yacht Club de Tahiti for quite some time and couldn't imagine sailing to Moorea without using the chute.

Once we got under way she noticed that the main was reefed and wanted to know why. Rather than trying to explain to her in my limited French that *Mahina* was too tender with a full main, I just unreefed it. The wind was very light. We were ghosting along at one and a half knots and it was very hot. After a while, Annick said in her funny way, "If I jump in, you stop for me?" I laughed and said, "Of course," and she promptly dove in and swam around *Mahina* a couple of times, climbing back aboard as we slowly drifted toward Moorea. She gave me a big hug which got me all wet, so I jumped in. From the water I could see that the oil spills in the harbor had given *Mahina* a thick, gooey, black boot top stripe; so I had Annick toss over a big sponge and some soap and I went to work on it.

About that time, *Natika,* a thirty foot racing sloop that Shirley was on started drifting past us under main and spinnaker, so I climbed back aboard and tried to see if *Mahina* could keep up with them. They moved a little faster than us, but I didn't feel like bothering with the spinnaker and Annick had curled up in the sun for an afternoon nap, so we just let them pass. In a few minutes their sails came down and they started powering. Since it was still midafternoon and we had only seven miles to go, we just kept drifting. A half hour later a nice fresh breeze came funneling through the gap between Tahiti and Moorea, and we were off and flying on a six and a half knot reach for Moorea.

We had an exhilarating sail past the deep valleys on the east end of the island, and tacked our way in through the gap in the reef all the way to the back of Cook's Bay. *Natika* and a sinking trimaran were tied to the rickety pier, but we preferred to anchor under sail in the middle of the bay. Annick took off for a visit to a friend who lived in the next bay, and Shirley and I walked to a little restaurant where for ten cents we bought a huge pomplemoose (sweet grapefruit) which we ate in a shady spot by the beach.

As we walked back to the boats, Shirley told me that she'd like to sail on *Mahina.* Later that afternoon, Annick came back from visiting her friend, and we walked around to Papetoi Bay where I had heard there was good snorkeling and a beautiful anchorage. I was very surprised to see *Papillon* anchored in a tiny cove with a stern line to a palm tree on the beach. *Papillon* was a beautiful, old ten meter racing sloop that had been converted for cruising. I had met Scott and Suzanne, the owners, in the Marquesas a couple of months earlier. They invited us aboard and we found out that they were headed for New Zealand with brief stops at Huahine, Raiatea, Bora Bora, and Rarotonga planned.

After an excellent dinner of rice and fish that Scott had speared underwater, Scott and Suzanne and Annick and I hitchhiked to Captain Bligh's. We had heard that it was the hottest night spot on Moorea (also the only one) and we were interested to see what it was like. We arrived a little early and had a good time talking and watching people arrive. The music was a wild combination of Tahitian, French, and American songs played full blast from a record player with huge speakers. I danced a few dances with Annick, then spent the rest of the evening dancing with some very beautiful Tahitian girls. The walk back to *Mahina* after the dance was beautiful, with a sliver of a new moon shining across the lagoon.

The next morning, Scott and Suzanne came over to *Mahina* to help Annick and me sail from Cook's Bay to Papetoi Bay where Papillon was anchored. There were two ways we could have made the trip. The first would have been to sail through the pass and outside the reef and come in through the next pass. The second way was to sail about a mile through a twisting dredged channel inside the lagoon that ended up in Papetoi Bay. I chose the second route since Annick said she had done it in her boat before and that the channel was dredged for three metres (about nine feet).

We started out smoothly, then a strong gust of wind put our rail under and our knot meter past six and a half knots. I knew we should get some sail down in a hurry, but in the excitement of trying to stay in the narrow, zig-zagging channel, there wasn't time for me to leave the cockpit. We were flying from marker to marker and around corners when there was suddenly a jolt and *Mahina* heeled over 60°. I thought for sure that it was all over for *Mahina,* but our momentum carried us over the coral head that had grown in mid-channel and we continued on our way. Annick immediately started pumping the bilge, but fortunately we weren't taking any water.

As soon as we had anchored in Papetoi Bay alongside *Papillon,* and had tied the stern line to a palm tree on shore, I put on a mask and dove down to check for damage to the hull. To my amazement I found that we had hit the coral head so hard that part of it was stuck on

Cook's Bay, Moorea

Friends giving Annick and me a tow

the front of the keel and had to be chiseled off with a big screwdriver. I was very thankful then that *Mahina* was a full-keel fibreglass boat.

Later that afternoon, Shirley from the *Natika* came by and we got together with Scott, Suzanne, and Annick to talk about our situation. It was decided that since Scott and Suzanne needed crew and would be arriving in New Zealand much earlier than *Mahina,* Annick would sail with them on *Papillon.* Shirley decided that it was time to get away from her Captain Bligh, so she left to go back to *Natika* to pick up her belongings.

Two mornings later Annick flew back to Papeete to quit her job and pack her sea bag. She was back in Moorea in a couple of days, bringing with her a friend of hers from Paris named Julie. They, along with Scott and Suzanne, helped me sail *Mahina* in through a narrow pass and to a beautiful anchorage in front of the Club

Med. There was only a foot and a half of water under the keel when we anchored. The water was very warm and clear, so we all jumped in and spent the rest of the morning snorkeling.

We had a fantastic five course lunch at the Club Med, which is the most exclusive resort on Moorea, and went water skiing after the feast. Later that afternoon, Scott, Suzanne, Annick, and Julie walked back to *Papillon* which was anchored in the next bay, and I watched the sunset across the lagoon from the beach.

The next day Shirley decided that life aboard a 27 foot boat with no head and where you had to wash clothes by hand was too rough for her, so she caught an inter-island trading boat back to Papeete.

I spent the next days snorkeling a lot. I had a great time exploring some little islands nearby and met some very friendly people on a trimaran named *Chamaru* from Seattle. Charles and Mary Sturkey had built *Chamaru* when they were living in Sasebo, Japan. They would finish their world circumnavigation when they reached Suva, Fiji. *Chamaru* was fifty feet long with a twenty-four foot beam and one of the most comfortable boats I've ever been on. I later got to know them well; and Abraham, their Filipino crew member, became a best friend of mine.

On Tuesday, February 28, Julie came by and said she needed a ride back to Papeete; so we pulled up anchor and sailed out the narrow channel. The twenty mile sail back to Papeete took all day. We had to beat into fresh twenty-five knot trade winds and short, choppy channel seas. It was just getting dark when we finally made Papeete Harbor, and we were quite thankful that some friends came out in a dinghy and took our stern line to the quay while we dropped the bow anchor, trying to back in without bumping the boats on either side of us. We were both starved and didn't have much money, so we had dinner at "le trucks." "Le trucks" are little vans with an assortment of hot Chinese and Tahitian foods and desserts. For less than $2.00 US I had rice and Chinese vegetables and orange juice and a huge piece of chocolate cake. It had been a long day and we really slept well that night.

The next morning Julie went home to her fare (bungalow) in the mountains and I hitchhiked across town to the Customs warehouse to pick up my new sextant that had been shipped from Seattle. After some talking, I managed to get it out of Customs for less than $1.00 duty. Next stop was the police station where I tried to get my visa extended for another three months. The large Tahitian official that handled visas was the only unfriendly official I met during that part of the trip, and boy was he unfriendly! Each day that I went in to ask if they had my passport and visa ready, he asked me to fill out the same forms and pay him another $5.00. This got pretty tiring and expensive, so I eventually gave up and left Papeete without another visa and my present one nearly expired.

On Tuesday, the *Krysten Perle,* the beautiful twenty-six foot lapstrake folkboat I met in the Marquesas, pulled up to the quay. Rick and Dave and I had a lot of fun together in Papeete. Since we were all short of cash, we had a great time cooking up exquisite dinners for each other on our boats instead of going out to the neat little restaurants that Papeete is so famous for. Their folkboat was so small inside that we had to sit in the cockpit to cook and eat; when it rained, we usually had dinner aboard *Mahina.*

One afternoon we hiked way up a beautiful valley to a waterfall and walked back to the boats in a warm tropical rainstorm.

On Tuesday, March 4, Bret, a good friend of mine from the Tuamotus, came into Papeete on a beautiful eighty-five foot schooner which tied to the quay alongside *Mahina*. They had just come from Huahine and Bret told me that he had met Annick and that she wanted off *Papillon* and back on *Mahina*. That was the best news I could possibly receive; I had been kicking myself for ever suggesting that she leave *Mahina* and sail on *Papillon*. So, without any delay, I paid my bill at the harbormaster's office and set sail for Huahine, about a hundred miles WNW of Tahiti.

The trip took almost exactly twenty-four hours, and I stayed up the entire time watching for ships. As the sun rose over Huahine, I changed the lapper for a smaller working jib so I wouldn't be over-canvased when it was time to beat my way up the pass and into the lagoon. I had long before gotten used to sailing in and out of passes and anchorages since gas was about $1.20 a gallon and I didn't like to rely on the engine.

There were five boats anchored off the main village of Fare. I anchored between *Papillon* and *Sandpiper* and took a stern line to a palm tree on the beach. *Sandpiper* was a CT-41 ketch from Bremerton owned by a dentist and his wife who were on an extended vacation. I learned from *Papillon* that the night before, the wind had come down through the valley at over fifty knots, causing all the boats to drag and one to go aground. This, plus the fact that my 25 pound CQR anchor was in over eighty-five feet of water, helped me to decide in a hurry to also put my twenty-two pound Danforth off the bow with all the chain I could spare.

Fare is a clean, beautiful little town with a funny old hotel. In the hotel we met Joe, an American from New York City, who had been living on Huahine for a year and thought it the most beautiful place in the world. We sure couldn't disagree with him! Annick told me later that day that she thought she wanted to move back on

Mahina but wasn't sure; she wanted to wait and see how things worked out on *Papillon*.

On Friday, March 7, I sailed on *Macubah*, a CT-41 from Vancouver, B.C., to Avea Bay on the south side of Huahine. *Macubah* drew over six feet, and there were some anxious moments as Brooks, the skipper, threaded his way through a maze of coral heads. After we were safely anchored and had had a good lunch, I caught a ride on a passing truck back to Fare where *Mahina* was still anchored.

Fare looked like an entirely different village when we arrived. The weekly inter-island copra schooner from Papeete was in for a brief stop and there were people everywhere. People had set up little stalls on the wharf and were trying to sell melons, chickens, pigs, and vegetables to the people on the ship. The pigs and chickens made quite an uproar, adding to the confusion.

The next morning I filled the water tanks, bought

Copra schooner leaving Fare, Huahine

some gas, and sailed to Avea Bay where *Papillon, Macubah,* and *Sandpiper* were anchored. Seven of us got a ride on a dump truck the next day to the village of Maeva which was a sacred place with a meeting house built on stilts over the water. There were twelve stone platforms, under which were the bones of the high priests; and there were extensive stone fish traps in the lagoon. After we got back to the boats that afternoon, Scott, Suzanne, Annick, and I went underwater spear-fishing out near the reef and came back with enough fish for an excellent dinner.

On Tuesday, March 11, I sailed out the pass at Huahine and sailed slowly across to Raiatea in light air. I entered the reef through Passe Teavapiti and sailed past *Papillon* and *Chamaru* which were anchored off the town of Utaroa. Utaroa is the second largest town in French Polynesia (Papeete is the largest); it has air service to and from Papeete twice a day. I was hoping to find an anchorage that was described to me by a friend in Papeete as being near the airstrip. All the other anchorages on Raiatea are very deep — about eighty or ninety feet, which isn't very safe — but my friend's is only about fifteen feet deep.

I entered a bay that I thought to be the one described to me, but when I was still out in the middle, I ran hard aground. At the time that the keel first hit the coral shelf *Mahina* was doing three knots, and her momentum was enough to carry her up on the coral until the bow was over three feet out of the water. I tried putting the engine in full reverse and rocking back and forth, then tried pushing off the coral with my twelve foot sweep oar, but it was useless. I soon realized that the tide was going out and if I didn't get *Mahina* off pretty quick I would be spending the rest of the night in a very awkward position. The only other thing I could think of to do was to row out a stern anchor and try to winch the boat back off the coral, so I started pumping up the Avon. Before I had gotten very far, I was quite surprised to see about twenty little boys and two men **walking** out to the middle of the bay where *Mahina* was aground.

They were all laughing and thought it great fun. The two men said "bonjour," then lifted up the bow and pushed as I put the engine in full reverse. With a nasty scraping sound, *Mahina* slid slowly back into the water. All the people that had gathered on shore to watch cheered and waved. Then the men pointed out a better anchorage to me. About then I wished that I had bought the two large scale charts of Raiatea instead of just the chart that covered all of the Leeward Society Islands. The charts were approximately $5.00 US each, so I had attempted to save money by buying as few as possible in Papeete.

Early the next morning I moved *Mahina* to the small bay by the airport that I had missed the previous afternoon in the poor light. I spent five days anchored there alongside *Papillon*. We found an excellent selection of provisions in Utaroa, and on some items the prices were actually cheaper than in Papeete. There were a couple of inexpensive Chinese restaurants in town and an old movie house, so we had some real fun evenings.

On Monday, March 17, I left Raiatea and had a pleasant day sail to Bora Bora, about fifteen miles northwestward. I took along friends I had met on Huahine as passengers. Henry and Caroline were from Vancouver, B.C., and were hitchhiking their way around the Pacific. We sailed through Teavanui Pass and anchored in front of the Oa Oa Hotel, tying a line to a piling on the beach. I had heard that Hans Flesch, the owner of the Oa Oa, was friendly towards yachts, but I was surprised when he asked me to the bar for free drinks and insisted that I put a picture of *Mahina* and a story of the trip in his scrapbook. He was on his second scrapbook; it was fascinating to read of yachts from many different countries and their adventures. There were a couple of yachts that were in each of the two books; they had sailed around the world in the time between. Hans went through the books and pointed out five of the boats that he knew had since been lost. Three of the five had hit the reef at Rarotonga, where I was headed next, and sunk. Hans offered me free use of his dock, showers, and washing machine. The hotel was made up of eight small thatched huts and one large hut where the restaurant and bar were. I was quite surprised to learn that the rates were cheaper than most hotels in Hawaii.

I was very excited to find that there were six letters and three cassette tapes waiting for me at the hotel desk. That was more mail than I had received in many months, and I shared it with friends there who hadn't received any. There was a birthday card from my mom and dad, a letter and a classical music tape from my brother Paul, a post card from my other brother David who was in Germany, and a long letter from my sister saying she was getting married soon and couldn't I come. I spent a little over a week anchored in front of the Oa Oa Hotel. During that time I read several books, bicycled around the island on my folding bike, went snorkeling in the lagoon with friends, and did some work on *Mahina.*

One day, the French foreign minister came to Bora Bora. With him came a host of French officials and a TV cameraman. The local gendarme dressed up in a fancy white uniform with gold braid, and all the school kids sang French songs they had been taught that week, waving little French flags as the minister stepped off the boat. It was a very hot and humid afternoon, and he looked as relieved as the islanders did when he finally finished his long speech in which he said that French had decided **not** to grand independence to French Polynesia. After the speech, quart bottles of cold Hinano beer were passed out to the islanders. I think that is the only way they could get the islanders to listen to his ridiculous speech. The Tahitians are angry at the powerful French government which refuses to grant Polynesia independence since the French nuclear bomb testing grounds are in the Tuamotus.

There is an organized Freedom Fighters movement in Tahiti; and New Zealand, Australia, Fiji, and the Cook Islands have made protests about the nuclear fallout to the United Nations. Even so, I found the islanders on Bora Bora to be very friendly. There were over 6,000 American troops stationed on Bora Bora during the last part of WW II and many of the older men would say things like "Hi, Joe!" or "Where you going, buddy?" as I rode by them on my bike. I stopped and talked with a couple of men who were very anxious to tell me what it was like when the Americans were on Bora Bora. They said they wanted the Americans to come back and make the French leave because the Americans didn't try to run their lives as the French do. They told me the name of a friend of theirs in San Francisco who had come back to visit them after the war was over and wanted to know if I knew him since I was from America. I explained to them that America was a big place with many times more people than Papeete.

They told me how to get to a place in the mountains where there were hidden underground buildings left from WW II, so I hiked up an overgrown trail until I came to a small clearing. There was a whole complex of water tanks and underground bunkers that had long since been abandoned to the frogs and birds. It was a spooky place, and I was glad when I got back down to the beach and out of the jungle.

I got back that evening in time for an excellent French dinner at the Oa Oa, complete with wine and a flaming dessert. That night there was a fantastic lightning and thunder storm. We all stayed awake, anxious to see if our anchors were holding us off the reef. We saw a jagged bolt of lightning hit a little motu (island) less than a quarter of a mile away, and then, just before dawn, a bolt hit on the shoreline about a half mile away. We found out later that morning that it had hit a canoe, killing one man and badly burning another as they were trying to pull their canoe up on the beach.

I got a letter from my friend Bret in Papeete saying that he wouldn't be able to sail to Rarotonga with me as we had previously planned. He had stayed in Papeete a while longer finishing work on a National Geographic contract. I decided to sail immediately for the Cook Islands. Since the *Chamaru* was just leaving for there also, I rowed out to tell them I'd be right on their tail. Charles gave me a walkie-talkie and we made a schedule of times that we'd listen for each other, and then they left. I rowed back to *Mahina,* said goodbye to friends at the hotel and on the two other yachts there, folded up the Avon, pulled up the anchor, and sailed out the pass.

Chapter 11

Bora Bora-Rarotonga

3/27 1515 Moving well under main and genoa. Rice and chicken soup for dinner.

2100 Beautiful full moon and a sky full of stars. Ghosting along at three and a half knots.

3/28 0200 Vane steering well. I'm getting a good sleep every couple of hours. Large swell starting to pick up from the south. I wonder what is going on down there.

1200 Shot four sights with my new Tamaya sextant. It is much easier to use than the plastic one that was warped by the heat. It is quite a bit heavier and is easier to hold steady. Had a late breakfast and finished reading **Tales of the South Pacific** by James Michener.

1800 Big squall astern with lots of rain. Whisker pole down and jib sheeted in hard behind the main so it is blanketed. This is much easier than dropping the jib and then raising it again when the squall passes.

1910 Lightning very close on all sides. The sky is very black and one of the flashes of lightning hit the water just off the starboard bow. I connected one jumper cable to a backstay and one to a shroud with the free end dragging in the water. I hope that this will work to ground the mast in case it gets hit. I remembered the last lightning, in Bora Bora, which had fried a guy. That would be most unpleasant!

2200 Three large squalls with lightning have passed and are disappearing over the horizon. The moon is out again and there are light clouds.

3/29 0100 A small brown tern landed on the vane and threw it out of alignment. I shooed him off by yelling and shining the flashlight at him.

0700 An apple and can of pears and a beautiful sunrise for breakfast.

1300 I'm waiting for a squall that is just a few hundred yards off the beam. It is dark and raining very hard over there. Hope it stays there — I have slicker and sou'wester hat on in case it doesn't.

1400 Here it is! Lots of wind and rain. Yuck!

3/30 0845 Sunny morning. Good to dry out after last night's many squalls. Sheets and towels out to dry in the sun. Busy day working out two moon shots and two suns. Made a tape to send home — much easier than writing a letter. Have been reading about Samoa. Thinking about sailing there after Rarotonga instead of to Fiji.

2020 Huge black ugly squall coming, so I took down the pole and jib and sat and waited for it. Turned out to just be a little sprinkle and slight gusts of wind.

2110 Strong wind and heavy crossed swell; very black, ominous clouds to windward. No lightning tonight — I'm sure glad for that!

3/31 0000 Just brought the DR position up to date. Only 30 miles to go to the northern Cook Island of Mauke. The pilot describes Mauke as being "low and circular, about two and a half miles in diameter with the trees reaching a height of about 150 feet." There are no anchorages and the population is about 700. It would have been nice to anchor, but I first would have to clear Customs in Rarotonga. ETA Mauke approximately 0530. There seems to be a fair current setting southward. This would go along with the NNW winds I've been having. Where are the SE Trades?

0100 Drinking black tea and trying to stay awake so I don't bump into Mauke by accident.

0510 Clouds clearing. Should see Mauke soon.

0635 Mauke sighted bearing 130°. That doesn't figure right with the DR position.

0830 Mitiero sighted bearing 310°. The current has pushed me about fifteen miles west of where I thought I was. Instead of staying to the east of the Cooks, I must go in between them now because of the current. I hope there is good visibility when I pass Atiu.

1000 Wind and seas building. Running under double reefed main. Hanked on the storm jib just in case it keeps building.

1230 The worst looking squall I've ever seen is rapidly appraoching from astern. Main down and storm trysail hoisted. Seas are very rough and still building. Barometer is nosediving.

1300 Boat balanced between storm jib and storm trysail — Joshua is steering well. Finally got below to dry off and rest.

1630 Barometer finally stopped falling. It seems that I'm experiencing some of the fringe of Hurricane Carol that is causing a lot of damage and is sinking ships around Fiji. The radio said it is heading this way.

4/1 0100 Still being battered by one squall after another. I'm very tired but happy to see that the barometer has started to rise slowly. Broad reaching at five knots under triple reefed main and storm jib.

0600 Getting low on provisions. Tried making a

crazy concoction of cold corned beef and carrots and ketchup. I could only manage a couple spoonfuls of the stuff. I was starting to feel weak as all I'd eaten in the last twenty four hours was some cheese and pears. DR position shows about fifty miles to go. RDF bearing on Rarotonga is 243°. If I can maintain at least four knots I'll be in Avatiu Harbor at 1700 tonight. It will sure be great to sleep an entire night without getting up.

1100 I am worried that I may not be able to get into Avatiu Harbor as the wind and swell is out of the NW making it a lee shore. The pilot states that when the wind is northward of east the harbor can be very dangerous.

1315 Rarotonga sighted between the squalls on the horizon. Yahoo!!

1500 No more squalls — only about thirteen miles to go! I am motoring, but am getting low on fuel.

1700 Within approximately three miles of shore. Very large swell out of the NW. I must save the little remaining fuel to get in the harbor, and there isn't enough wind to get me in before dark, so I set the storm jib and hove to for the night under storm jib and triple reefed main. With the sails set this way I'm drifting away from the island at about one knot. Went below to relax for the first time in a few days and came on deck to see the sun setting behind what looks like one of the most beautiful islands I've seen. It is very jagged and green and looks inviting, especially after four days of squalls. I just hope I can get in the harbor.

4/2 0530 Replaced the storm jib with the number one jib, shook one reef out of the main, and headed for Rarotonga. I am picking up the island's one radio station very clearly and find the mixture of New Zealand and Maori songs really interesting. A little plane just circled overhead, then headed off toward Aitutaki.

0845 Swells still large, but wind has almost died completely. Motoring slowly toward Avatiu Harbor. I can see the wreck of the 98 foot schooner *Yankee* and the fuel storage tanks that the pilot mentions.

0910 **0910** Alongside the tiny opening in the reef that makes up the entrance to Avatiu Harbor. Inside the harbor I can see the *Chamaru* tied up alongside the seawall. A man in a canoe waves to me as he paddles by on his way out fishing. I decide to give it a try and turn and head in under full throttle. Just as I was surfing through the tiny gap in the reef, the engine coughed and made noises like it was going to quit. I pulled out the choke and it roared to life and suddenly I was safe inside the tiny harbor where the water was as smooth as glass. Abraham motioned me to tie up alongside *Chamaru* and started putting out fenders. In a minute I was safety rafted alongside and was cleared by the very friendly Customs men who were already aboard *Chamaru*.

Avatiu Harbor, Rarotonga

Rarotongan boy

Chapter 12

Beautiful Raro

Soon after I was cleared by Customs, I met Father George. He is a very friendly Dutch Catholic priest who has been living on Raro for many years, and yachts are his hobby. He insists that every skipper write a couple of pages in his notebook. He has been collecting stories and photos of visiting yachts for twelve years and has nearly filled his second notebook. Some interesting yachts entered in his notebooks are *Whisper,* the first small sailboat to circumnavigate the Pacific; the *Dove,* Robin Graham's second boat that he sold in Los Angeles on completion of his world circumnavigation; and Irving Johnson's *Yankee* on its first visit to Raro. On its second trip to the South Pacific, under new owners, she was lost on the reef near Avarua Harbor on Raro. *Yankee* has since been pushed up by the waves until she now is in very shallow water, and her masts have fallen off.

After reading Father George's books, I walked into town with Charles and Mary Sturkey off the *Chamaru.*

This was the first time I'd seen cars driving on the left, an indication of the New Zealand influence. I found food prices to be about one third less than in French Polynesia and the selection of food (mostly imported from New Zealand) was excellent. The first night in Rarotonga, Charles and Mary and Abraham and I were invited to the "island night" at the old hotel in the middle of downtown Avarua. For just over two dollars we had a fantastic dinner of marinated raw fish, breadfruit, lobster salad, baked fish, rice, and arrowroot and banana pudding. It was a buffet, so Abraham and I went back for seconds and thirds.

After dinner, a dancing team from the other side of the island performed. This team had won first place in Tahiti the previous year in the team competition. Their dances were much faster and more suggestive than the Tahitian dances I saw on Moorea. After they had performed three dances, they got everyone out of the audience that they could and had a dance contest. The winner got a big bottle of wine. After the dance contest, all the visitors to the island were interviewed by the host. We later found out that the entire evening was broadcast to all the Cook Islands on the local radio station. They wanted to know all the islands I had stopped at, was I going to visit other Cook Islands, and how did I like Raro? When the host asked Abraham where he was from, he said "the lost atoll," and the people there didn't know what to think since he was Filipino but looked like them.

The next morning, Father George came by the dock where *Mahina* and *Chamaru* were tied up and insisted that we go for a tour around the island with him in his pickup. Our first stop was the village of Titikaveka where Father George had a little house and church. The church was a simple frame structure with woven mats on the floor and hand-made wooden benches for pews. In the front of the church was a large painting of Mary and baby Jesus done by a local Maori sister. Mary looked like a Maori woman and had a flower lei around her neck. Father George then made us coffee in his tiny house and told us some stories. One was of a single-hander who had fallen asleep on a very calm night and had been awakened by local men who walked out to see if he was okay. The boat had been left high and dry on the beach by the tide!

He also told us of four yachts that weren't so fortunate and were lost on the reef in the night. There was a beautiful white sand beach in front of the church and enough room to anchor. The reef is close to the island in most places, except for Titikaveka which has one of the best lagoons for snorkeling and swimming. We made a brief stop at the village of Arorangi, then Father George proudly showed us their new jet airport, built by New Zealand.

That afternoon I met Rolff, the skipper of the only other yacht in the harbor besides *Chamaru* and *Mahina*. Rolff was a German-Australian who was involved in the Greenpeace movement that was protesting the French nuclear tests in the Tuamotos. He had sailed non-stop from New Zealand to Rapa, in the southern Tuamotos, then to Pitcairn and past the test sight island of Muraroa, and to Tahiti. His purpose was to collect samples of marine life to test for radioactive content. Rolff was much more fortunate than the crew of a New Zealand protest schooner which had just been seized by the French Navy.

That night Rolff and I went to the movie, an outdated Hollywood western which the people enjoyed immensely. It was hard to hear the words because of the racket the kids made cheering.

On Saturday, after I had biked out to Titikaveka Village and paid a visit to Father George, Rolff and I got up enough nerve to go to the dance. It was held in a large, dark hall. We paid 35 cents to get in, then went and sat down on a bench along the wall to see what was happening. There was a band on the platform with a repertoire consisting of "Proud Mary," "Country Woman," and a couple of other oldies along with some Maori songs. About halfway through the dance, Rolff and I met Tereu and Rosy, two cousins from the northern Cook Island of Rakahanga. We had heard rumors of the boldness of the girls from the northern islands, but were quite surprised to find the rumors true. After the dance, the girls insisted that we continue the evening with them. Another cousin of theirs invited us all to her house where she lived with a guy from New Zealand who was on an extended vacation. We sat around and talked for a while, drinking some horrible coconut toddy. Very vile stuff! After an hour of talking and drinking, Rolff and I were getting pretty sleepy and suggested we start heading home as it was two in the morning.

When we got to the harbor we found out that the girls had decided to spend the night with us — we had had no part in the decision. We had a bit of a space problem because that was the one night that Rolff's crew member, Susie, decided to sleep on board Rolff's boat. Since it was a Tahiti ketch, there really wasn't room to bring another lady on board, so I took out all the sails in *Mahina's* forepeak and stowed them on deck. I made the forepeak up for Tereu and me and gave Rolff and Rosy the main cabin. Raro's harbor is only a break in the reef with a tiny bay behind it. The swell comes straight through the mouth, bouncing off the seawalls causing the boats in the harbor to roll in four directions. Polynesian women are not noted for their seamanship, and Rosy was no exception. Within ten minutes she had succumbed to seasickness, all over the starboard bunk. Rosy was very upset and crying, so Rolff took her ashore in the dinghy and walked her home while I tried to clean up the mess without getting sick myself. The next morning Tereu was afraid to go ashore, for fear she might be seen and get the reputation of being a "loose" woman. She eventually borrowed a pareu (a cloth to wrap around her), climbed out the forehatch, dived into the water and swam across the harbor. I rowed ashore and met her down the road with her clothes. As we walked into town, she told everyone she met that she had been swimming. At seven o'clock Sunday morning? Well . . .

I hurried back to the boat, picked up my bike, and headed for Titikaveka. I had told Father George I would try to make it to his Sunday morning service and was glad I did. All the singing was in Maori and the people harmonized beautifully. Father George's brief sermon was also in Maori. After the service, Father George and I were invited to dinner at Robbie's house. He was a New Zealand man, now manager of the local fruit cannning plant, which was Raro's largest industry. He and his Maori wife had just gotten back from a holiday in New Zealand, and they proudly showed us snapshots of their trip. New Zealand looks like a rugged, beautiful country. We had a fantastic many-course meal served by Robbie's daughters. Afterward, we sat on the veranda overlooking the shoreline, talking and watching the tide come slowly in.

When I got back to *Mahina* that afternoon, I saw that the *Matahiva,* the Cook Islands copra schooner, was pulling up its gangplank and getting ready to leave. I quickly got in the dinghy and rowed out to where I had dropped my bow anchor and pulled it up so that it wouldn't be run over as the *Matahiva* left. When they left, they took with them the thousands of little black copra bugs that had been plaguing the inside of *Mahina* since we were tied up next to them. I had a quiet afternoon reading and writing letters as everything in town was closed.

The next morning, Monday April 7, I went to the fruit cannery and bought some fruit. I ended up with 24 quarts of orange and pineapple juice, ten cans of fruit salad, and thirty cans of crushed pineapple, all for less than eleven dollars US. Some of the cans were dented, so they couldn't sell them to the stores on the island, so they sold them to the yachts instead. I went back another day and bought 48 more cans, so that when *Mahina* left Raro, she was the closest to her waterline she had ever been. That afternoon I went to a wholesale grocery store and bought a couple months supply of soup, canned vegetables, canned butter, powdered milk, and oats.

Just before dusk a beautiful Morgan 52 foot cutter named *Silversword* sailed slowly through the pass and into the harbor. There were six people on board, all from Honolulu. Jay and his sister Kathy and four of their friends had left Honolulu a year earlier and sailed through Micronesia to Suva, Fiji. They had to rebuild their engine in Suva and spent six months waiting for parts. From Fiji they sailed to the Tonga Islands where they had a great time diving and trading for baskets and tapa. When they arrived at Niue Island, halfway between Tonga and Raro, they were placed under quarantine restrictions and had to sail three miles offshore every night because they were coming from islands infested with a fly that was causing an epidemic of Denghe fever. Jay was very happy to be in Raro where they could sleep all night.

On Tuesday morning, I went to the government dental clinic. I had a wisdom tooth that had been quite painful, and I had heard that there were good dentists in Raro. So, rather than having it pulled in Tahiti where it would have been expensive, I waited until I arrived here. The dentist was a Maori man who had been trained in

New Zealand. His equipment was castoffs from New Zealand and looked ancient, but he did a quick job and had the stitches in before I knew it. The girl at the desk sheepishly asked if $1.35 was too much to pay. I assured her that it wasn't, and left, happy to have that over with.

When I got back to *Mahina* that afternoon, I was very surprised to see Bret, my friend from the Tuamotus and Tahiti on board waiting for me. He had stopped at Raro on his way to Fiji and New Zealand and had been asked by a Customs officer as he got off the plane where he would be staying. Bret did some quick thinking and, figuring I'd probably still be here, told the officer he'd be staying on the yacht *Mahina*.

On Wednesday, April 9, I went to the hospital to try and get my Vaccination Certificate back. While the health officer was clearing me for entrance to the Cook Islands, he noticed stamps from Eritrea and Khartoum and decided that I should have a yellow fever shot again. He kept my Vaccination Certificate to make sure I would get the shot. No one knew anything about this when I got to the hospital, so after an hour of waiting and trying to find the medical officer, I pedalled five miles back down the hill to the out-patient clinic on the other side of town. After some asking around, I found a man who had my Certificate on his desk, so I asked for it back. He couldn't understand why the medical officer had taken it, and I wasn't about to explain, so he gave it to me.

That afternoon, Bret and I went with our six friends from the *Silversword* to "island night" at the old hotel. Afterwards, we went to the Banana Court, the only night club on the island, and had a lot of fun dancing.

Bret and I rented motorcycles and went exploring some of the mountain roads. It was fun, but they were so loud after our bicycles that we took them back after a couple of hours.

On Sunday, I went back to Father George's church

with half the crew of the *Silversword*. Father George was so happy that we came that he said a special prayer asking for safety for all the yachts in the Pacific. After the service we were all invited to a feast; the *Silversword* people went, but I took off and bicycled around the island. I still think that Rarotonga is the most beautiful place I've ever been. The west side of the island has rugged green peaks, the highest being Te Manga at 2,140 feet. The interior of the island gets more rain than the coast; however, most of the people prefer to live along the coast where the climate is perfect. The temperature is usually in the 80's in the daytime, and it occasionally gets down as low as 70° at night. The near constant SE Trades keep the island ventilated so that it isn't muggy at all.

The people on Rarotonga have got to be the friendliest anywhere. Everyone that I rode past smiled and said a cheery "hello." Once when I stopped at a little store in a small village for an ice cream cone, it ended up being a three hour affair. There were six men of the village relaxing and drinking beer when I came in. After she gave me the ice cream cone, the lady running the store insisted that I sit down and talk with them. The men wanted to know where I had come from, why I was sailing alone, if my "mamma" and "papa" were alive and how they were, how many brothers and sisters I had, what I thought of Rarotonga, and so on. One of the men had been trained as a pharmacist in New Zealand and had returned to Raro. Many Cook Islanders move to New Zealand where jobs pay much more, making a shrinking population in the Cooks. The men wish that their children would be content with the old ways and not leave the island, but they realize that times are changing. When I finally got ready to pedal back to *Mahina,* the men saw that the light on my bike wasn't working, and all six of them came out to lend assistance fixing it. Fantastic people. Simple and honest.

On Tuesday morning Bret left on the plane for Fiji and we made plans to meet in New Zealand. I spent the day filling tanks and stowing food. In the late afternoon I biked out to the beach at Titikaveka for the last time, sorry to leave such a beautiful island and its wonderful people after being there only two weeks. When I arrived back at the harbor, I stoppped by the *Silversword* to say "hi" and they told me they had just been given a tour of the *Toa Moana,* a New Zealand ship that was unloading food and supplies for the Cook Islands from New Zealand. I've always been fascinated with big ships, so I took the opportunity and just walked up the gangplank. I started looking around on deck, and a man named Jimmy came by and asked if I'd like to see around the ship. He took me to the pilot house and showed me the controls. He said the ship was built in Holland and powered by two German diesels. There was an intercom system on the bridge so that the captain could call any of the officers in their quarters and could talk with any part of the ship. The engine room was huge and noisy, but absolutely spotless. Next, Jimmy showed me his quarters. He had his own room with desk, bed, and a shower. It was all maple paneled and looked very comfortable.

Jimmy then asked me if I'd like to come to the galley for tea. I thought when he said tea that he meant tea to drink but I was in for quite a surprise. First he handed me a plate heaped with cold cuts of beef, chicken, and turkey. Next came a plate full of cheese, then he brought out the most fantastic salad I've ever seen. It had lots of crisp lettuce (which I hadn't had in six months), crushed pineapple, juicy slices of tomato, and big chunks of lobster. It was fantastic! After all that we finally had tea.

Jimmy said that he had immigrated to New Zealand from Northern Ireland ten years earlier. He told me that the standard of living was much higher in New Zealand than in most places in Europe. His wife and two little boys often went sailing with him in his 22 foot sloop which he kept moored on a river near Aukland. Next to football (rugby) sailing is the most popular sport in New Zealand, according to Jimmy, and everyone there either has a sailboat or is building one. He apologized for having to go on watch, but promised to come over to *Mahina* when he got a chance. I later learned that the "old man" of the *Toa Moana* was young (just over 30) and that everyone on board admired him, something which was reflected in crew morale. Sounds like an ideal job!

On Wednesday, April 16, I had lots of last minute jobs to do before setting sail for Aitutaki. I checked the post office for the last time and was overjoyed to find a cassette tape from my mom and dad and sister. I got my passport stamped for clearance to leave, and went around and said goodbye to all my new-found friends.

Toa Moana

Chapter 13

Storm and Near Shipwreck in the Cooks

4/16 1030 Leaving Avatiu Harbor on Rarotonga under power.

1130 Turned engine off, ghosting along at three knots under main and lapper. The sky looks dark and the barometer is falling.

1800 Raining lightly, heavily overcast. Thinking about whether I should head home or for New Zealand. Listening to an interesting play on Radio Australia.

4/17 0130 Good night; just enough wind to keep Joshua steering well. I'm getting lots of sleep.

0800 Some of the overcast is gone and it's actually trying to be sunny! Large swell coming in from the north.

0900 Tried to work out a sight with the boat rolling heavily. Got mad and slammed the coffeepot down on the stove, breaking the piece of metal that holds it to the wall. Pretty stupid, John! Gave up sailing — doing more rolling than anything else — and powered for one and a half hours.

1815 Hove to for the night. Should be about thirty miles off Aitutaki. Had a good sleep.

2100 Radio beacon on Aitutaki is bearing 310° and getting weaker. The wind and current seem to be pushing us slowly away from the Island.

4/18 0600 Made sail for Aitutaki.

0710 Land ho! I can just barely see the outline of the low string of islands that are long the south side of the lagoon. Engine, motorsailing into the wind so that I won't have to tack.

0910 Large squall with lots of wind and rain is completely blocking the island.

1025 Squall has passed. Small island of Maina is bearing 325°. There are also breakers bearing 340°.

1105 Island of Maina is directly abeam.

1200 Gybed and ran up east side of Aitutaki's fringe reef.

1300 Tacked by wreck that is shown on the chart and sailed past a pass, which was where I expected it to be. The reef is very low and completely submerged in places, so I have to guess where the pass is. The head Customs officer in Rarotonga gave me permission to land at Aitutaki and told me to sail back and forth in front of the pass and wait for the pilot launch to come out and lead me in.

1700 Gave up waiting for pilot launch to come out after sailing back and forth in front of the pass for four hours. I shot off a smoke flare to try and get their attention, but no one came out. I could just barely see people on the beach near the wharf, three quarters of a mile away, so I'm sure they could see the sails. The wind has shifted to NW, making this a lee shore, and that may be the reason the launch won't come out. Also, there are frequent heavy squalls, making sea conditions pretty rough. I am very tired and wet and would really like to be anchored safely inside the lagoon, but going in there without a pilot is totally out of the question. Set sail for Palmerston Atoll, 200 miles WNW.

1815 Drying out and catching up on log. Still pounding head into large seas, but wind is starting to die down. I guess *Mahina* and I are headed for Palmerston or Pago Pago. Listening to good music on Radio Australia. I'm very tired; hope to get some sleep soon. These are crazy squalls; they just keep coming over the horizon, bringing more rain and wind. The bananas given to me in Rarotonga are all starting to get ripe at the same time. For lack of a better place to stow them, I just lashed them to the lifelines on the foredeck. They have gone through a bit of a beating up there, and some are a squishy mess. At least there is no shortage of fresh fruit.

4/19 0000 Sea still rough. I can see a few stars between the squalls.

0325 Hove to and got a good long nap.

0630 Looks like a huge squall is going to hit us. Swells are huge and barometer is nosediving. Main down, under working jib alone.

0930 Very rainy and grey. Still under jib alone — rolling quite a bit in the rough, uneven seas. Talked to myself on tape recorder. Hey! Distance between Palmerston and Pago Pago is only 500 miles. Not bad at all.

1630 Wind very strong and increasing. Doing five and a half knots on a reach into large, crossed seas.

1700 Motion becoming too severe; all sail down and lying a-hull under bare poles. It is a relief to be able to relax. I have lashed the helm down so that *Mahina* is taking the breaking crests on the stern quarter where they can't do much damage. Twice, boarding seas have filled the cockpit up to the lazarette hatches. Sure glad *Mahina* has a small cockpit. Things are starting to get very wet and stale below. I've been through one squall after another for the last three days and have had to keep all hatches and vents closed tight because of the heavy sea conditions. My books are starting to get moldy and the sheets that I've been sleeping on are salty and never get dried out. Since I got mad and broke my Sea Swing stove I had no way to cook as it is much too rough for my two-burner non-gimballed Optimus. I had been eating cans of soup and vegetables cold, and once I fixed tuna salad with mayonnaise and vegetables. Not appetizing at all, but I must keep going through the motions of eating so I don't get weak.

2030 I was asleep on the lee bunk and awakened suddenly as *Mahina* was literally picked up and thrown down on her beam. I was bombarded with binoculars, a flare gun, and all the tools out of my tool box when this happened. These things had been in the shelf on top of the opposite settee, and the force sent them hurtling down on me. I immediately opened the hatch and went on deck to check for damage. Finding nothing apparently wrong, I crawled back inside and went to sleep, unaware of the damage done by the huge sea.

4/20 0700 Hoisted storm jib and came back to the cockpit to unlash the tiller, only to find that the rudder was stuck over hard on one side. No amount of pressure on the tiller would move the rudder, and I was afraid to push too hard as the bronze tiller head fitting has been developing a crack. I decided that the only way to find out what was wrong was to dive down with a mask on and take a look. Dropped the storm jib, dropped 100 feet of floating half inch line overboard, and jumped in for a look. This was very dangerous to do as the seas were still large and, without sail up, *Mahina* was rolling quite heavily. It would have been all over for me if I timed it wrong and *Mahina* had come down on top of my head while I was underwater. However, the water felt warm and good. I immediately saw that the rudder was jammed much farther to port than it is supposed to be, and was split from the top, halfway to the bottom. I climbed back aboard, and all at once the seriousness of my situation hit me.

It would be about 650 miles downwind to Pago Pago, or about 65 miles to windward, pounding into these huge seas to get back to Aitutaki. I was sure that I would be able to repair the rudder or build a new one in Pago Pago, but I had no idea if there would be materials and equipment available to make the repair in Aitutaki, or, for that matter, if I'd be able to get in through the reef if I did make it back there. I decided to give Aitutaki a try.

0915 Hoisted storm jib and started pounding toward Aitutaki. I am dragging 100 feet of half inch line off the leeward stern cleat to keep *Mahina* from heading up into the wind. Tried to set Joshua, but his main rudder has become very stiff, a result of some new grease I put in him hardening up.

1300 Raining hard and seas still very rough. Hard to keep heading high as large rolling breakers are throwing the bow off.

1830 Aitutaki radio beacon strong and bearing 105°. Only thirty miles to go. I am getting very tired since I've been out in the wet cockpit for the past eleven and a half hours.

2200 Storm jib down, lying a-hull under bare poles. I hate to take sail down because I know the wind and current will start pushing *Mahina* away from the island, but I am exhausted and must get dried out and eat something and get some sleep.

4/21 0400 Wind and sea conditions still above Force 7.

0730 Radio beacon on Aitutaki bearing 135° and stronger. Hoisted storm jib and started the pounding routine again.

1450 Land sighted through the squalls on the horizon.

1600 Land closer and bearing 115°. Yahoo!

2200 Very tired, but don't want to take the jib down and lay a-hull now that the island is close, because I'd hate to have to spend another day out here if the current pushed us away again. Getting short naps while *Mahina* steers herself.

4/22 0045 Lights sighted bearing 160°. I thought these were the lights of the *Toa Moana* which could still have been anchored off Aitutaki, unloading food and supplies, but later I found out that they were lights on the wharf.

0300 Started engine to charge batteries and to see if it was still working. After running for a couple of minutes, it died. I disconnected the fuel line at the carburetor, and saw that there was no gas coming through the line, so I disconnected the other end at the tank, blew the dirt out of it, cleaned the sediment bowl on the tank, and took the carburetor apart and cleaned it. By the time I got everything back together, two hours had passed. It is very difficult to work in the small engine compartment with the boat being tossed around by the large seas.

0700 Engine started. Motorsailing toward the pass at four knots. Engine running good.

0730 Arrived off pass. Went fairly close to a small outboard fishing boat and asked the men on board to send the pilot launch out to tow me in when they went in. They seemed not to understand, and took off at full speed through the pass and toward the village, waving for me to follow them. At this point I really wanted to get the boat inside the lagoon, so I went through the gap in the reef and tried to follow them.

The channel was very narrow, about fifty feet wide, and the current coming out looked like rapids on a river. As soon as I was in the pass, the current caught *Mahina* and started her veering from one side of the pass to the other, completely out of control. I decided quickly it would be impossible to get in without a tow, and tried to turn the boat around, using the rudder on the vane. Suddenly, *Mahina* was caught in a violent eddy near the reef, and it looked like she would ram the reef and surely sink. I threw the engine in full speed astern, and, just before the bow would have hit the reef, the engine dug in and held us off. I let the boat drift out of the pass, and when we were just clear of the reef, I dropped the bow anchor quickly. I had been very reluctant to anchor, as it is 85 feet deep right up to the reef, and the depth indicator was showing that there were coral heads up to fifteen feet tall on the bottom. I let out all the bow anchor chain that I had — seventy feet — and let as much anchor line out as I dared. I was afraid that the line would become wrapped around one of the giant coral heads on the bottom and chafe and break. As soon as the anchor was cleated off, I raised an orange distress flag and shot off a 25mm parachute flare, hoping someone on shore, three quarters of a mile away, would see it and send the launch out. I continued to send flares up every half hour for two hours. During this time the wind had increased so much that it blew my orange distress flag to pieces, so I stood on the bow waving my red windbreaker. I also took my Emergency Locator Beacon out of the liferaft pack and turned it on, hoping that the airport on Aitutaki might be monitoring that frequency since that was the day of the weekly flight from Raro to Tahiti.

After two hours of flares and distress signals with no results, I decided that the only way I was going to get a boat to tow me in was to go in myself and ask them to come out.

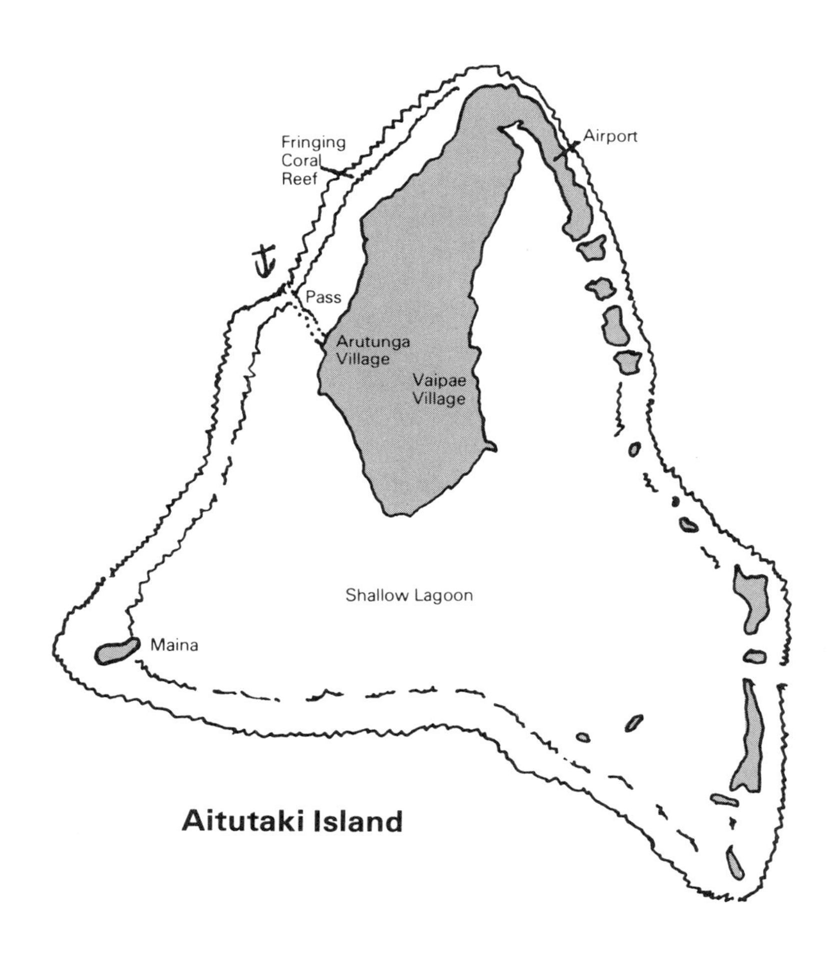

Not for navigational use

Chapter 14

Aitutaki Interlude

I had been told in Raro that the current in the pass at Aitutaki flowed out at three to five knots continuously, so I wasn't sure if it would be possible to row in or not. I pumped up the Avon, put in an extra set of oars, a life jacket, and flares and put on my thick wool Navy pants and boots in case I had to pull the dinghy over coral. I put my flute, camera, passport, and a box of special slides in a plastic bag, leaving *Mahina* for what I expected to be the last time. As soon as I untied the dinghy, the current started pushing me out to sea. By rowing very hard, I was able to make it to the reef, about fifty yards away. I stayed as close as I dared to where the waves were breaking onto the reef and worked my way slowly to the pass. I remembered a little suggestion I had read in the Pilot concerning the passes in the Tuamotus which had helped me in getting into Rangiroa. As soon as I was in the pass, I stayed as close to the coral on the side as I could, even scraping along the bottom in places. This way I got a little back current that made it possible to row the three quarters of a mile to the shore. Half way to the shore I tried to cross the channel to get to the other side where it looked like it would be easier rowing. In the middle of the channel, the current caught the dinghy and sent it spinning back toward the entrance as I desperately tried to get across. I finally made it over and got into calmer water where I was able to row the rest of the way.

When I got to shore, some little boys helped me pull the dinghy up on the beach and I ran toward the nearest building which was the post office. I found the most important looking man and told him the situation I was in and requested assistance towing *Mahina* in. Mr. Jake was not a man to be hurried. He explained to me that before they could send the launch out, they would have to find the Resident Agent and ask his permission. It turned out that the Resident Agent was up on the mountain checking out the island's only well, and it was a full two hours before Mr. Jake came back to the harbor with the launch pilot. They tried to start the launch, an interesting 35 foot steel tug with a big shiny new diesel, but found it had a dead battery. After some discussion, they decided they would try and borrow a battery somewhere on the island and drove off in search. All this time *Mahina* was anchored on the edge of the reef with strong winds trying to blow her out to sea. I fully expected to see her disappear over the horizon at any moment. Finally, after two and half hours, Mr. Jake and his men got the boat running and we headed out to where *Mahina* was anchored.

The ride through the three quarter mile long channel was very fast; the five knot current was behind us, and the launch pilot had the throttle wide open. We shot through the tiny break in the reef and were suddenly in open water. With some difficulty, because of the strong winds and heavy seas, the launch came along side *Mahina,* and I jumped over. There was a heavy thud as boats collided, and two men off the launch came aboard *Mahina* to help handle lines. They started to pull up the anchor while I warmed up the engine to help us get through the pass. When the anchor line became taut, they cleated it off on the bow and I put the engine in forward and tried to break the anchor out. Pull as we could, we couldn't budge the anchor, so the launch came along side and motioned for us to hand the anchor line to them. They fastened it to their tow cleat and ended up using all eighty horsepower of the tug to break it out. It took three men to haul the anchor and chain up once it was free, as the anchor was a 25 pound CQR with 70 feet of 3/8 inch chain down 85 feet. After they had the anchor aboard, they came by close again, and we passed them a 5/8 inch nylon tow line. With that fastened to the bow, we took off.

Just as we got into the pass, a large swell from astern picked up *Mahina* and sent her surfing toward the launch which was in the trough ahead of us. Just before we would have rammed them at seven knots, the skipper opened the throttle and the launch shot ahead, causing a violent SNAP as the line became taut. Once we were inside the channel, it was much easier going; however, I could see sharp, jagged coral heads on each side of the boat as we threaded our way through the narrow channel toward the wharf.

A causeway was built by New Zealand workmen between the island of Aitutaki and its surrounding atoll during World War II for the U.S. forces stationed there. Aitutaki was one of the stopovers for Allied planes flying between Tahiti and New Zealand. Now, however, all that remains of the causeway is a sand and crushed coral portion less than a quarter mile long which, protruding out into the lagoon is used as a dock. When we got to the end of this wharf, the launch let the tow line off, and I dropped a stern anchor over and threw a line ashore where a man tied it around a rock. As soon as all the lines were secure, I went inside *Mahina* and collapsed. Six days of continuous storms and squalls had totally exhausted me physically and mentally.

Soon a group of little boys gathered around the bow and wanted to come aboard. I pulled the boat forward toward the shore and they eagerly scrambled aboard and all came below to see what *Mahina* was like inside. I gave them the last of my raisins, which they called grapes and ate like candy. I asked them to show me where I could take a shower, and all ten boys escorted me to the town's water tank. The only water faucet was under the tank and was too low to use as a shower, so one of the boys ran to his house and got me a plastic bucket. They all watched intently as I shampooed my hair and scrubbed down. After going back to *Mahina* and changing to clean shorts and shirt, I set out to explore the main village of Arutunga where I was anchored. At Donald's, one of a chain of stores established across Polynesia in the early 1920's, I met Papa John. He was an enormous white haired man, the son of a German trader who was one of the first white men to settle in the Cook Islands. His father had married an island girl and had been the storekeeper at the Donald's store on the island of Mangaia (pronounced Mung-eye-uh) for many years.

Farther down the road I saw a house with a little shack close by that had "ZK 1 CL" painted on the side and a giant beam antenna on a tower in the yard. I knocked on the door and asked the woman who answered if there was someone who was a radio operator there. She said that her husband was and that he would be back from work soon and asked if I would come back at around 7:00 PM. I had met some Maori men in Raro who were ham radio operators, and my thought was to try and contact them and pass the word to Charles on the *Chamaru* in Pago Pago that I had run into trouble and wouldn't be in Pago as soon as we had planned to meet.

I walked back to the house with the big antenna at seven and met Kurt. He was a Dutch carpenter who had immigrated to New Zealand fourteen years earlier. He was very friendly and offered to do anything he could to help me get *Mahina* back together again. We were able to contact Charles, who was anchored in the lagoon at Suwarrow Atoll, about 600 miles WNW of Aitutaki. Kurt told Charles that I had been delayed and was attempting to make repairs, and I would meet them in Pago Pago later than we had originally planned. We also were able to contact Sue and Eleanor, friends of mine on a thirty foot sloop who were in Raro. They relayed information of *Mahina's* condition to my parents in Seattle via a ham operator there.

After we had finished sending messages, Kurt and I spent a very enjoyable three hours talking and getting to know each other. Kurt told me that he had met his beautiful wife Manuae, who was from Aitutaki, in Auckland, New Zealand. Manuae was working as a dietitian in an Auckland hospital when Kurt met her. They lived for nine years in a nice house in suburban Auckland before Kurt got the bug to move on again. Then they moved to Aitutaki where he had just finished building their very comfortable, small house on the beach. They had a beautiful four-year-old daughter named Eleesha who was soon going to start school. Kurt, like so many people I met, eagerly asked what life was like in America. He wanted to know how much he'd be making for carpentry, what it would cost to rent a house, and what the people were like. He had somehow gotten the idea that there was smog and too many cars everywhere in America, and I explained to him that it is just in the major cities where things are crowded and un-

Nana's girlfriend

Can we come aboard?

pleasant. He said that they hope to stop in Los Angeles and go to Disneyland on their way back to Holland to visit his mother. On many islands I found that Disneyland was one of the best known features of America.

Kurt understood how worn out I was and was a very understanding friend. It was 10:30 PM by the time I started back toward *Mahina.* Everyone had gone to bed and the village appeared deserted.

The next morning, Wednesday, April 23, I enlisted the help of two little boys and, with great difficulty, removed the rudder. The bolts that held the tiller on were rusted and took a lot of Liquid Wrench and patience to work loose. After the tiller and rudder head fittings were removed, I put the proper tools to remove the rudder in the dinghy and put on my mask, fins, and scuba tank. I tried to secure a line to the rudder so that it wouldn't sink when I loosened it, but there wasn't any place to fasten a line to. With visibility of only about one foot, and a strong three knot current, it was very difficult to remove the bolts holding the bottom of the rudder in. I was also nervous about sharks as the boys told me that less than a year ago sharks had eaten a man who was fishing in the lagoon not more than twenty yards from where we were. When I finally got the last bolt out, the rudder dropped down three feet and stayed there. Once it was free, its weight — about 85 pounds — started taking me to the bottom, and the current carried me away from the boat. With much effort, I finally made it back to the Avon which was tied alongside *Mahina,* and the two little boys who were in the dinghy helped pull the rudder aboard. I was exhausted and shaking from the cold, so it really felt good to be up in the warm sunlight again.

From the dinghy, we lifted the rudder ashore with the help of a crowd of little boys who had gathered to watch, and set it down on a large, flat rock. The damage was obvious, but how to repair it was not. There were two mild steel rods that had been welded to the stainless steel shaft. These rods went into the center of the rudder and kept the shaft from turning. The problem was that the rods should have been stainless, like the shaft; this would have made for a much stronger weld. When the welds broke, the shaft turned inside the rudder, causing it to split partly open. I tried to split the rudder the rest of the way open using long screwdrivers and a tire iron borrowed from Public Works, but I found that I couldn't because the center of the rudder was filled with a mixture of resin and sand that had bonded perfectly to the inside of the fibreglass rudder shell.

That morning, I cabled to find out about getting a new rudder and shaft sent from Sweden. When I got the answer a week later, I found that a new rudder would cost about $120 and shipping from Sweden to Papeete, Tahiti by air would be about $500. I would still be faced with getting it from Papeete to Aitutaki. Cost made that alternative out of the question.

At noon, the pastor of the Mormon church came by and asked if he could help. He looked at the rudder for a while, then grabbed the stainless steel shaft as I held the rudder and slowly twisted it out. Once it was out, I could see the broken welds, and I got a better idea of how to fix it. I spent the rest of the afternoon at Public Works trying to find out if they had any welding equipment and knew of any welders who could weld stainless steel. I eventually found out that there was one man there who thought he could fix it, but he told me that he had been out of oxygen for their gas-welder for four months and wasn't sure if there would be more coming on the next ship. He suggested that I go out to the airport and see if they could fix it.

The next morning I bicycled to the airport which was five miles away and on the opposite side of the island. The men at the repair shop there were very helpful, but told me the same story Public Works had about being out of oxygen for their gas-welder. After a short conference in Maori between the supervisor and the chief mechanic, they told me that they would try and weld the rudder shaft using their electric arc-welder. They said that they would send the dump truck by early Monday morning to pick it up.

When I got back to *Mahina,* I met Bruce and Jenny who had stopped by on their motorbike to look at the boat. Bruce was a young doctor from New Zealand who had chosen to do his internship with the small clinics in the Cook Islands, instead of in the big hospital in Auckland. His pretty wife, Jenny, was a high school teacher in New Zealand. She was helping out teaching in the schools on the islands that Bruce went to. They were both very warm and friendly, and they came back later for dinner. Bruce told me that he crewed on a schooner quite often in Auckland. Jenny said that she didn't like to go sailing on it because she was often the only woman on board and the boat always reeked of whiskey and pipe smoke.

After a dinner of soup and sandwiches (the bread was hot and just from the baker — delicious!) we went to the movies together. An outdated Hollywood western was showing; and by the racket the kids made, you could tell they loved it. The movie was shown in an old village hall crammed full of backless wooden benches. The walk back to *Mahina* through the village in the bright moonlight was beautiful; a gentle tradewind breeze which was filled with tropical fragrances was rippling the surface of the lagoon.

The next morning was New Zealand Memorial Day, and there was a small parade and church services all morning in honor of the soldiers who fought in World War I and World War II. I spent the morning aboard *Mahina* reading some books and magazines I had borrowed from Kurt and catching up on my letter writing. That noon, Bruce and Jenny invited me over to the house that they were staying in, and Jenny fixed lunch. They didn't have much, just some melons and cold chicken that had been given them by the islanders, but we had a good time.

After lunch I decided that I wouuld try and see if I could bicycle around the island. After I passed the airport, I took a wrong turn and ended up in a maze of trails that didn't go anywhere, so I backtracked to the long, rugged beach on the windward side of the island, near the airport, and watched the sun turn the sky a million shades of pink and red as it set over the horizon. Later, there was a bright, tropical moon out to help me find my way back to the village where *Mahina* was anchored.

The next morning I tried going down a different road, and discovered it was the road that went around the island. I stopped at the village of Tautu on the other side and bought a can of cold orange juice. There was a group of men sitting on the stone fence in front of the church, and one of them asked me if I had come on a yacht. I stopped and talked with them for a while, and they told me about their island.

Once, many, many years ago a tiny village on the island was attacked by enemies, and all the villagers were killed and devoured by their captors. All, that is, except for one man who had been out fishing in his canoe in the lagoon. That man returned to his village and soon married a girl from the attacking village. After a few years, he gathered his family and friends together and plotted a tasty revenge. Before that came to pass, however, the London Missionary Society arrived in force to teach the islanders the ways of civlization, putting an end to the fisherman's plans.

The effect of the LMS, with its strict "blue laws," is still felt on Aitutaki. A hundred years ago, when the LMS first arrived, men and women had no sense of shame in being seen about the island together. They soon learned that this sort of behavior was unseemly and took to walking only in groups or alone. You can still feel the LMS's presence everywhere on the island today.

That night, I got up enough courage to go to the local dance. I had gotten the impression that I should be pretty careful with my social life on Aitutaki. A few nights earlier, an older man came by and asked if there were any girls aboard *Mahina*. His visit made me decide to be cautious about spending time alone with any of the island girls. I sat with some friends I had met earlier, and everyone waited to start dancing until the last hour of the dance; but I still danced with quite a few pretty girls before the night was over.

The next day was Sunday, and, aside from the many church services that morning, the island was dead quiet. In mid-afternoon I was awakened from a nap by two ladies knocking on the bow. They came aboard and told me that they were out looking for whiskey. One of the ladies showed me an empty bottle in her purse, and they told me that they had been looking all around at their relatives' houses and hadn't found any. She said that many people on Aitutaki make a sort of "bush whiskey" out of coconut toddy and some other mysterious ingredients. Even though the three churches preach strongly against it, on a Sunday afternoon stroll through Arutunga village one could see some pretty laid back islanders. One of the women who visited me was the wife of a retired American colonel who lived on the island, yet she and her friend were laughing and giggling like a couple of schoolgirls. Her friend, who looked about 45 and was toothless, gave me a last minute bit of advice before they left on their quest for whiskey. She said, "Don't trust the girls here. Just fucky-fucky them and throw them off, otherwise they steal from you." With that, they roared off on their overloaded Honda 50 motorbike.

The next morning, before seven o'clock, the dump truck from the airport came by and picked up *Mahina's* rudder. They said that they would fix it themselves; but, since I wasn't too excited about that idea, I rode out to the airport on my bike as fast as I could. I didn't have to worry about anything being done in a hurry at the airport shop. The workmen went through a slow-motion routine of opening drinking nuts and scraping the custard-like insides out to eat for breakfast before starting work. I set about cutting out chunks of fibreglass on the leading edge of the rudder so we would be able to weld the rods back to the shaft. After scrouging around through the junkpile, I came up with a four by six inch scrap of 3/16 inch steel and cut a slot for it in the front of the rudder. I figured that if we welded it in place on the shaft, even if both of the rods broke again, the plate would prevent the shaft from turning and keep the rudder functional. After we shoved the shaft back inside the rudder and lined everything up, the chief mechanic welded the three pieces of metal to the shaft very carefully. By the look of awe on the other mechanics' faces, it was obvious that welding was something that just didn't happen every day. After the metal cooled, I put putty on the cut-out fibreglass pieces and put them back in place over the welds. Then came the first of many layers of fiberglass resin and cloth. The directions on the resin which I had picked up by chance in Tahiti called for a full twelve hours drying time in between coats. I came back that afternoon and tried to sand down the first coat in preparation for the next, but it wasn't hard enough and just gummed up the sandpaper, so I left it for the night.

That evening, the *Lorena,* a sistership of *Toa Moana,* anchored off the pass. The men in the storage sheds near the wharf had quite an assembly line worked out to pack the many boxes of bananas that were to be shipped to New Zealand on the *Lorena.* Two men made the wood crates and one man painted "Aitutaki Bananas" with a stencil on the finished boxes. Eight men were washing bananas in fifteen foot long metal tubs. At the end of each of the tubs were piles of empty crates, with four people packing bananas into them. From there, the banana crates were carried to a cart that wheeled them the short distance to the small barge tied up in the harbor. It was quite a busy operation. Early the next morning the unloading of supplies from the *Lorena* and the loading of bananas started. I hung around the warehouse for a while, hoping to get a ride out to the *Lorena* on the tug. I finally did, taking my cracked bronze tiller head fitting with me, hoping someone on the ship would be able to repair it.

Once I was aboard, I met Denis, the second officer, who had been told by yachting friends of mine in Raro that *Mahina* was anchored at Aitutaki with a broken rudder. He offered the use of the machine shop on board and I showed him the cracked tiller head fitting. He thought that they would be able to fix it, and he went to wake up the captain, who, according to Denis, was the best welder on board. While the captain was brazing up the crack, Denis and I went to his quarters and talked about New Zealand and the Pacific Islands.

After we had talked a while, Denis took me down to the machine shop in the engine room. The captain had just finished making the repair. He had riveted a small piece of bronze over the crack and then brazed around it. Denis gave me the last can of fibreglass resin from the ship's supply room. I was almost out of resin and didn't know where I'd get more as none of the stores on the island had heard of fibreglass. I watched as the *Lorena*'s cranes finished loading the small, flat barges that the tug had brought out through the channel. As soon as the next one was loaded, the tug came alongside and I scrambled down a swinging rope ladder and jumped onto the tug as they picked up the tow line for the barge. As soon as I got back to shore, I biked out to the airport and went to work on the rudder.

I was really in luck as the airport shop had just received a powerful 6,500 rpm commercial grinder. It made smoothing the rudder down in between layers of fibreglass cloth much faster and easier than doing it by hand. The next morning I went through the grinding routine again and put the fourth and final layer of fibreglass cloth around the edges of the rudder. I was very glad to be done with the fibreglassing because it is a very messy job, and I had to shower after each time I worked with it to get the tiny, itchy particles out of my skin. The Mormon preacher had said I was welcome to use the shower in ther garden shed, so I pedaled to the church and showered each afternoon so I wouldn't bring the glass particles aboard *Mahina.*

One evening the Mormon missionary asked me to have tea (dinner) with him and his wife. All they had was breadfruit and some canned corned beef since he hadn't caught any fish that day, but it was nice to be with them. He said that he and his wife hoped to make a trip back to the Temple in Salt Lake City that fall, and on the way they hoped to stop at Disneyland. His wife sounded much more excited to see Disneyland than the Temple. That night "The Hospital" with George C. Scott was playing at the movies. I don't think the people there understood it at all, because most of them walked out before it was over. Westerns were much more popular on Aitutaki.

The next morning I went out to the airport, sanded the rudder down for the last time, and painted it with a coat of anti-fouling paint. I spent the afternoon waxing the cabin top and oiling the teak. A beautiful girl named Nana came by and watched and talked to me as I was getting *Mahina* ready to go to sea again. She told me that her father had gone to New Zealand and got a good job and asked her mother and her to come and join him there, but they decided they would rather stay and live on Aitutaki. That evening I took her to the dance and we had a lot of fun.

After the dance, I said good-night to Nana and went home to *Mahina* and went to bed. Just as I was falling asleep, I heard a knock at the bow and stuck my head out the hatch to see Nana and three of her girlfriends. They had gone home and put their brothers and sisters to bed, changed into their nighties, and come to *Mahina* for a visit. I made tea and put on the only tape I had of Maori music, and we sat around talking. The girls wanted to know about my family and all about my sister who was soon to be married. At about one in the morning I said that I was tired and would like to go back to sleep; so, after many goodbyes, the girls started heading toward shore. I asked Nana if she would like to stay for the night, and she shyly said "yes." We sat in the cockpit for a while watching the moon set across the lagoon before going to bed.

The next morning Nana and I talked about her sailing on the *Mahina*, but she decided that that was out of the question as she even got seasick in her brother's canoe in the lagoon. I told Nana that I was seriously thinking of selling *Mahina* when I got to Samoa, and I had already been approached by a pilot from Western Samoa who was interested in buying *Mahina* as soon as I arrived there. I also told her that if I sold the boat I was thinking of coming back to live on Aitutaki and be with her.

A young man named Roy came by for breakfast. Roy was from Palmerston Island, my next planned stop, and he had earlier told me he would help with putting the rudder back on *Mahina*. After breakfast we put the rudder in the Avon, and I put my tank and mask and fins on and got in the water. With great difficulty we maneuvered the rudder shaft into its opening and moved the rudder back and forth until it was all the way up. Trying to hold the clamp in place was quite a juggling act, but I finally got it all back together. I was very glad to have the scuba tank; it would not have been possible to remove the rudder and put it back on without the tank. After I was all done putting it back in, I checked and found that there was only about five minutes of air left in the tank. When I had put all the tools away, I went up to the Post Office and sent a cable home saying that the rudder was all fixed and not to try and ship a new one from Sweden.

That evening Kurt and Manuae and their daughter Eleesha came by for custard and tea. We had a nice time talking in the cockpit together.

I spent the next day filling water and fuel tanks and tuning the engine. The water came from Papa John's big cement rain water storage tank behind his store. The store was about a half mile from *Mahina,* and to carry the forty gallons of water and fifteen gallons of fuel, I lashed two jerry cans together and hung them across the seat of my folding bike and pushed them down to the boat. Much easier than carrying. I found that, with new spark plugs and a little tinkering with the carburetor, *Mahina*'s engine was running better than it ever had.

That afternoon I biked out to the beautiful beach by the airport and watched the sun set there for the last time. It was very sad knowing that I'd be leaving Nana and the other good friends I'd made during the two weeks I'd spent on Aitutaki; but I had, and still have, a strong feeling that I'll be back there before too long.

The next morning I did a million last minute jobs, like getting my passport stamped to leave, folding up the Avon, and going around to say goodbye to my friends.

The hardest and saddest thing to do was to say goodbye to Nana. I told her that I might be back and . . .

I was very anxious about going out through the pass; but I had timed the high tide right, so there was at least a foot clearance under the keel in the unmarked channel, although the channel was hard to see. The *Matahiva* from Raro was anchored off the reef unloading food and supplies. I pulled alongside and said "hi" to Bruce, the captain. He was an American yachtie that liked Raro so much that he had pulled his boat out of the water two years earlier and left it out while he worked as the captain of the Cook Islands' only inter-island schooner. He had married a beautiful girl from Puka-Puka in the Northern Cooks and seemed quite happy with his present lifestyle.

The road on Aitutaki

Chapter 15

Aitutaki-Tutuila

5/6 1130 hours log 8,286 After I said goodbye to Bruce, I hoisted sail and drifted slowly away from Aitutaki at three knots. I was not anxious to be sailing again, and much rather wished I was going to be staying and living on Aitutaki; but there just wasn't any safe place to leave the boat as hurricanes come through every year or two and really do a bit of damage.

1500 Still doing only three knots in very light air. I wish I could get moving faster so I wouldn't be able to see the island any more. I sure wish Nana had come. I have a sore back from pulling up the anchor and took two aspirin for it, even though I don't believe in taking aspirin. I found a Raiatea-to-Samoa chart that I had forgotten I had. It is large scale and I won't have to use plotting sheets. Maybe that will make the trip seem to go faster. The forecast I got from the airport just before I left said that there would be high clouds and a four to six foot swell from the south and that's exactly what it is doing now. It also said that in about three days I might run into the same convergence zone that gave me lousy weather before. I hope it weakens before I get that far.

1830 Had scrambled eggs for dinner and watched a beautiful sunset. Wind light, but there's still a heavy swell out of the south.

5/7 0100 Boat steering itself on a broad reach at four knots. I'm getting good sleep and waking up every couple of hours to check the course.

0600 Still dark. The sky is so overcast that I can't see the sunrise.

0810 Passing through small rain squalls. I can see a few patches of blue between the clouds.

1100 Finished working out a fix from two sun shots, checked the battery, tightened the bolts on the tiller, and caught up writing in the log. The rain squalls have all passed and the sky is blue and the sun is drying everything out. *Mahina* is moving well at five knots and there is a heavy swell from the NW starting to pick up.

1600 Just took another sight and got another fix. We are making good time and have only about 110 miles to go to Palmerston Island. I expect that we will have about fifteen miles of drift in the next 24 hours, so if we can keep sailing at five knots, our ETA at Palmerston will be for 1330 tomorrow. That would be great.

I have heard a lot about Palmerston and met some of the Marsters family on Raro and Aitutaki and am very anxious to see the island and how the people live. Palmerston, a small island of about five by three miles, was uninhabited until 1862 when an English seaman named William Marsters settled on it with a group of islanders and tried to set up a coconut plantation for a Tahitian businessman named Brander. Unfortunately, Mr. Brander died and his relatives didn't have enough money to pay William Marsters for his labor and the supplies he had bought for the plantation from passing ships, so they gave him ownership of the island instead of payment. Will Marsters married two women from the island of Tongareva in the Northern Cooks, and later in life married a third woman from Manihiki, also in the Northern Cooks. From the three women he had seventeen children and 54 grandchildren.

The first European to discover Palmerston was Captain James Cook. When Cook was ten days out of Raiatea in the Society Islands, on June 16, 1774, his lookout sighted tall coconut palms on the horizon. Soon they sailed along the coast trying to find a safe anchorage. Finding none, they continued on toward Niue Island, which they reached four days later. Cook named Palmerston Island after the Viscount Palmerston who was first Lord of the British Admiralty and had served for forty years in the House of Commons.

I was anxious to anchor off Palmerston, wind and sea conditions permitting, and go ashore to meet the Marsters family who I was told were very friendly and rarely had visitors. There is no pass through the reef that is deep enough for anything other than canoes and longboats, so I would have to anchor off the reef in a very exposed place. It would be safe as long as the winds remained out of the east and southeast, but would be a trap if the winds shifted around like they did when I was at Aitutaki.

5/8 0415 Wind increasing steadily. Working jib down and storm jib hanked on forestay but not hoisted. *Mahina's* main is triple reefed and we are still doing six knots. Seas are building and already twelve to fourteen feet. It looks like we are back in the same convergence zone that gave us so much nasty weather last time. I sure hope that everything holds together this time.

0700 Wind is blowing a steady 35 knots with gusts higher. Running at over six knots under storm jib alone. It is very wet and miserable outside and I'm glad that

Joshua is steering well so I can be inside where it's dry, listening to Radio Australia and reading a book about Palmerston. I had a good breakfast of hot oatmeal to start the day off.

1500 Wind still increasing. According to my DR position, we have about fifteen miles to go until we reach Palmerston, or about three hours worth at five knots. That would have us arriving at Palmerston at 1800, only an hour before sunset. That doesn't leave enough time to anchor — the light would be bad for trying to find a good place — so I've decided to go on. I considered heaving to for the night and trying to find Palmerston in the morning; but Palmerston is a low coral atoll, only five feet high at its highest point, and therefore very hard to see on the horizon. With heavy, overcast skies tomorrow, I doubt if I could find it without another sun shot. Even in good weather you can only spot atolls like Palmerston about four or five miles off. Also, anchoring off the island with the wind as strong as it is and conditions as unsettled as they are would be dangerous. I would really like to meet the Marsters family and see what life is like on such an isolated island, but it isn't worth risking the boat.

1700 I just got the weather warnings on WWV shortwave. The forecast is for high winds and a line of thunderstorms and squalls 400 miles from a line running from the Ellice Islands to the Northern Cooks. I am right in the middle of that line. I wish this convergence zone would be pushed north by the SE trades.

1930 Wind increased until *Mahina* was screaming along under storm jib at up to nine knots. This is too fast for comfort and puts too much of a strain on the mast and the boat, so I went up in the rain and wind and dropped the storm jib and lashed it to the lifelines on the foedeck. When I was almost done lashing it, an extra large sea broke completely across the foredeck, and I had to flatten myself out on the deck and hang on for dear life. At least the water is warm. It would be terrible to go through this outside of the tropics. Went inside and dried off with a towel and thought about how nice it would be to be with Nana now. I hope I can sell the boat in Samoa and come back to live with her; then I don't think I'd ever go sailing again. Maybe on a canoe in the lagoon, but that's all. Praying that things will work out. Some people don't know how much they should appreciate just being on land where you don't have to worry about whether you are going to make it to the next island or not.

2030 hours Went to bed and had a good sleep even though the boat was being tossed about by the big seas.

5/9 0630 hours Time to wake up! Storm jib hoisted. Wind has diminished a little, but is still strong enough to keep me down to just a storm jib. There is a very large crossed swell, making for a bumpy ride. I made oatmeal and forced it down — I wasn't really feeling hungry — but it is really important to keep my energy up. Vane is steering well and I think that the sun is going to break through the overcast soon. At least we are moving in the right direction toward Samoa now.

1300 Sun's finally out. Had a great bucket shower and shampoo in the cockpit and now am all squeaky clean! The sun feels so good and warm. I am anxious to get to Pago Pago to see the Sturkeys and Abraham again.

2000 Good soup for lunch. It was fish chowder from New Zealand that I bought in Raro. The swell has gone down considerably and I now have a double reefed main and No. 1 jib up.

2110 Just turned engine off after running it one and a half hours. The wind has died completely and left *Mahina* wallowing in lumpy, crossed seas. The sky is pitch black and there is lightning on all sides. It is sort of scary. I am anxious to go to bed because I'm very tired.

I've been steering most of the time since 6:30 this morning since the swells have been large and the wind light. Good night!

5/10 0700 Sails up. Wind light — doing three and a half knots under main and lapper. I just listened to the weather on WWV and there were no warnings for the South Pacific. I think that the ridge of low pressure that has been causing lousy conditions for the past couple of weeks may be breaking up, or else we may have finally got around it. I sure hope so. It would be nice not to have any more lightning and squalls with high wind and big seas for the rest of the trip to Samoa.

0900 FLASH!!! I just heard on the Samoan radio station that there has just been an earthquake in Chile registering 7.8 on the Richter scale! There is a Pacific-wide tsunami watch (tidal wave), but they don't know yet whether a tsunami has been generated. I very quickly pulled out Bowditch and found that what I suspected is true. I am in the best possible place if a tsunami occurs. The wave, perhaps as much as 100 miles wide, would be moving at more than 400 knots; but the wave height would be less than three feet, so there would be a good chance I would never notice it.

1230 Tsunami watch cancelled. Sun burning off the clouds and the wind is super-light. Powered two hours. Got a good fix from three LOP's. Position was ten miles north of DR position. I guess the large swell from the south pushed us a little off course.

1900 Joshua steering well on a broad reach in light air at about three knots. Thinking about Nana and a peaceful, beautiful life on Aitutaki.

2300 The main's gybing just woke me up from a great four hour nap. The wind has become too light for Joshua to cope with as there are still some sloppy seas. I guess I will try and stay up and steer by hand tonight. I don't want to lose time by taking everything down and going to sleep for the night.

5/11 0300 Ran the engine for two hours to charge the battery and to get us moving. I have only used one of three five-gallon gas tanks so far, so I might as well make use of the engine since it's working and the wind is so light.

0700 Beautiful sunrise and only a few light high clouds! Had the last of the bananas and the uma (custard-like meat of a young coconut) of one coconut for breakfast. Tasted pretty good! Not quite like an omelette with lots of fresh vegetables, but better than cans, for sure.

1100 For something to do (since I've finished reading all the Readers' Digests that Kurt gave me) I added up how much money I have put in *Mahina.* I keep remembering more things; now the total is nearly $16,400! I hope I can get most of that out when I sell her in Samoa. I wonder if Harry, the Polynesian Airlines pilot, will buy her. I think he would take good care of her and not just leave her rotting in Apia harbor. He mentioned sailing down to Niue and Tonga during his vacation.

1250 Just finished working out sight from two LOP's. Looks really great. Only about 220 miles to go until I should sight Tau in the Manua Island group. The Manua Islands consist of three islands: Tau, Ofu, and Olesaga. They are about eighty miles east of Tutuila and come under the government of American Samoa; however, much of their government is conducted on a local level through the chiefs and the family systems. I would like to stop and visit there, but the law requires that all ships entering the territory clear at Pago Pago on Tutuila before going to any of the outer islands. Maybe I can stop at the Manuas after I leave Pago Pago. Hope so!

The wind is light and from dead astern, with the swell

on the stern quarter, making confusing conditions for Joshua. When a wave throws *Mahina* off course, Joshua just doesn't have quite enough wind to pull her back. Wish I could go below where it's cooler and read, but I guess if I'm going to make Pago Pago soon, I'd better keep *Mahina* steering a good course. I'm sure thankful for the dodger to sit under; without it I would be very hot sitting here in the bright tropical sun.

1400 Still out in the cockpit stuck on the tiller. I just had a coconut for lunch. The juice inside was cool because I keep the nuts down in the bottom of the cockpit locker. Very refreshing. I just heard on the American Samoan radio that today is Mother's Day. Well, mom, happy Mother's Day — sorry I forgot to send you a card.

1830 Beautiful sunset and the swell is getting smaller. I just wish that there was more wind so that Joshua could steer and let me be lazy. The barometer has started rising; maybe we're in for some more good weather. I'm going to try and stay awake all night tonight again so we'll cover more miles.

5/12 0530 Squall with lots of wind and rain is descending on *Mahina.* Whisker pole down and jib dropped.

0800 Squalls have all disappeared over the horizon. Beautiful sunny morning. I wrote a letter to Dick and Ann, my best friends in Seattle, while trying to steer and keep an eye on the compass. I gybed three times before I finished the letter. I wish the wind would shift a little one way or the other. Instead of running, I've been tacking down wind, broad reaching. With the wind directly astern as it is, if I steer a course straight for Pago Pago, *Mahina* loses a knot and the sails flap and bang. I am starting to get pretty tired and tense as I've had very little sleep in the past two days, steering almost around the clock.

1400 Caught up on navigating and on writing in the log. Only 135 miles until I should be able to sight Tau, and in 235 miles *Mahina* should be inside Pago Pago harbor. Pago sounds like an interesting place; at least, by its radio station and what I've read about it, I think I'll like it there!

I feel God taking care of me. The squalls have been going around us instead of over us. I was feeling uptight, so I read a couple of chapters in **The Prophet** and opened the Bible to Psalm 37. "Trust in the Lord and do good; inherit the land and practice faithfulness. Have your delight in the Lord and He will give you the desires of your heart. Commit your way to the Lord; trust in Him too, and he will bring it about . . . Be still before the Lord and reserve yourself to Him . . . But the gentle shall inherit the land and shall delight themselves in plenty of peace." I really feel a source of strength and peace from reading this. I feel much closer to God and His creations when I am out here where there are no distractions. Sailing alone has made me appreciate people and the beauty of the earth more than I ever have before.

5/13 0010 Fantastic night. Large bright tropical moon with just a few light wisps of cloud and NO SQUALLS! Yahoo!

0700 Fiery red sunrise and oatmeal for breakfast. Only 175 miles until we will be anchored inside Pago harbor. The WWV forecast said no signigicant weather for the South Pacific. Finally, that ridge has weakened.

1400 Just finished getting fix from four LOP's. They all crossed at exactly the same point, so good job on navigating, John! The sun is out in full force, and there are no squalls in sight. *Mahina* has been averaging four knots in light air. Unfortunately, there isn't enough wind yet to make Joshua work, so I'm still stuck out here in the cockpit. I should sight the Manua Islands in only 69 miles. At this speed, that would work out to be some time before noon tomorrow.

1800 Another brilliant sunset. Wind is holding steady. Maybe I can get Joshua to steer so I can get some sleep.

2200 AHHH! Just got a great two-hour nap. Feel much better. These moonlit nights in the tropics are beautiful beyond description. There is a steady flow of phosphorescence behind *Mahina* and the spray that comes on the foredeck. It never gets very cold — sometimes I put on a shirt at night, but never more than that and shorts. The air smells so clean and fresh.

5/14 1100 LAND HO!!! West tip of Tau bearing 330° and right where it was supposed to be according to my navigation. Not a bad job at all, John! Good fresh trades from dead astern, and swells on the stern quarter — too much for Joshua to cope with — so I ended up steering from 0700 to 2000 without a single break. I could tack downwind and get Josh to steer, but I am anxious to get to Pago Pago as fast as I can since it's only 70 miles away. Had a squeaky-clean shower and shampoo and am getting the cockpit scrubbed down and ready for civilization. Manua Islands are directly abeam. The largest of the three is Tau, which is roughly six miles across and 3,000 feet at the highest point. They are all very green and lush looking. I would estimate that I am about seven miles away from Tau now.

1500 I am tired of steering and being out here in the hot sun. A whole school of tiny (four inch long) squid just flew over *Mahina,* leaving a mess behind. One missed and landed in the cockpit. He sort of oozed out a black ink-like mess where he splat-landed. Almost there. Yahoo!

1700 Wind increasing steadily. No. 1 jib up instead of lapper, and main reefed. Only 55 miles to go. At this rate we will arrive at 0300.

2000 Wind and sea conditions up to Force 5. All

sail down and lying a-hull with only 33 miles to go. Time for a nap.

5/15 0015 Tired of being tossed around so hoisted a double-reefed main and started heading for Pago.

0125 All sail down again because I don't want to get too close to a lee shore with this strong eastery wind. Less than 25 miles to go!

0220 Light sighted bearing 270°. Headed for it and it turned out to be a small (thirty foot) fishing sampan. Swells are large and still building. Fifteen to eighteen feet. A jet just flew over. It looked like it had just taken off from Tutuila and was still climbing. I could barely hear it; it looked like a toy as it disappeared behind the clouds with its little blinking lights. Rolling along at three to four knots under a deeply reefed main.

0450 Rotating aerobeacon at the airport sighted, approximately ten miles away. Hove-to under main and waiting for dawn.

0610 Sunrise, and the island of Tutuila is dead ahead, about eight miles away. There are some nasty looking squalls on the horizon behind me. Hope they don't decide to visit just when I'm trying to find my way into the harbor. Double-reefed main hoisted and *Mahina*'s doing three to four knots.

0700 Just noticed a tear in the next to the top batten pocket. I have been hoping that it wouldn't get any bigger, but each time I look it has grown a couple of inches. It's now about a foot long. I guess it'll just keep growing unless I take the sail down, so I'll drop the main and go under storm jib.

0800 Wind increasingly lighter, so rather than change the storm jib for a larger sail, I started the engine. It's running fine and we are very close. What looks to be a very rusty large fishing boat just passed by.

0830 log 9,048 Just crossed Taema Bank, a shoal area of four to eight fathoms off Pago Pago harbor entrance. I'm headed for the buoy that marks Whale Rock. After passing that to port, the Pilot says that I can turn and head for the inner harbor.

0900 I pulled alongside what looked to be the Customs House, according to the chart and Pilot; but, since there was no one around, I decided to anchor alongside the *Nightingale,* tied to a mooring buoy near shore. I knew Bob and JoAnn from Tahiti, Moorea, and Bora Bora; and Laurie, their crew member, was also a good friend of mine.

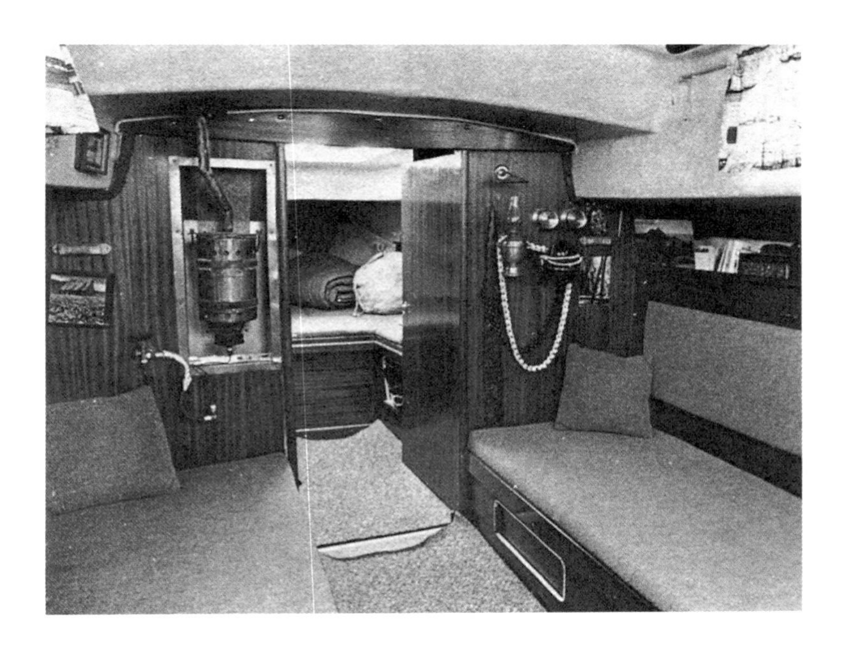

Chapter 16

Pago Pago

As soon as I had the anchor down, Bob rowed over and said hello. I noticed that he had a large, nasty scar on his back that wasn't there when I last saw him in Bora Bora, and asked what happened. He said that in a gale the jib sheet that was not in use got caught in the prop, and he dove down to cut it off. His boat had quite a crop of barnacles, and when it came down on him, they really cut him up. Fortunately, JoAnn was a nurse and was able to fix him up.

Bob told me that they had arrived only two days earlier in Pago, and he said to wait where I was for Customs. I thanked him for the information and went back to stowing sails and tidying up things below. Before long, a Land Rover with three young uniformed men pulled into the boat launching ramp, on the shore nearest *Mahina*, and motioned for me to come ashore. They very politely told me that they were Customs and Immigration officers and asked if I would move *Mahina* over to the Customs dock. I told them that since *Mahina*'s anchor and chain were already down and were heavy I'd rather not. They could not be persuaded to come out to *Mahina* in the Avon because, they said, once they were rowed out to a yacht and the dinghy tipped over, getting them all wet. So, I proceeded to pull up anchor and motored slowly to the Customs dock.

Before the officials came aboard, I put on a Maori tape that I bought in Raro, and that really relaxed things. When the men came aboard and heard the island music, they decided it was time for a siesta, since they had just eaten lunch. Instead of asking Customs questions, they asked if I was lonely traveling alone and if I have a girlfriend. I told them about Nana and showed them a picture of her. They all approved immensely, thinking it a good thing that my girlfriend was an island girl. When the man from Agriculture finally came, they all quickly filled out their little slips of paper and said goodbye. The head Customs officer thought that I should come by his office for a beer soon. I wasn't surprised at their friendly attitude, for I had learned a long time earlier that if you are friendly and open to them, officials will usually be the same.

After going back to the anchorage area, I rowed ashore and tried to cash a travelers check at the bank, since I had no US money. There was a branch of New York City Bank, but they wouldn't cash my $20.00 travelers check because I didn't bring my passport along for ID. I thought that was pretty funny since I had an account with the bank in the states. I had never had any trouble cashing travelers checks before, even in the tiniest store in the Marquesas.

On the way back to where I had left the Avon, I met George, an American yachtie who had bought a boat in Pago that had been damaged by a drop from a hoist. He was also a pilot who had flown extensively in Africa.

When I heard that, I immediately asked him if he'd ever been to Sudan, where I was born. He said yes, but told me that he and the plane had been captured at gunpoint when he landed at Khartoum for fuel. He didn't recommend sailing there until another government, tolerant to foreigners, came to power.

As it was getting toward dinner time and we were both hungry, we caught a bus down to an interesting Chinese restaurant named the Golden Dragon on the other side of the bay. No sooner had we got in and sat down than the lights went out. The waitresses acted like nothing had happened and brought out little gas lamps for the occupied tables. George said that the power generators given to Samoa by the US had not been taken care of properly, and that the power often went off a number of times in a day, ruining all the food on the island that was under refrigeration.

That night I really slept well, thankful to be anchored and not have to go out and check the course all the time, or worse, steer all night as I had been doing the last few days before I arrived here.

As soon as it was open the next morning, I went to the telephone building and tried to place a call home to my parents. After a half hour wait, the girl behind the window pointed to the second booth and said they would try my call. I was really surprised to hear my brother Dave answer the phone as last I knew he was going to school in Germany. He was equally surprised to hear me calling them. I talked with my mom later and told her about Nana and that I was thinking very strongly about selling *Mahina* and going back to Atitutaki to live. I also told her that I had already put an ad in the local paper to sell *Mahina* and had a prospective buyer lined up. Before long, fifteen minutes had gone by, and a huge bill run up, so I had to say goodbye. I told them I would call them again as soon as I decided which way I was going.

That evening, I took my friend Laurie to the Golden Dragon for dinner. I had met her in Tahiti where she lived and worked as a travel agent. We had a great dinner, and afterwards we caught a ride to the only movie theatre in Pago Pago. All that was showing there, and all that ever showed there, were Chinese kung fu movies. I wasn't too excited about going, but Laurie said she had fun going to them in Tahiti, so why didn't we try it — we could always walk out.

After paying our dollar each to get in, we sat down and waited for it to start. While I was gone to get ice cream cones, Laurie looked around and discovered that she was the only woman in the theatre. The men there were almost exclusively Korean and Chinese. Some of them, whom Laurie had met when the *Nightingale* was hauled out at the marine railway, stopped by and said hello. It was surprising to notice the difference between the Samoans and the Koreans and Chinese. The Samoans seemed a bit resentful toward Americans for pouring the money in, and were at times rude and even hostile, while the Oriental people there were always very friendly and kind. The fact that Laurie was Chinese-Hawaiian may have made a difference.

The show was about a kung fu girl who took on a small army avenging her father's death. Not a word of it was in English, and there were no subtitles; but it was interesting, and the countryside — wherever the movie was filmed — was spectacular.

We caught the bus back to town for a quarter after the movie. An entire book could be written about the busses on the island of Tutuila. Almost all of the busses are owned by families, and they are painted all kinds of bright colors. Most are trucks that have had a wooden box with benches down the sides built on the bed. All the drivers pride themselves in having a tape deck, which is usually played continuously at full volume.

The next morning was Saturday, and I decided to take Roger, an Armerican teacher, up on his offer of using his washing machine. I packed all of the clothes I had on board into a sailbag and took off bicycling toward the village of Nuuluii where Roger and his pretty wife Chris lived. The ride along the coast of Tutuila was spectacular, reminding me a lot of Highway 101 in Oregon and northern California. On one side of the road cliffs went almost straight up, and on the other side it was a short drop-off to the beach where the waves were crashing in. Chris and Roger had gone motorcycling up in the mountains and weren't home, so I put the clothes in the washer and started reading a new Time magazine. It had been nearly seven months since I had read a news magazine from the States and it was interesting but depressing. After all the clothes were out of the dryer, I packed them up and started heading back. Traffic was a little heavy, and I think that every family that owned a car that could move and gone out for a Saturday afternoon drive.

Mike and Joanie Hitchcock, teachers in the town of Leone, came over to the *Chamaru* on Sunday shortly after I did. Charles had talked with Mike by ham radio when we were all in Raro and arranged to have him collect mail for *Mahina* and *Chamaru*. Mike brought two boxes with him; one was a ham radio and the other was the antenna I had ordered from Seattle when I was in Raro. I wasn't sure if I was going to keep the boat or not, so I just left them on the *Chamaru* for Charles to play with until I decided what I was going to do.

Early the next morning I started heading toward Leone to pick up the mail that Mike and Joanie had forgotten. It only took two busses and 75 cents to go the twenty miles out of Leone. It was all the second bus could do to make it up the hills, and by the time we got to

Leone, it had a long string of cars behind it. The driver was very friendly, and said that some of the busses have regular routes picking up the same people and taking them to and from work every day. Some, like him, just cruise back and forth on the island, picking up anyone that is standing by the side of the road. It seems like a pretty simple transportation system, and it was working well.

When I got to the school it didn't take long to find Mike. He was teaching a chemistry class of high school seniors and trying to eat lunch at the same time. I spent the rest of the day there, fascinated by watching how the classes were taught. Mike really had the respect of his students, and he didn't put up with any bullshit; but the kids were enjoying the class and learning a lot at the same time. Mike's wife, Joanie, who was teaching biology in the next room, came by to say hi.

Mike told me that within a week of graduation, seventy percent of the students leave Samoa and either go into the US Army or to Hawaii or California. He said that Samoa's number one export is Samoans, and that there are more Samoans living on Hawaii and in California than on Samoa. A family of eight or ten isn't considered large, and since most of the kids send money back home to their parents when they are working in the states, it's an encouragement for the parents to have large families. Unfortunately, however, American Samoa is small and can't come near to supporting all the people, so it's a growing problem. After school was over, Mike and Joan drove me to their nice house by the airport. There I met their two daughters and their thirteen year old boy, Tim, who later became crew on the *Mahina.*

When I stopped by the post office, I met Laurie and a new-found friend of hers named Grace who was from Vancouver, B.C. and had been on a working holiday in New Zealand and Australia for the last year. She said she might be interested in sailing to Hawaii instead of flying there as she had planned. That, plus the fact that the Air New Zealand office was just above us, led me to stop in and inquire about the cost of a ticket from Aitutaki to Pago. It turned out that it would have cost over $300 for Nana to join me in Pago — I had just cabled her about doing exactly that — since she would have to fly to Fiji, then to Apia, Western Samoa, before arriving in Pago.

Abraham, Grace, Laurie, and I took the cable car on Tuesday across the harbor and to the top of Rainmaker Mountain where there was an educational television station. The view from the mountain top was fantastic. We could just barely see the smudge of Western Samoa, 45 miles away, and the view down the northern side of Tutila was one I won't soon forget. While we were captivated by view, the cable car came up with a load of Samoans going to a village on the north side. There were no roads to the village; and, since it was easier than hiking up the muddy mountain trail from Pago Pago, the villagers rode the cable car to the top of the mountain and then walked down the trail on the other side. One man was carrying a frozen tuna that was about four feet long and looked very heavy. After we got back down off the mountain, the four of us caught a bus to the Golden Dragon for dinner. After an excellent Chinese meal, Laurie proposed that the four of us plan to meet at her home in Papeete in exactly five years.

On Wednesday morning I got to work early cleaning *Mahina*. Thinking that whether I sold the boat or kept going, I'd need to clean some things out, I put clothes and books that I wasn't presently using in a box and mailed them home. After going to the post office, I went back to *Mahina* and spent the rest of the morning straightening up storage lockers. That afternoon I went shopping at Burns-Phillips, one of a chain of stores throughout the Pacific. It looked just like a big department store in the states with its rows of electric gadgets and junk.

When I got back to the dock, I found I had a visitor. Jack was the publisher of one of the local newspapers whom I had met while placing an ad for *Mahina*. He said he was interested himself in buying a sailboat and had come by for a look. After I had him aboard for a tour, he went home to talk it over with his wife; they'd tell me their decision later. Yahoo! One prospect for *Mahina* already!

That evening the Sturkeys went to a school program in which a friend's daughter was dancing. Abraham and I hitched a ride out to the theatre, and when we saw that it was still playing the same kung fu movies, we decided to go to the dance program instead. Ute's daughter, Elizabeth, was dressed in a fancy Samoan outfit complete with feathers and headdress.

After she danced, Abraham and I went up and put money in her hat for her to give to her school.

After the dance was over, Abraham and I sat outside on the porch of the hall and talked about my situation. It was then that I decided to sail *Mahina* the 6,000 miles back to Seattle, instead of selling her in Samoa. I knew that almost all of the trip would be going to windward and probably part of it would involve beating into the trades, but I still wanted to go for it. I valued Abraham's advice since he'd come to be one of my closest friends in my travels around the islands. He could see that it was a point of pride with me to finish what I had started nearly a year before.

I picked up my new ham radio and antenna early the next morning and started figuring where to install it and how to fasten it down. By noon I had made a wood base for the radio and a strap to hold it in place in the bookshelf over the starboard bunk. Charles came over and helped connect the power supply leads to the battery and tried to help figure out a sufficient ground system. The next morning, Abraham came over and gave me a hand putting the antenna together. It turned out to be about eighteen feet tall instead of the six foot height I had expected. When we finally hoisted it up and tied guy lines to the backstay, *Mahina* looked more like a yawl than a sloop with an antenna.

That afternoon, the *Folly III* came into harbor and anchored nearby. Suzanne and Eleanor were two college professors from Los Angeles in their mid-forties who had given up teaching for sailing around in their older, full-keel Cal 30 sloop. I had met them briefly in Papeete and Raiatea, and we had a real good time talking together in Raro just before I left. They were sailing for New Zealand but were doing so in a relaxed, easy manner. When I told them that Charles had just helped me install a ham rig on the *Mahina,* they were pleased that we'd now be able to keep track of each other better. The three of us went to the Golden Dragon that evening and had a great dinner. We yachties are all getting to be regular customers there.

Saturday morning I bought a 4 by 4 at the local lumber yard to use as a support post under the beam that supported *Mahina*'s mast. The original construction of the mast support on *Mahina* had proved greatly inadequate. The force of the mast had caused the beam, made of fibreglass and wood, to buckle, and this in turn caused the rigging to become increasingly looser. I hoped that jamming the 4 by 4 under the beam would transfer the load down to the keel and keep the beam from splitting completely. I also took the tiller and tiller head fitting off so I could take them in Monday morning and get a replacement fitting made out of bronze.

Through the help of George, a friend of Charles' on Whidbey Island, I was able to talk to my parents in Seattle and tell them that I had decided against selling the boat. I hoped to be back to Seattle by mid-September before the weather deteriorated in the North Pacific, and I had already started preparations to leave for Hawaii.

On Sunday, Charles and Mary and Abraham and I went out to the Hitchcocks' house in Leone for a dinner party for all the ham radio operators on the island. Mike and Joan's daughters fixed a fantastic Mexican dinner. That evening, I met Mike and Joan's friend Ron, an island grade school teacher who had just quit his job. When I told Ron that I was looking for crew to sail to Hawaii, he seemed very interested and said he would keep it in mind.

The next morning, Charles came over with some meters and finished tuning up my new radio. That afternoon I was able to get a call home through the phone patching of a ham operator in California. Now that I have my own radio working it should make passages a lot more interesting.

I busied myself making lists of provisions I'd need for the trip to Hawaii. When walking toward Burns-Phillips the next morning, Ron stopped and gave me a ride. He said that he'd like to sail on *Mahina* if the offer was still open. I told him that it certainly was still on, and we ended up going to Burns-Phillips together and buying $60 worth of provisions. I also bought a waterproof Timex quartz watch for $55 as Charles had bought one and found it kept better time than the *Chamaru*'s $600 ship's quartz chronometer. I had often worried about what I would do for navigating if my Zenith receiver ever broke down and wasn't able to give me the time on WWV, and the Timex seemed to be an accurate back-up at a reasonable price.

On our way out of the store, Ron and I ran into Mike and Joan, and we told them that Ron was sailing to Hawaii on *Mahina*. Mike thought that was great and said "Why don't you take Tim along as well? He'd really like to go." Without really thinking about it, because I didn't really think he was serious, I said "Sure. Send him over tomorrow." Well, Tim **did** come by early the next morning and swam out to where *Mahina* was anchored. He thought *Mahina*'s cabin was neat and asked what kind of things he should bring for the trip. I hesitatingly told him to bring shorts and shirts and a sheet and mask and snorkel. I wasn't really sure how it would work out having three of us in such a small space for such a long, rough passage to windward, but I decided we'd give it a try. Tim asked what kind of food he should bring, and I told him that he could supply the munchy things like nuts and potato chips since Ron and I had already bought most of the provisions. Tim really took it all seriously, and the next morning I found him standing on the dock with a case full of hundreds of packets of sunflower seeds and a case of 24 cans of Granny Goose shoestring potatoes. I explained to Tim that unless he was really crazy about sunflower seeds and shoestring potatoes he had brought enough to last for years. Then I rowed him and his mother out to *Mahina*. Joanie said she wished she could come to.

I spent that afternoon filling the water tanks and bending the mainsail back on. It had just come back from being sewn back together by a woman on shore who had a sewing machine and made a little money repairing yachties' sails. I took the tiller and fitting that needed to be replaced over to the marine railway on the other side of the harbor. It took quite a bit of chasing around, but I finally found a man who could make a new fitting. He said that he'd braze up a new fitting out of quarter inch bronze stock that would be much stronger than the original cast bronze fitting.

Then, the next day, Ron and I went back to Burns-Phillips, thinking that with one more person on board for the passage we might need some more food. We found that they were having a sale on dented cans of Chunky

Turkey soup, so we bought all they had (23 cans) at only thirty cents a can instead of the usual price of eighty cents a can. We also bought twelve one-pound cans of mackerel for just 25 cents a can. Not bad at all considering the high cost of food in Samoa. Saturday morning I changed the oil in the engine and cleaned the plugs and filled the gas tanks, getting the engine ready to go.

In the afternoon, a beautiful 62 foot yawl sailed into the harbor. I rowed over and met Steve and Linda, owners of the *Madeira,* and their crew member, Jacques, after they had cleared Customs. They had left New York a year earlier and had sailed through the Panama Canal, stopped at the Galapagos Islands, the Marquesas, and at Tahiti before sailing to New Zealand, where they had spent six months before sailing to Samoa. The *Madeira* was a custom one-off ocean racer built by Charles Morgan in Florida. Steve and Linda purchased her from the Annapolis Naval Academy which had raced her in several Trans-Atlantic races, giving her quite a record of victories. She was a very impressive boat, both on deck and below. The foredeck had a large sliding hatch that opened into a sail and sheet room that was separated from the rest of the boat by a waterproof bulkhead. All the halyards were led aft to the cockpit, and the boat was generally rigged to be sailed easily by two or three people. *Madeira* held the Galapagos - Marquesas passage record until recently when it was broken by a 104 foot schooner. Steve said that *Madeira* averaged between seven and eight knots on the trip from New Zealand to Samoa, all of which was to windward. Below, *Madeira* was finished off exquisitely in teak and maple. The owners' cabin was aft and had a double berth and desk. The entire stern bulkhead was a teak bookcase, filled three books deep with a wide variety of selections.

The Navy had taken the Loran out of the navigation station, but they had left numerous radios and electronics. Forward of the main salon was crew's quarters and the sail room. *Madeira* was the most comfortable cruising boat I had ever been on, and I can imagine that sailing her would be a dream. Four weeks after I was aboard her in Samoa, she went on the reef in front of the Tradewinds Hotel in Suva, Fiji, while trying to get to a safe anchorage during a week-long gale. Her skeg and rudder were smashed off, but *Madeira* was pulled off the reef before the hull was seriously damaged.

On Sunday, June 1st, the Sturkeys and Abraham and I were invited to the weekly Sunday afternoon picnic held by the local Filipino families. Louis, the financial manager of the marine railway, was a good friend of the Sturkeys and had offered to sponsor Abraham so he could settle in Samoa. Abraham was in a difficult situation. He had crewed on the *Chamaru* for the past five years and couldn't go back to the Philippines because of the political situation and couldn't live in the US without being adopted or marrying a US citizen. Abraham thought that he might have a better chance of being given permission to live in the US if he had lived in Samoa, an American territory, and proved himself first. Louis picked us up at the dock and drove us to a beautiful beach on the other side of the island. Abraham brought mask and fins and a spear gun and soon added to the huge variety of fish and different Filipino dishes displayed on the tables. There was a little going-away party for one of the group that was leaving for college in the states. The Filipino people were warm and friendly and the picnic was a lot of fun.

I took a bus to the marine railway early Monday morning and tried to find the man who was supposed to have had the tiller head fitting ready. I discovered that all he had done was to cut the stock. After telling him that I had told Customs that I was leaving the next day (not quite true) and must have the fitting finished today he found a man to bend one of the pieces and braze it up. After the brazing was done, I helped another man set up a milling machine to even it down; and then I drilled holes in it and rounded the corners on the grinder. By the time I was finished grinding it, it was long past quitting time, and the only people left there were the Korean mechanics working on a huge propeller and shaft off one of the fishing boats that was in drydock. As soon as I woke up the next morning I went back to the marine railway to pay my bill there. I was shocked to see that I owed $70 for the tiller fitting, on which I had done half the work, and a piece of metal to fix the Sea-Swing stove. Rather than argue, I paid, leaving me with exactly $3.23.

Korean fishing ships, Pago Pago

Chapter 17

Samoa-Christmas Island

When I got back to the dock where I had tied the Avon, I found Tim and Ron waiting patiently with sea-bags in hand. After a few quick good-byes to Mike and Joanie and my friends on the *Chamaru,* we pulled up the anchor and headed out of the harbor. When we reached the entrance, I shut off the engine and Ron dove over and scrubbed the barnacles off the paddlewheel for the log and knotmeter. When he got back on board, he said that the bottom was covered with barnacles and grass. I hadn't gone diving and scrubbed the bottom as I usually did every week because the water in Pago harbor was so terribly foul from fish guts dumped into the bay by the tuna canneries, making it a happy home for sharks.

6/3 1520 Log 9,051 *Mahina* is close-hauled and pounding some. I guess it will probably be like this for the next 3,000 miles or so. Ron and Tim both got seasick and are below asleep. I guess it will probably take them a while to get used to sailing when we are heeled over 20 to

25° all the time. There is a new moon out and lots of stars, making a beautiful sky overhead.

6/4 0600 Sunrise and the Manua Islands sighted.

0930 After a discussion, we decided to stop briefly at Ofu Island to scrub the growth off the bottom. It is to windward of us, so we started tacking.

1600 Every time we got close to Ofu and tacked to get in, the current carried us away. This light wind just isn't enough to cope with the current. Engine on to help us get in before dark. Ron has been to Tau, the neighboring island to the west of Ofu, but not to Ofu. I heard from someone in Pago that a small boat harbor had been planned for Ofu, but wasn't sure if it had ever been built. The Pilot mentions a large buoy that trading ships tie to, but I'd rather not spend the night scraping against that.

1645 In safely through a shallow, narrow opening blasted in the rock. They are in the process of building a breakwater and blasting and dredging to make this deep enough for the trading boats to come into, and it's really a mess. We tied up alongside a 26 foot plywood sloop that a friend of Ron's named Gary built in a garage in Pago. There are bulldozers and a dredging crane working, so this is a noisy, dusty place. Ron and Tim took off to see if they could find Gary, and I stayed and watched *Mahina.* A couple of Samoan men who work on the construction crew here came by and said hello. They were very friendly and wanted to know where we were headed.

When Ron and Tim came back from exploring, it was getting dark. We were all hungry, so the three of us working together came up with an excellent dinner of mashed potatoes and vegetables with turkey gravy made from Chunky Turkey soup.

We were awakened at 0600 the next morning by the shrill blast of a whistle, so we scrambled on deck to see the *Hamutana,* an inter-island trading boat, tie up to the other side of the same barge we were tied to. It was really interesting to help unload the wood and building supplies and to watch a group of men try to get a crate of squealing pigs on board. After the *Hamutana* left, Ron and Tim and I put on masks and fins and dove down to try and see if we could reduce the underwater park that had grown on *Mahina*'s bottom. Tim stayed close to Ron and I as we scrubbed, with his back to us and keeping an eye out for sharks, as the water was very cloudy from all the construction. In only an hour of hard work we had the bottom reasonably clean and climbed back aboard for a breakfast of pancakes. As soon as breakfast was over, I took off to explore the island. I was stopped by three little girls in the small village who insisted on seeing what I had in my knapsack. When I showed them my camera, they begged me to take a picture of them. In return, they gave me two giant fruits that they called oranges, but which tasted like sweet grapefruit.

When I got to the airport, a new small grass strip without any buildings, people were starting to gather for the arrival of the weekly plane from Tutuila. Rather than wait for the plane, I walked down to the end of the road where there was a beautiful beach and an excellent view of Olosega Island that was separated from Ofu by just a small channel.

On the walk back to *Mahina,* I met an old man who was collecting coconuts from his trees to dry for copra. He was very friendly and cut open a young drinking nut for me. The juice from the nut was very cool and refreshing after walking so far in the sun. When I got back to *Mahina,* Ron and Tim took off to explore the island while I stayed and watched *Mahina.* We were keeping someone on the boat all the time because Gary, the skipper of the sailboat that we were tied alongside, said that they were blasting every day, and once set off a charge without telling him that sent rocks flying 200 feet in the air very close to his boat. Fortunately, none hit his boat.

6/6 0840 After a quick breakfast, we said goodbye to Gary and cast off lines and motored very slowly out of the harbor. As soon as we were out of the lee of Ofu, we caught a nice trade wind that sent *Mahina* along at five and a half knots.

1540 Making a good heading of 60° which is exactly the heading for Pukapuka in the Northern Cooks. I copied a small chart of the island from an old book in the library. I met some girls from Pukapuka at the dance in Raro who were very friendly, and I really hoped to stop there. I also read a fascinating book called "Island of Desire" by Robert Frisbie. I had heard that Pukapuka was still one of the most isolated islands in the world, being visited only a few times a year by the Cook Island trading boat. The Pilot said that there were no anchorages, but I thought that if the wind was out of the east, we might be able to anchor in close to the reef with the wind holding us off. It would be risky at best, and either Ron or I would have to remain on board, ready to pull anchor immediately if the wind changed and started pushing *Mahina* toward the beach.

6/7 0700 Tim: It got dark pretty fast. I had to bring in the lure which I have been trolling all day. John fixed some dinner, but I couldn't eat any because my stomach doesn't want any. I tried to fall asleep, but it was scary. The boat was pounding and pounding and felt like it would fall apart — I couldn't sleep at all. I went on watch at 7 a.m. John and Ron are sleeping like babies because they were on watch all night. I had an apple for breakfast — the boat was moving slowly but surely. It was good to hear some rock and roll on the Samoa radio station.

0800 Winds starting to ease a little. *Mahina* has steered herself well through the night with the tiller lashed. After updating our DR position, it looks like we are going to manage a hundred miles a day quite easily, noon to noon.

6/8 0200 Conditions are better tonight than last night. We have hit some squalls, but they haven't been strong enough to make us reduce sail. Earlier this evening, after I had checked into the net, our friend George on Whidbey Island came on the air and told me that he had my mom on the telephone, so I had a good talk with her.

Every night at 0530 GMT, a ham radio operator named Robbie in Vila, New Hebrides, comes on the air on a certain frequency and runs the Pacific Maritime Mobile Network, or the Mickey Mouse Net for short. The first thing he does is to ask all stations to stand by for any possible emergency or priority traffic. After that, he has the vessels at sea check in. Most of the check-ins are from yachts, although there are some US Navy and Coast Guard ships that check in regularly. Also, I've heard oil tankers, freighters, and passenger liners check in. The advantage of having a ham radio and using the net is that Robbie tracks all the vessels and calls the appropriate places if any vessel is in trouble. Ron told me of one instance of where a ferro-cement sailboat sailing from Samoa to Hawaii developed a large crack and began taking on water faster than her pumps could manage. Tim's father, Mike, answered the distress call and contacted the Coast Guard in Hawaii who sent a plane that dropped high capacity gas pumps from the air which managed to keep the boat afloat until it reached Hawaii. It's also a lot of fun to keep track of where your friends on other yachts are, and it's a good way to learn what an island (approach, Customs, anchorages, etc.) is like before you arrive.

1630 Beautiful day — weather much improved. Fix from two LOP's puts us 75 miles WSW of Pukapuka.

The wind is from the east so we would have to go on the other tack and head ESE to make it to Pukapuka. I decide to pass the island, even though it would be interesting, because I don't want to be going south — not even for a few miles. It would be disappointing to get there and find that it would not be possible to anchor. I dropped the sails and Ron and I took turns jumping over the side with the bottle of Joy soap and had baths and shampoos. After the bath, and before we hoisted the main, I cut out a patch of Dacron and glued it over the top batten pocket with contact cement. The batten had chafed a hole in the batten pocket, and, rather than taking the main off and spending hours sewing a patch on, I tried the glue repair. It held well for nearly 3,000 miles to Hawaii, where I had a sailmaker replace the entire batten pocket. I now carry an extra can of contact cement on the boat all the time for such quick sail repairs. I spent the rest of the afternoon and into early evening sewing up the leech of the no. 1 jib. It had been made with red-colored thread which the sun rotted, causing the seams to open up. I ended up with a headache from sewing with only a small reading light as *Mahina* pounded along on her way.

2030 Tim: I just talked with dad, mom, and Kelly on the radio. It made me cry. Every time I think about mom, dad, and my sisters, I start to cry. I guess I'm homesick because I miss the people who love me very much. I can't help it — I'm just going to have to get over it. It's very lonely out here in the ocean. I don't see how John could sail by himself. I couldn't.

2200 Beautiful night. Only a few minor squalls. Wind and sea conditions Force 3 - 4. Earlier this evening Ron got a phone patch through to his girlfriend in Seattle. He had lived with her a year in Samoa and was missing her all the time.

6/9 0930 Beautiful light air morning. A great

relief not to be pounding any more. Sheets and towels and clothes strung all over the cockpit to dry. This morning I talked with Charles who is at Wallis Island north of the Fijis; with Al, who is near New Caledonia; and with Paul, who is the forecaster at the airport at Nandi, Fiji. I made all of these contacts through Charles' 40 meter morning net of friends. It's a lot of fun to talk with the yachts who are visiting other islands and hear what they are like.

1300 A school of large porpoises came alongside *Mahina* and spent about 15 minutes frolicking around us and making spectacular jumps out of the water. They are brown and large — fifteen feet — and not like the bottlenose dolphins I've seen before. I shot a lot of pictures and later found out that there wasn't any film in the camera. Too bad!

6/10 0600 Ron writes: Well, I had the first major injury of the voyage yesterday afternoon. It was all so undeserved, too. I had just gotten myself strapped into the high side bunk for a late afternoon nap when the microphone for the radio (which was supposed to be tucked securely in by the radio above my head) crashed down on my face, gouging out a chunk of flesh from my nose. It bled a lot and swelled up, but I fortunately was able to hold the piece of skin in place with a band-aid. This morning it looked like hell. It was quite an education seeing my face in a mirror for the first time in over a week. I don't think I'll shave until we get to Christmas Island. Our ETA in Hawaii is the weekend of July the fourth. John is thinking about maybe going straight into Honolulu instead of going into Hilo and slowly working our way over to Oahu. I had a nice mid-watch last night — bright sky — and I sighed a light on the horizon off the starboard beam — probably a fishing boat since we aren't in any shipping lanes.

I woke Tim up at 0200 and instructed him on what to

do on his first watch alone at night. I had a hard time sleeping on the high side. Sailing conditions continue to be fantastic with a good fresh SE tradewind pushing us along at a steady four to five knots. The cockpit is not the dryest place to be as head seas send intermittent showers of salty spray that sometimes find their way over or around the dodger. We've only had one squall in two days though, and we had an exhilarating fresh water shower in that this afternoon.

6/11 0900 Tim writes: I miss everyone back in Samoa. It's really good to hear that Kelly is taking good care of the clownfish in my aquarium. I've been trying to think of what to get Kelly for her birthday for the last few days. I know — maybe she'd like a skateboard so she wouldn't always be borrowing mine. John and Ron always talk about women. It's really different to be on a sailboat. There isn't much to do but stand watches, change sails, and read. You do a lot of thinking out here in the blue. I got a good sun tan. When I get back to Samoa I'll look like a Samoan. The sun is starting to sink into the ocean. I went to bed and missed dinner because I was too tired.

6/12 A lazy day that went by very fast. Biggest event of the day was at 1300 hours when we dropped the lapper and took turns jumping over the side and swimming and washing our hair. We had cabin biscuits and peanut butter for lunch today. Not really the most balanced meal in the world, but it was good. It looks like we will have no problem finishing the 25 pounds of cabin biscuits that we started out from Samoa with. The problem is that *Mahina* is being sailed by a bunch of munchy-freaks. I have been too lazy to take any shots, and we are just going on DR.

6/13 0900 Tim: I slept okay. Last night, John said that I stunk, so this morning I went for a quick swim. Ron cooked oatmeal for breakfast but I didn't feel like eating any, so I just did the dishes when they were through. After I was finished cleaning things up in the galley, I set the trolling line. No sooner did I have the line out than a huge tuna grabbed the lure and jumped at least three feet out of the water. What a sight! I rushed to pull in the line, but soon found out that the tuna had snapped the line and taken the lure. It looked like it was a forty to fifty pound fish. I was really mad. After a while, I washed my clothes. They were really smelly and took some time to do. In the afternoon we dropped the jib and took turns going swimming. It sure did cool me down! The sunset was beautiful, so I took a picture of it. I sure hope that it turns out. John fixed dinner and I fell asleep afterwards listening to a Hawaiian radio station.

6/14 A slow day; not too much happening. I finally got around to taking a couple of sights and getting a fix. Our position as of 1625 was S 01° 17' W 162° 13'. That puts us about 330 miles SW of Christmas Island. Tim is reading "Two on a Big Ocean" by Hal Roth and greatly enjoying it; Ron is reading "Watership Down," a book of mine that is a story about rabbits, and I'm reading "Territorial Imperative," an anthropological book of Ron's.

6/15 0100 A black line of squalls is on the horizon headed our way.

0200 Ron: After I'd been in the sack for just over an hour, I woke up with a real rip-snorter of a squall in progress. After a while, John went up in the spray on the foredeck and dropped the jib, and we sailed the rest of the night under reefed main alone.

0630 Ron: As we head NE into the glowing light of a cloudy sunrise , the light reflection gives the water surface a molten metal grey color. The seas are no longer small gentle rollers, but are instead mountainous storm seas — fifteen to twenty feet — the largest we've seen thus far.

0930 Tim: I couldn't sleep last night because the weather was bad. When I went on watch, the swells looked like tidal waves. The wind was blowing hard, too. The boat was pounding and I was afraid and wanted to be home in Samoa. I hate this weather. This morning I couldn't eat breakfast. The sun was shining, but the wind and waves were still like monsters. I sure hope it clears off. A lot of spray was coming over the top of the dodger and whoever was on watch would get soaked to the bone. All of my clothes are wet.

1430 Sun out and conditions improving slowly. Got a fix that puts us at S 00° 22' W 161° 22', or about 260 miles SW of Christmas. Our course is such that we would not quite be able to make Christmas Island if we continued on this tack. I don't want to have to try to tack east when we get close to Christmas because I've been told that the current sets westward by Christmas Island at over eighty miles a day, making it close to impossible to go east. So we put *Mahina* over on a port tack headed SE, with hopes of getting enough easting to reach Christmas on the next tack. It will take some getting used to being on this other tack after ten days on the starboard tack. Cooking, navigating, and dishwashing are entirely different.

6/16 0900 I turned on the radio to talk to Charles at our regular morning scheduled time, and I could hear him but he couldn't hear me. He called us a couple of times, and I turned up the gain all the way; but I just wasn't getting out. The meter on the radio that shows the power output was hardly budging at all. I checked all the connections going into the radio and the battery, then went into the cockpit to check the antenna. It was easy to see what the problem was. A wood crate full of anchor chain had slid across the back of the cockpit when we tacked and slammed into the base of the antenna, smashing all the terminals. After a couple of hours I got everything put back in order and the radio worked.

6/17 1200 Ron: Salt water sores are a real bummer. I've developed a nice crop of them on my butt, and my hands have at least a half dozen wart-like growths from being wet all the time. They'll go away, but I wish they were gone now — they are literally a pain in the ass. The captain (who has just caught up the navigation) is yelling elatedly that we've been doing better than anticipated on this tack and even though we are moving away from the equator again, we're making excellent easting. Tomorrow we should be able to get back on the NE tack and go like hell for Christmas Island. We should arrive there on Friday and ETA for Hawaii is about July 7. I think John will be heading right into the Ala Wai Yacht Basin and haul out as soon as possible. I'll be trying to find a berth on a Trans-Pac boat headed back to the West Coast.

1800 Tim: This was a good day! The sun was out and the winds were cool and light and the seas were calm. It sure was beautiful. I wish mom and dad could be here. We had shoestring potatoes, Spanish peanuts, and peanut butter and cabin biscuits for lunch today. It was crazy, but good. I started reading a book last night, using a flashlight when I was on watch out in the cockpit since the boat was steering itself. It is called "Sisters in the Sun" and is about two islands in the Northern Cook group. I really enjoy books about the South Pacific. John always teases me and calls me "the kid" — but I tease him back. In the late afternoon I helped him work on the forepeak. We tightened screws and tried to soak up some of the salt water that leaks in with sponges and towels. After that we worked on the antenna some more and I watched land birds flying around the boat in crazy circles. John and I pulled down the jib and filled the forward tank from one of the jerry cans. Then the three of us went swimming. The water felt cool and refreshing.

The sun is just starting to set and is making the sky very beautiful. Ron is making mashed potatoes and chicken stew for dinner. It sure smells good!

6/18 0700 Ron: Well, there's no question about being able to make Christmas now. During the night the wind shifted to SE and we were able to grab enough easting until now we're only about one degree (sixty miles) west of where we need to be. We are about 190 miles SW of the island and reaching along at over six knots. Since the wind shifted to SE, we were able to ease the sails a little, so that now we are close reaching instead of being close hauled. *Mahina* is not pounding at all now; it's surprising what a difference it makes just falling ten or fifteen degrees off the wind. Anticipation is running high among ship's company. I've been planning my second shave of the passage for several days now. I think that it will happen tomorrow. We are all very curious as to what awaits us day after tomorrow, but there is no remedy for that but to wait. Last night was a beautiful night with a half-moon and brilliant Venus softly illuminating a gently undulating seascape. I had lots of time to think on my watch (I **always** have lots of time to think on my watches) and I seem to be totally preoccupied with what I'm going to do when I get back to the states.

1600 Tim: I found a recipe for brownies in a cookbook of John's and decided to give them a try. They were really good, and I couldn't keep John's fingers out of the dough. They disappeared real fast after they were done cooking in the pressure cooker. I made the rice to go with the chicken stew for dinner tonight, but I didn't put enough rice in and so the rice turned out gooey. But it still tasted good.

6/19 0845 Ron made us grits for breakfast which we ate with milk and honey since we were out of oats. I caught up with our DR position and found that we have only 78 miles to go. That would have us arriving at about midnight tonight — if the wind holds. I am going to have to spend a lot of time today on navigation because I don't want to miss the island. I have been told by people in Hawaii and Samoa that Christmas Island is one of the hardest islands in the Pacific to find because it is very low (average height is five feet) with no hills or lights. Before we left for the Marquesas, I met a couple of boats in Hawaii that had tried to find Christmas Island for up to three days but eventually had given up. The problem is that there is a current setting west at up to eighty miles a day to the south of the island and along the shore, and to the north of the island runs the Equatorial Counter-current at up to thirty miles per day, setting east. Also, often a convergence zone is formed between the northern limit of the SE Trades and the southern limit of the NE Trades, causing the weather to be overcast for weeks at a time.

1650 This has been a beautiful day. The winds and seas are the lightest they have been for the entire trip, but we are still doing over five knots. I just shot the last sun sight of the day — the sun was only 11° above the horizon, barely high enough for an accurate shot. The moon is clearly visible, so I just took a moonsight. I'll cross that with the last sun sight and will get a fix that should tell us how close we are to the island.

1815 Only fourteen miles to go! I was very hesitant about making a landfall on such a low island at night, so I talked on the radio with Charles about it. He said that as long as we didn't get too far east, ending up in the Bay of Wrecks where the current makes it almost impossible to get out, we shouldn't have any problem. I didn't think that we would have to worry about being too far east as the current had already started setting us westward at over two knots according to my navigation. Charles had visited Christmas Island about three months earlier and gave us some very valuable information about where to anchor and what the channel into the lagoon was like. He said that the Customs officer must clear us first, and then they would tow us in through the five and a half foot deep channel because the current was very strong. I decided to try for landfall at night and sail back and forth in front of the island if we couldn't find a place to anchor. If we hove to for the night, chances would be very good that the current would carry us away from the island, making it very hard to get back against the four-knot current.

2100 After poring over the plotting sheet that I'm using and rechecking the last four LOP's, I decided that we should be within three miles of the island and sight it very soon. Ron is steering and he was very happy when I told him that we were almost there. Just at sunset we saw three flocks of land birds heading exactly the way that we were. I had used birds before for reference when getting close to an island, and they were never wrong, so I don't suppose they will be this time.

2110 After standing on the cockpit seats and staring toward the horizon ahead of us, I caught a whiff of a land smell. Ron said he smelled it also, and I decided that it smelled like coconut trees. Excitement is high, but the kid is below asleep. He doesn't plan to come out until he can see it.

2115 LAND!!! YAHOO!!! What I thought to be a low dark cloud on the horizon turns out to be an island. We must not be too far away as I can see the white breaker line. The moon just came out from behind the clouds and the water looks like silver. A school of fifteen or twenty small dolphins just joined us at *Mahina*'s bow for a spectacular escort toward the moonlit island. All of our yelling and the squeaking from the dolphins finally woke the kid up and he is in the cockpit yelling and carrying on like the rest of us.

2130 log 10,466 We are here! I have had the depth sounder on and have been keeping an eye out for the bottom as our chart shows that this approach to the island hasn't been charted. We were reaching along at over six and a half knots in the glassy-smooth water when all of a sudden I saw the sandy bottom, and the depth sounder started showing ten feet. I put the tiller hard over immediately and Ron dropped the jib, because we didn't want to run aground. I started the engine and left the main up. Ron sighted a weak light on the horizon near where we thought the village of London was, so we headed for it.

Coconut Palms
London
Banana Village
Cook Is.
Paris
(abandoned)
Lagoon
and
Salt Flats
Poland Village and Plantation
Bay of Wrecks
Southwest
Point
Coconut Palms
Low lying scrub land with some trees along coast
Christmas Island
Southeast
Point
Not for navigational use

Chapter 18

Christmas Island

The light Ron spotted turned out to be the anchor light of the fishing schooner *Pursuit,* from San Francisco. We motored past them — their lights were all out — and went a little closer to shore before stopping the engine and dropping the main and anchoring. The water was so clear and the moon so bright that we could see the bottom even though the water was 35 feet deep. I waited until we were on top of a small patch of white sand before I dropped the anchor so that it wouldn't get stuck in the coral. Tim had fixed us a coffeepot full of hot chocolate which we drank before turning in for a very restful night's sleep.

I woke up the next morning at 0600 to see the *Pursuit* raising anchor and heading out to go fishing. By 0730, Ron and Tim were up and we had a good pancake breakfast. As soon as breakfast was finished and *Mahina* cleaned up a little, we all put on our masks and fins and jumped over the side. It felt so free and good to be back in the water, surrounded by colorful formations of coral and a thousand different kinds of fish. It reminded me a lot of diving in the Tuamotus. Ron worked his way in to the shore, but Tim and I didn't feel like swimming through the surf breaking on the coral reef, so we had a good time swimming around in the coral forests and chasing some parrot fish that must have been four or five feet long. After an hour of snorkeling, Tim and I started back toward *Mahina*. Just before we got to the boat, a grey reef shark about six feet long made a pass at us. I think Tim and I set a record for swimming the last twenty yards back to the boat. When we got back aboard, I pumped up the Avon and headed toward shore while Tim stood anchor watch. As I got close to shore, I met Ron swimming back to *Mahina*. He said that he met a little boy that told him the captain should come ashore to meet the Customs man. I told Ron about the shark and asked him if he wanted a ride in the Avon back to the boat. He said no, that he had swum around sharks before in Samoa and wasn't afraid of them. Later we learned that the local people won't go swimming there because of the sharks.

The surf wasn't too high, so I didn't have much trouble landing the dinghy on the beach. The first person I met was a nice New Zealand guy named Doug. I told him that we wished clearance and to come inside the lagoon, and he said that he'd try to round up the doctor, Customs man, and the island policeman. I walked around the village while I was waiting for the men. The houses are made of plywood and have corrugated iron roofs. There is no soil anywhere, just white coral sand. There are many coconut palm trees growing and some scrubby little bushes around. The people are very dark and their features are not Polynesian. They are Micronesian, from the Gilbert and Ellice Islands. When I got back to where I had left the dinghy on the beach, the Customs man and the island policeman were waiting. They spoke a little English and told me that the doctor was on his way and would be there soon. The Customs man told me that we were only the fifth boat to visit Christmas Island this year.

The doctor arrived shortly, and we proceeded to launch the Avon through the surf with four large men in it. Just as we got to the breaker line, an extra large wave picked up the bow of the dinghy. I pulled on the oars for all I was worth and the Avon literally stood on its transom as we crashed through the surf. The island men thought that it was great fun. When we got out to *Mahina,* Tim had made some Hawaiian punch to serve our guests. Entry formalities were very short — the Customs man asked how long we wished to stay, and stamped our passports; the doctor looked at our vaccination certificates and smiled, and that was it. Pretty simple. The men were very friendly and relaxed, even more so once we got the formalities out of the way. They wanted to know where we had come from and where we were going. When Ron and Tim told them that they lived in Samoa, the men nodded approval.

The doctor said that both of the island boats were out doing a fishing survey, so there was no boat available to pull us through the channel and into the lagoon. He said it was almost high tide, however, and that the current shouldn't be too strong. The policeman and Customs man pulled up the anchor and stood bow watch with Ron and Tim, looking out for coral heads near the surface. The doctor said that at high tide five and a half feet could be carried through the channel and thought *Mahina* would have no trouble since she drew only four feet. The doctor stood on the cockpit seat beside me and directed me through the channel. The current was coming at us quite strongly. Because of that, plus the weight of four people standing on the bow, *Mahina* was only doing a scant two knots as we went into the channel. We eventually got into a quiet little bay just inside the lagoon and anchored in fifteen feet of water on a white sand bottom. The men said that they hoped we would enjoy our stay. We thanked them very much for their help and rowed them ashore.

After taking a stern line ashore and tying it around an old post, we went to the island government office building, which was really a small, nearly-empty shack. There, our friend the Customs man changed our US money to Australian money. He had to cable to Tarawa, the administrative headquarters for the Gilbert and Ellice Island Colony, from which Christmas Island is administered, to get permission to cash my traveler's checks, so I borrowed $20 US from Ron until the answer came back. With a few dollars now in our pockets, we headed across the street to the bulk store where we proceeded to buy more canned butter and powdered milk and some peanuts and crackers to munch on when we went exploring. We walked through the village of London, which wasn't very big, and stopped at a beautiful white colonial house on the beach, where we met Jan Grant. She said she and her husband Dave had been on Christmas for a couple of months, taking the place of the plantation manager who was on vacation at his home in Scotland. Jan and Dave and their two small boys moved from Scotland to New Zealand twelve years earlier. After having spent over nine years in New Zealand where Dave worked as a refrigeration engineer, they decided that it was time to move on. He got a job working for the British government at Tarawa, in the Gilbert Islands, where they had lived for the past two and a half years. Jan said that Tarawa was much more crowded than Christmas Island, with over 7,000 people living on a small atoll. She invited us in and gave us ice-cold drinks of lemonade which really tasted good as it was very hot outside. There are only a few trees for shade and the coral sand is glaring white.

At about five that afternoon her husband Dave came home. He was glad to see some new people to talk with and showed us on a big map on the wall where the towns of London, Poland, and Banana were. He also showed us the site of the joint US - British nuclear bomb testing of 1958. It was starting to get dark, so Dave gave us a ride back to *Mahina* in his Land Rover, which was one of the five cars on the island. For dinner we had curry stew over rice that was so good that we all ate too much and fell asleep immediately.

The next morning after breakfast, I rowed the folding bike ashore and took off to explore. Ron and Tim took their cameras and headed for a large complex of abandoned military buildings. The road that I biked on was perfectly flat and very hot, without shade. The asphalt was still in very good condition since it rarely rained there. The road was over a hundred miles long and went from London to Poland, along the perimeter of the entire island. The only thing keeping it from being a complete circle was the pass in between London and Poland to the interior of the island, which was covered by salt flats and marshes and inhabited only by land crabs that grew up to eight inches long. I tried to find the abandoned US base — over ten miles away — but I was getting very tired from the sun, so I turned around.

When I got back to London village, I stopped by one of the two village stores. I asked the girl inside if she had any cold drinks, and she said no. But while I was looking at the very few things that they **did** have, her brother Matthew gave me the last can of lemonade in the store as a gift. I asked if they had more that I could buy for Ron and Tim, but Matthew said that it was the last they had. Soon their mother came in and insisted that I come into the house that was attached to the store. She was a large woman, without teeth, and she was carrying a tiny baby. Since she spoke only Gilbertese, she explained through her son Matthew and through sign language that I was their guest and should come to their home often. She brought a beautiful shell lei out of another room and put it around my neck. Matthew brought out a portable cassette player and played me some Gilbertese music that he had recorded at a traditional dance. Matthew knew a little English and told me that he came to Christmas Island fifteen years ago with his family from Aranuka Atoll in the Gilbert Islands. He worked on the copra plantation during the day, as did two hundred men on the island. Matthew said it was hard and heavy work and that the sun was very hot.

After we had been talking a while, Matthew asked if he could see *Mahina,* so I rowed him out. As it was getting toward dinner time, I started fixing spaghetti; and just as it was ready, Ron and Tim came back from exploring the old army buildings. The four of us had a great spaghetti dinner.

Afterwards, Matthew told us that there was a dance and asked us if we would go with him. It was held in a round meeting shed with a cone-shaped roof that came so low at the edges we had to duck to get in. Once inside, we paid our twenty cents and sat down on the floor and watched the goings on. The music was cassette tapes played at full volume on a small stereo. The songs were old American pop songs like "Wooly Bully" and "Simple Simon Says." There were about forty young people there dancing a mixture of everything from the twist to their native dances. After Ron and I had sat out a couple of dances, two pretty girls came over and asked us to dance with them. As Ron and I weren't about to pass up a good thing, we accepted and had lots of fun. We traded girls for the next dance, and all of the younger girls started making eyes at Tim. He wasn't about to give in, unfortunately, even though he was soon surrounded by girls stroking his blond hair and smiling at him. Ron and I tried to encourage him to give it a try, but he couldn't be persuaded. Afterwards he told us that he had a stomach ache and didn't think that the girls were very pretty. I tried to explain to him how relative beauty is, but he didn't go for it.

When the dance was over, Ron tried to persuade one of the local lovelies to go for a walk with him to the boat, but she didn't understand what he was asking her and was embarrassed because everyone was watching her and wondering what she would do.

On our way back to *Mahina,* we were escorted by two young men who wanted to know more about where we were from. One of them, who was only twenty-one, was the head of the union for the plantation workers and seemed very intelligent. His friend, the son of the commissioner of the Line Islands, was a bit drunk and kept insisting that we drink some of his warm Australian beer. Ron and Tim helped him out, but I didn't feel up to it.

Ron and Tim slept in while I went to church the next morning. I wore the best clothes I had — some holey jeans and a clean shirt — but I was surprised to see that all the men wore white shirts, ties, and black slacks. The singing was in Gilbertese, with harmonizing, and was very beautiful. I couldn't understand a bit of what was said, but it was sure interesting to watch. Everyone except the minister sat on the floor which was covered with woven mats. After the service, the women and children children left; and the men had what seemed to be a sort of discussion time, asking the minister and each other questions. I asked the man next to me what they were talking about, but he didn't speak English, so I never found out.

After church, I stopped by Matthew's house. He introduced me to his father, Isaiah, who sat down and rolled a cigarette and tried to talk to me. He said, through the help of his daughter, that he was a foreman on the plantation and had been on the island for about fifteen years. He wanted to know where we had come from and where we were going; and when I told him that Hawaii was our next stop, he brought out an old, well worn Sears catalog. He carried the catalog like it was his most prized possession, and opened it to a page with electric blenders on it. He said, through hand gestures and the interpreting of his daughter, that he wished that I would buy a blender for him at the Sears in Hawaii, and mail it back to him. He wanted it so that he could make ice cream to sell in his store. I asked him if the current was 110 or 220 volts but he didn't understand. I asked Dave later, and he told me the electricity in the village of London was 220 volts and came from an ancient generator left by the British forces following the end of the nuclear tests. It is only run for a couple of hours in the morning and three hours every evening.

Isaiah repeated the invitation to come and rest at his house any time I wanted, and his wife brought me some fried fish for lunch that one of her little boys had caught. When I asked her how many children she had, she gestured with her fingers that she had seven. About that time, Ron and Tim came by and said that they were going to pay a visit to Dave and Jan Grant and asked if I'd like to come along, so I said goodbye to Isaiah and his wife and family.

When we got to the Grants' home, they insisted that we have hot showers, a luxury we certainly didn't turn down. Later, Jan asked us to stay for dinner, another luxury we eagerly accepted. Dinner turned out to be a pretty fancy affair for such an isolated island that hadn't seen a supply ship in nearly six months. There was soup and crackers for starters, then steak and onions and baked potatoes with canned butter, and apples for dessert. Dave said that the food had been a gift from the fishing schooner *Pursuit* that we had seen anchored off the island. They carried a freezer full of meat and a lot of fresh food for the time that they would be spending working on the fishing survey for the government and ended up giving some of it to the two imitang (white) families on shore. After dinner we had tea and cookies and had a very enjoyable time talking island life and politics as we watched the moon rise across the lagoon.

We told Dave that we would be very interested in seeing the other villages of Banana and Poland. He knew of a truck going around the island sometime during the next week to pick up the copra from the plantations, and he said he'd try to arrange a ride for us. We were very surprised the next morning to be wakened at 0730 by Dave honking his horn on the shore closest to *Mahina.* Dave said that the copra truck was leaving for Poland in ten minutes and that if we wanted to go we should hurry and meet it in front of the bulk store.

After rolling the kid out of the forepeak and gobbling down the last of the brownies he had baked the day before, we tumbled into the dinghy and hurriedly rowed ashore. The first stop the truck made was the packing shed about a block away where we helped load the truck high with empty burlap bags for the copra. Then we stopped at a house where we picked up a young mother and her small child who were going to visit some friends of theirs that lived in Poland. The next stop was the great village of Banana. True to its name, there were a couple of banana trees struggling to grow in the harsh environment. Aside from the coconut trees, the land was sandy and bare and very hot. There were about twenty identical little houses in Banana, all in a neat row along the road, and all painted olive drab with paint left by the Americans.

After unloading some bags, and a letter for the

foreman of the plantation, we were off on our way to Poland. The road between Banana and Poland was about eighty-five miles long and very hot. The driver took a shortcut across some of the dried salt ponds in the middle of the island, and we drove past the Bay of Wrecks where the surf was crashing in great waves on the beach. Just before we got to Poland, we passed a small pickup driven by the only white person on the island that we hadn't met. Fred was so surprised to see us waving to him from the back of the copra truck that he nearly ran his truck into the ditch when he turned around to look at us.

When we got to Poland, we were an instant attraction as they rarely have any visitors there. All of the little boys and girls came running after us, and, when the truck finally stopped at the only tiny store on that end of the island, we were surrounded. Tim was the biggest curiosity since he was small and had blond hair. The store owner gave us three warm cans of lemonade but wouldn't let us pay for them. They were very refreshing. After finding out that the truck would be loading copra for about an hour, the three of us took off with an escort of little Gilbertese boys for the beach that Dave Grant had told us had puka shells.

Ron writes: We walked down the road until we saw a side road toward the shore. We then came out onto my fantasy of an atoll beach. Sparkling, unmarked white sand under a brilliant sun with wild, white surf breaking across the reef. The Pacific was shaded from dark blue to light aqua as you looked from deeper to shallower water. The beach stretched north and south as far as the eye could see.

After we had collected a few puka shells and taken pictures of each other, we decided to head back. We didn't want to miss getting a ride on the truck back as it only came once a week, and walking the distance would have been impossible in the hot sun. When we got back

Tim and friends looking for shells near Poland

John, Tim, and Ron

to the shed where the truck had just finished being stacked high with bags of copra, the foreman of the plantation asked us to go with him to his house for a rest.

Tonga Fou told us that he had come to Christmas Island seventeen years earlier and had been there while the atomic testing was going on. Tonga said that the tests were held at 60,000 feet about forty miles south of the island. He said that there were about forty tests in all and that the US left in 1963 and the British in 1964. He told us that along with managing the copra plantation's forty workmen, he was responsible for seeing that things went smoothly in the plantation village. For example, he told us that at four that morning the water line going to the village from the windmill and well had broken, and that they had been working on repairs all morning. They filled containers and brought them to the village in Tonga's Land Rover so that there would be water for washing and cooking breakfast.

Soon it was time for the truck to make the long trip back. We rode in the cab since the back of the truck was piled high with copra bags and little black copra bugs. The trip back to London was very hot in the crowded cab, so we all ended up falling asleep.

When we got back to *Mahina* it was late afternoon; we had lunch and then took a genoa bag full of dirty laundry to Dave and Jan's house to wash. I had seen the shiny washing machine in Jan's kitchen and assumed that when she told us to bring our washing we would be doing it in the machine. When Jan said that the washing machine and refrigerator ran on 110 volts and that there hadn't been any 110 volt power in the island since the Americans left and that the shiny applicances were just to look at, I filled up her sink full of soapy water without a word and started scrubbing. When I was on the fourth rinse and scrub, Jan sent Marjo, her kitchen girl, by to help. I had met Marjo at the dance and she was very friendly and eager to help, even though she didn't speak any English. After the washing was done, I joined Ron and Tim and Jan and Dave on the veranda for tea, and we had an interesting talk about politics in New Zealand, Britain, and the US.

The next morning after sleeping late and having a pancake breakfast, we headed back to the Grants' house to finish as Jan would say, "a wee bit o' washin'." We spent the afternoon filling water tanks and buying a couple of gallons of kerosene that we badly needed for the stoves and lamps. I had planned to buy five gallons of gas so that we'd be leaving with all tanks full, but when we got to the store with our cans and found that gas was over US $2.50 a gallon, I decided that if we ran out of wind on our way back to Hawaii, we would just wait. After so much work, we decided that it was time to take it easy again, so we all took off in different directions.

Ron: When I was finally able to get away for good, I took my shell bag and had a beautiful, solitary walk down the open beach in front of London. I picked up lots of shells, no real treasures, but just mostly had lots of time to think and contemplate a spectacular sunset. A brilliant, orange fireball descended through dark purple bands of clouds and hesitated slightly before sliding into the mighty Pacific.

When Ron and I met on the shore near *Mahina,* we remembered that we had been invited to Doug and Jeanette Gibson's for cocktails, so we walked through the village where the cooking fires were going and the children playing quiet games of hopscotch on the sandy paths. When we arrived, we were surprised to see not only Doug and Jeanette and Dave and Jan, but Uta, the commissioner of the Line Islands, and his wife. Everyone was dressed very nicely with all the ladies wearing beautiful long skirts and flowers. Soon after we arrived, Fred, the man that we had passed on our way to Poland, arrived with his friend George. George had just flown in on a small plane that came to check the self-transmitting weather station and was going to relieve Fred who had been living alone in a tiny house near the Bay of Wrecks ten weeks. They were both marine biologists and part of a newly-formed Hawaiian company that was setting up a brine shrimp farm in the salt ponds in the center of the island. The shrimp are frozen and shipped by plane to commercial hatcheries in the States where they would bring a very high price. The company, Environmental Consultants, Inc. of Honolulu, was formed by a group of University of Hawaii graduates who had convinced the Gilbert and Ellice Island government to underwrite the costs of setting the operation up. The exciting part about the whole project was that as much of the work as possible was done by locals, with usually only one scientist on the project at a time. George said that they were training the Gilbertese in all aspects of the operation and hoped to phase themselves out except for advisory help within a couple of years. It was good to see an American company that wasn't out to make a buck at the expense of the local population, but was instead providing a much-needed new source of income.

After having an excellent, spicy tomato soup, there was potato salad followed by steamed rice and peas. The main course was shish-kabob — huge hunks of fresh-caught lobster and beef and onions — done over an open fire. It was excellent! After dinner, the servants brought tea and coffee and liqueurs (Drambuie) and we had a great time talking. At about 10 p.m. George and Fred and Jan and I left because we were getting sleepy.

Ron writes: After they left, I stayed to hold up the Yank national pride by drinking with the Scots. Uta and his wife from the Ellice Islands were there; he's the commissioner from the Gilbert and Ellice Island government to Christmas Island. With him I discussed the similarities between the Ellice and Samoan languages. All in all, it was a very enjoyable evening which didn't end until well after one a.m. Dave, Doug, Uta, and I seem to be the hard core drinkers of the party.

Thursday was a day for doing odd jobs in order to be ready to sail again. Ron took the hacksaw and went searching through the abandoned warehouses for a piece of metal to use as a backing plate behind the antenna. Tim organized the forepeak and I took all the food and cans out of the shelves and storage space, scrubbed the insides, and sprayed them with a bug killer in hopes of eliminating the cockroach population that had found its way onboard. We had showers at Dave and Jan's for the last time and went to bed early in preparation for the many activities of the next day — departure day.

We were very busy Friday. George, the biologist from Honolulu, came by before breakfast with some information for their lab in Hawaii. We were able to get a ham operator in Honolulu who patched us into the ECI lab and George gave them the information that they needed on the progress of the operation. As soon as he left, we all went ashore and Tim folded up the bike and cleaned the sand out of the Avon while I took our passports to the Customs man to get clearance to leave. It turned out that the regular Customs man was in Australia receiving training, and the temporary officer had never had a ship arrive or leave while he was there, so I had to help him type up the forms. He gave me an impressive looking blue certificate with a stamp that said "H.M. Customs, Gilbert and Ellice Islands."

In the next room was Uta's office; I went in and thanked him sincerely for letting us visit the island. I told him that his was one of the most friendly islands that I'd ever been to, and he said that we were very welcome to come back and visit and hoped we could stay longer next time. An amazing man. It seems that when most men are put in a position of authority, they wind up being aloof and snobbish. Not Uta!

After buying some island crafts like mats, hand-made eel traps, woven purses, and a shark-tooth sword, we bought a few last minute food items and went to the post office. Charles on *Chamaru* had told us over the radio to make sure that we bought some of the Christmas Island Christmas cards that they had at the store and to take them to the post office and get them stamped Christmas Island, as it is a very rare postmark. When we got to the post office, we found the door open, but no one inside. After walking to a nearby house, we found the post-master, woke him up, and asked him to come sell us stamps. The stamps were colorful pictures of island activity such as weaving, fishing, and harvesting copra. He made a big affair of pounding the postmark stamp on the letters as he rarely had any business. The police station,

Longboat for unloading ships, Christmas Island

next door to the post office, was also empty, so Ron and I took turns taking pictures of each other sitting on the porch in front of it. After that, we stopped by the Grants' house and said goodbye to Jan and Dave, who gave us a ride to *Mahina*.

There were two things on our list to do before we left. The first was to check the rigging. Instead of rigging block and tackle to the mast and pulling myself up, I just hoisted Tim up in the bosun's chair using the halyard winch. He took a look at the spreaders and said that he didn't see any cracks or problems, so I lowered him, deflated the Avon, and hoisted anchor and headed out through the channel.

The channel out of the lagoon was only five to seven feet deep and the coral heads on the bottom were very visible, so I went very slowly and Ron and Tim kept a sharp lookout on the bow. Once we were clear of the lagoon, we anchored near *Pursuit* where we had anchored eight days earlier on arriving at Christmas. We spent an hour scrubbing the barnacles and grass off the bottom. We seemed to acquire them easier and easier as the bottom paint was scrubbed off. Then we rowed over to the *Pursuit* to meet the people that we had heard so much about from Dave and Jan.

Steve and Barbara Rigsby, the owners, were very eager to have us aboard. They lived on the *Pursuit* with their nine and fourteen year old boys and huge Airedale named Scotty. *Pursuit* was an impressive 65 foot steel fishing schooner built by a Tacoma, Washington, shipbuilder under Steve's supervision. Her engine room was spotless and well laid out, with a huge Cummins diesel for a main engine. Steve said that he had never had any problem with it. There was also a small Perkins diesel that ran the refrigeration compressor when the main engine wasn't on. *Pursuit* had a 22 ton capacity hold in which the fish were kept frozen by a mixture of icy salt water that was constantly sprayed over them. The forepeak of the ship was storage for groceries and equipment not in use, but Steve said that he planned to get it finished off into sleeping quarters for the boys. The pilot house was very well laid out and had excellent 360° visibility. It was equipped with over $20,000 worth of electronics, including radar, Loran, five radios, and Weatherfax. Steve showed me how to work the Loran, something I've always wanted to learn about, and Barbara got a weather map for me from the Weatherfax machine. Steve said that the entire hull was half inch steel and the house three-eighths. He said that he had had a variety of wood fishing boats since he and Barbara started fishing the West Coast in 1958, but had never felt as safe as he did in the *Pursuit*.

The interior of the cabin and galley was all finished in oiled teak and was nicer than any yacht I've ever seen. The galley was large and well laid out, with a refrigerator-freezer, a diesel stove, two sinks, and a large countertop. Barbara insisted that we stay for dinner since they had received some fresh supplies from another boat that just arrived from Honolulu that afternoon to take part in the fishing survey. We had tender roast beef, fresh carrots, and rice for dinner. After dinner, Steve showed us slides of fishing on the West Coast and in Alaska, and I brought over some slides of the Marquesas and Tahiti, making for an enjoyable evening.

Chapter 19

Christmas-Honolulu

It was 0130 by the time we got back to *Mahina*. Since we were anxious to be in Hawaii before the sixty-odd transpac boats arrived, we decided to leave right away; so by 0230 we had started the engine and pulled the anchor up and were motoring northward along the coast, trying to get out of the calm spot in the lee of the island.

6/28 0245 Log 10,480 Hoisted sails as we passed the northernmost point of the island. Ron was very tired coming off watch. The wind is light and out of the SE, so *Mahina* is on a broad reach and won't steer herself.

0900 Sunny morning. No. 1 jib down and lapper raised. Main unreefed. Tim caught some fish last night while fishing with the Rigsby boys; but I had to throw them overboard because they smelled bad. It sure doesn't take long for things to spoil in the tropics.

6/29 2200 Ron: Today was a lost day. Everyone spent their off-watch time sleeping. I spent about two hours sitting on the foredeck just enjoying the warmth of the late afternoon sun, the calmness of the sea, and the solitude of my own thoughts. I'm really looking forward to getting to Hono, but now John is talking again about going to Hilo first. I need to get to the Ala Wai soon after the Transpac boats arrive to be able to line up a crew position back to the States. My last watch had a little of everything — a rain squall and lots of clouds slowly clearing to a star-speckled sky, and then an early moonrise. There was also a pod of about fifteen dolphins that came by for ten minutes or so.

6/30 0600 I made a list of things for me to do today: sew up blue shirt, sew split in the leach of the No. 1 jib, practice Morse code, catch up writing in the ship's log, and get a weather report from the ham operator at the Nandi Airport in Fiji.

1300 Very light air. Thirty-six miles in the last 24 hours.

7/1 0800 Ron: Some heavy news last night. I finally got a phone patch into Mom and found out that Dad had another heart attack this weekend. He's already out of intensive care unit and apparently recovering well. That obviously changed their plans for going back East for the family reunion this weekend. My brother Don went anyway; I hope he's able to have a good time. Meanwhile, back in this convergence zone, the weather is lousy! Rain off and on all night and light variable winds — really hard to sail anywhere in this stuff. We've been sitting still most of the time — maybe covering a mile or two in an hour — but once in a while we'll get a solid wind current that will blast us along at four and a half to six knots for an hour or so. We saw a big fish on the surface yesterday — probably a shark — about eight feet long.

1200 Tim: I slept like a baby last night. It is still overcast but the wind had picked up a little and we are doing almost three knots now. Ron fixed oatmeal for breakfast and I did the dishes. We took it easy the rest of the morning. I did some bird watching, John talked on the radio but couldn't get hold of my dad. The sun finally came out and said "Hi!"

7/2 0900 I think that we have finally found the beginnings of the NE trades. We've been doing four knots close-hauled for the past three hours.

1200 Tim: I finally got another bite on my trolling line. This one was much bigger than the last one that got away, and it put up a great fight. The line cut my hands, so I put on Ron's diving gloves and put the line on the jib sheet winch. We didn't get the fish aboard because he bit right through the 300 pound test line. I should have put a steel leader between the lure and the line. Oh well, I'll get him next time.

1600 Ron: We had a nice swim and shampoo this afternoon until John got spooked by the reflection of the hull in the water and yelled "shark!" Even though there wasn't one, that kind of dampened our enthusiasm for swimming. I really feel the need for more exercise and to cut down on how much food I gorge myself with. I feel super slow and bloated all the time.

7/3 0900 Ron: Seas sixteen to eighteen feet. Wind 25 plus knots. Wow! What a night! This was without a doubt the worst pounding of the trip so far. The slamming of the waves has been incessant with several terrific crashes per minute. Also, the heavy spray in the cockpit is back. It's impossible to go out there without getting wet in a few minutes. The pounding is beginning to tell on the people too. John's mood is as cantankerous as hell, and Tim is just quieter. I'm tired after a restless night with little sleep and the motion has my head and stomach off-balance. Bad radio propagation last night to Seattle so I wasn't able to talk with my girlfriend Terry, but we got a patch through a strong Southern California station that enabled me to talk to Mom for a while. Dad's recovering very well and should be home in a week — that's a week ahead of schedule! And wonder of wonders! Grandma is going to fly out to California with Don for a two-week visit. That'll be her first trip in an airplane, and it sure would be nice to see her.

7/4 1000 Just talked with Tim's father Mike who is in the Tonga Islands on a radio expedition. He said that they were two days late arriving because the tug that he was riding on ran into heavy seas and lost an engine. Mike set up his radio and strung up an antenna in a tiny old hotel on the beach. He was having a good time working US stations who didn't have a Tonga radio contact yet.

1400 Ron: This was a nice quiet Saturday — the last of this cruise, I hope. Our latest fix puts us about 350 miles south of the Big Island so we should sight it on Tuesday. I must say that I'm ready for it. I'm not sure what I'll be doing next Saturday night, but I'm sure that it will be more fun than this. We should pull into Hono some time Thursday. I'm really anxious to get my mail and talk to my friend Jay. Hawaii AM stations are really booming in this afternoon. It's kind of weird to listen to the Fourth of July festival activity in the Diamond Head Crater — we're so close and yet still so far away. Tim baked a chocolate cake in the pressure cooker this afternoon — quite an accomplishment under these conditions!

7/5 0700 Bad news! When going up to the forepeak to straighten things up, I noticed that the support beam under the mast was bent worse than usual. Upon close inspection, I found that one of the two supports on the main bulkhead had sheared its glue bond, breaking a three-eighths inch stainless steel bolt, and had been forced through the fibreglass cabin sole. Also, the main port bulkhead had started to warp seriously at the top. All I could think of to do was to replace the broken bolt and put the jam post I had made in Samoa alongside the damaged beam to transmit the load to the cabin sole.

1400 Conditions looking pretty good. We have covered 140 miles in the past 24 hours, which is excellent considering that we're still hard on the wind. The seas are down to eight to ten feet, which is still a little bumpy, but at least we're not pounding as bad any more. I knew that all that pounding was going to damage something. I just hope that the bulkhead and mast support hold together for a few more days.

7/6 1400 Fix shows that we've done another 140 mile day. The seas are down to six to nine feet, and we've

been able to fall off a little. We're no longer close hauled but now are close reaching. Much more comfortable. When I was talking with Mike Hitchcock this noon, a station off the coast of Mexico cut in. The operator was the captain of a 20,000 ton freighter off Baja that was currently in an 85 knot hurricane who had heard me give our position to Mike. He said that it was headed our way and recommended we get into port as fast as possible. I assured him that we didn't want to be clobbered by it and were carrying all the sail we possibly could for Honolulu. Later, I was able to get a weather forecast through a patch at the sub base at Pearl Harbor to Fleet Weather Central. They said that the hurricane was headed our way at fifteen knots, but that they expected it to blow itself out before it reached us. We are all very anxious to get in and hope to sight the island of Hawaii just before sunset if we can hold this record-breaking speed another day.

7/7 0800 Ron: Beautiful morning! Bright sunshine, light winds, smooth seas, and fluffy white clouds — a perfect day to be alive and sailing into the Hawaiian Islands from the south.

1500 Tim: All of a sudden the trolling line tightened up. I saw the fish jump out of the water and got the gloves on and started pulling him in. He didn't put up much of a fight, and I finally got him in the cockpit. It was an eight pound Ahe, an excellent-tasting Hawaiian fish. I cleaned him in the cockpit and what a mess it made! Blood and guts all over the place! I fileted it and dipped the filets in a batter made out of eggs and then dipped them in flour and fried them. Ron cooked rice to go along with it, and it turned out to be one of our best meals so far. I wish mom was here to help us eat it. I guess we can have the rest for breakfast.

2315 Sighted a light bearing 270°. It slowly came by and passed us. It was a container ship. I woke Ron and

Tim up to see it, but I think that they would have rather slept. I tried sending Morse code to them with the flashlight, but they didn't answer. It looked like they may have been hove to, waiting for space to tie up in Hono. I think I can small land. Yahoo!!!

7/8 1000 Ron: Sunrise brought the island of Hawaii right under the sun. It was already well abeam, so it must have been in sight range for hours — but it was too dark to see it. No help from the moon either, this time of the month. The swell was pretty rough and the breeze was freshening, so John pulled down the lapper and hoisted the No. 1 in the growing glow of the sunrise on the eastern horizon to the raucous strains of "Roll Me Over." Since the boat was rolling heavily, that seemed like the natural song to sing. After the sun was up a little while, the island disappeared in the haze and the land so close to us has scarecely been visible all morning. Today is a fine day for getting a tan. Tonight will probably be a restless, sleepless night for us. We're all eagerly anticipating the landfall in Hono tomorrow afternoon.

1400 Tim: I woke up from a short nap and decided it was time to finish scrubbing out the pressure cooker. When I looked at the trolling line, I saw it jerk hard and I knew I had something. I put on the gloves and we winched him in on the jib sheet winch. It turned out to be a dolphin-fish. It was about four feet long and very pretty — blue and green. We would have only been able to eat a little of it, so I took the hook out and let him join his friends that were waiting for him beside the boat.

1630 I just got another weather forecast. Hurricane Carlotta is down to tropical storm force and is at 17°N 162°W. But Hurricane Delice is packing winds of 105 to 125 knots and is headed west at ten knots. Her position is 16°N 106°W, so we won't have to worry about her for a while.

2300 A very cold night — the cabin thermometer is

down to 68°. This is the coldest weather any of us have experienced in the past year so the blankets and sweaters are out in full force tonight. We are now steering for the lights of Hono instead of by the compass. Almost there!!!

7/9 0600 Sunrise and Oahu ahead and Molokai on the beam. Earlier this morning we could see lights of jets coming in to land at Hono airport.

1000 Just talked with Mike on the radio and he was very excited about our landfall—not as excited as we are! There are two long white military ships off the starboard beam that look like Russian naval vessels, with two Coast Guard cutters shadowing them. Back to the world of games!

1130 Sighted Diamond Head and started steering for it. We can see the rows of hotels along Waikiki. We are busily scrubbing down the cockpit and generally getting *Mahina* presentable.

1300 Just passed the Diamond Head buoy. We are getting the usual blast of wind coming down the valley and are surfing along at seven to eight knots. The Boeing hydrofoil just passed real close to us. It is very fast and quiet and looks like something out of a James Bond movie. We are surfing by all the hotels now. There are a couple of new ones since last year. We saw some Hobie Cats out playing around in the surf.

1320 Sails down and motoring up the channel. The range lights are brighter than they used to be, and make entrance easier.

Chapter 20

Hawaii Again

1330 Log 10,515 miles Arrived at Texaco dock in the Ala Wai Marina. First thing Ron did was to go to a vending machine nearby and buy three ice cream bars. They were so cold that they hurt our teeth. The attendant at the gas dock was very unfriendly and it was all I could do to persuade him to let us leave *Mahina* tied up to the empty dock. We were waiting for the man from Customs and for a call back from the Harbormaster's Office telling us if they could find a slip for us to tie up in for a few days. When the Customs Officer arrived, he was very polite and looked at our passports briefly and asked Ron to pay duty on his camera and portable stereo which he had bought in Samoa.

After filling up the gas tanks, we motored slowly across the harbor to Ala Wai Marine, where I had scheduled a haulout appointment for *Mahina* over the radio a couple days before we arrived. Pete, the owner, had said that we could tie up alongside his tugboat if there was room, but when we got close, we saw that there wasn't any room there. Quite a few boats that were being worked on were rafted to the dock. Not knowing quite what to do, we motored slowly back toward the Hawaii Yacht Club even though it looked full. When we passed the visiting boats tied up in front of the Club, a crew member of a boat from San Francisco motioned to us that there was room for us to tie alongside their boat. I dropped a stern anchor while Ron and Tim got fenders and dock lines ready.

After we had tied up, Bernie, the Hawaii Yacht Club's harbormaster, came by. He was a little grouchy because we had tied up without asking him, but when we told him that we couldn't stay tied to the gas dock and had just completed a 3,000 mile passage, he was very understanding and said that we could stay. I went in to the Yacht Club office to fill out their papers and get the card keys for the head while Ron and Tim cleaned up *Mahina* a little and headed for the shower.

After we had all taken nice fresh water showers, we started out the gate, headed for the nearest restaurant. Just as we were leaving, a man in a very big hurry came rushing by and asked where the *Mahina* was. I told him that we were off the *Mahina* and that she was tied up at the end of the line of visiting boats. With that, our newfound friend pulled out his wallet and flashed a gold badge that said US Customs on it. I told him that we had just cleared Customs and asked him what he wanted. He said that he wanted some information from me, and opened his attache case to get some papers. Inside were two pistols, one holster, and extra ammunition. The officer came aboard and proceeded to tear everything apart from the forepeak to the cockpit lockers. I told him that if he was looking for drugs he would be very disappointed because I never had any on board.

After finding nothing, he started firing off questions

like an interrogator. He first wanted to know every stop I had made since leaving Seattle. Next, he wanted to know the name of every single yacht I had seen in the past year. I told him that he was getting a little ridiculous, and that if he wanted information about a boat to tell me the name of the boat and I would tell him if I had seen it or not. This made the Customs officer mad, so I told him the names of a couple of yachts I had seen. When asked the purpose of the interrogation, he replied that there had been some strange instances of boats turning up without skippers recently. I asked him to name the boats involved, which he did, and I had never heard of any of them. After some more brusque and unfriendly questioning about where I was headed next and when I was leaving, he departed. We were all very relieved to see him go.

By chance we found the little restaurant that I had gone to just before I left Hawaii a year earlier. It was a small steak house named Buzz's on a back street off the tourist track of Waikiki. We went there for their salad bar. For $2.50 each, we each got as many shots at the table loaded with different salads as we could handle, plus fish and a baked potato. Ron and I went back to the salad bar twice; the kid went back once. The next morning we all took hot showers again, just because they felt so good.

When we were back in the boat getting dressed up to go shopping and girl-watching, Ron looked out of the forehatch, then ducked his head down and said, "Oh no!" I stuck my head out the main hatch and was surprised to see three uniformed Customs agents with pistols and handcuffs on their belts headed our way. In a few seconds they were aboard and went through the same searching and questioning routine as the day before. When I asked the reason for all the questions, they said that a new branch of the US Customs had recently been formed in Hawaii whose sole purpose was to track all yachts in the Pacific. When asked if they didn't think that they were going a little out of their jurisdiction, they said "Absolutely not!" They went over *Mahina*'s registration papers and our passports, and then took the ship's log and went through it to see if the islands I said I had stopped at matched what was in the log. After over an hour of searching (even checking the bilges) and questioning and finding nothing that they could hold us on, they left. I was not at all happy to be subjected to that kind of harassment without reason. We were all US citizens and had never carried anything illegal on board, so it didn't seem at all justified. Before leaving Hawaii, a year earlier, I had heard that the French Customs in Polynesia could be rough at times, but they were always polite and never harassed us. So, what a welcome back to the old US of A!

After we put everything back together that the agents had pulled apart, we went across the street to the Ala Moana shopping center. Tim ran into a girlfriend of his from Samoa whose family was moving back to Hawaii, and Ron called a pilot friend from Samoa who had just gotten a job flying tourists around the island. I needed a haircut badly as I had been cutting my own hair for the past year and it was getting pretty shaggy, so I went in the first place I saw. It turned out to be a pretty fancy place, but the woman who cut my hair was very friendly. Her name was Mona, and we went to see "Jaws" together when she got off work.

The next day — Saturday — I spent airing everything out on *Mahina* and shopping for charts to get me back home since I had traded most of my North Pacific and West Coast charts for charts of the Marquesas. That night I went out dancing with Greg, the crewmember on the boat that we had tied up alongside. We went to Captain Nemo's, one of the best night clubs, according to

Greg. The band was too loud, and it was more of a pick-up game than a place to have fun. I left pretty disappointed because it wasn't anything like when I had gone dancing in Moorea or Raro or Christmas Island.

On Sunday morning, I took everything out of the forepeak, including the cushions, and bolted down the plywood that made up the bunk. It had originally only been screwed in, and it kept working loose every few days when *Mahina* was going to windward, so that everything bounced around up forward. I found that eight or ten well-placed bolts with big washers on them kept everything from working loose on the trip back.

For dinner I took Tim out to a good cheap Chinese restaurant that I had been to the two other times I was on Oahu. Ron had moved in with Jay, his pilot friend, and wasn't around any longer.

On Monday morning I caught a ride with some people from the yacht club who said *Ragtime,* the first place Transpac boat, was about to cross the finish line. We hiked down on the hillside just under the Diamond Head Lighthouse as a spinnaker appeared on the horizon. *Ragtime* went surfing across the finish line at seventeen knots, on a blast of wind she caught off the mountainside. Half of her hull was lifted out of the water by the spinnaker.

That afternoon as I was working on the vane, an older man in a small cabin cruiser came by the dock trying to pick up a pretty blond. He couldn't get close enough to the float because of all the dinghies tied up to it, so I told him that he could pull alongside *Mahina* to take on his passenger. While she was boarding, he told me he was going out to watch *Ondine* come across the finish line and asked if I'd like to go. Without any hesitation, I hopped aboard and we were off. *Ondine* came screaming across the line, and instead of dropping her 'chute then, she carried it on by Waikiki Beach. Just as she was passing the Royal Hawaiian Hilton, the wind increased, causing her to take a partial knockdown, her spinnaker bellying out in the water. Up close she was a spotless and shiny baby blue ketch that looked much larger and more powerful than *Ragtime.* Evidently, in the lighter air that prevailed, *Ragtime* sailed just a little quicker.

Back at the dock where the racers tied up, watching the crew getting garlanded with flowers by pretty girls, I met a friendly lady named Trish who lived on a Viggen, a 24 foot sloop made by the same company that made *Mahina.* Her boat was like a *Mahina* that had just shrunk a little. Trish came over for dinner, and we fixed an omelette that couldn't be beat.

The next morning, Tim went to stay with a friend of his from Samoa for a few days before flying home.

That day I went grocery shopping for the trip back and filled the water tanks. When Trish got home from work, we took off and went biking all over the city and stopped at a couple of nice parks.

When Ron and a girl named Marla came by the next day and asked to sail to Maui with me, I told them that I would be stopping at Lanai for a few days; but that was all right with them. It was 2330 by the time everyone had all their stuff together and we had cast off lines. Once we got outside the harbor, I went below to finish stowing things and Ron went to sleep, leaving Marla on the tiller. I had told her to call me if she saw any lights headed our way, so when I returned on deck, I was shocked to see the "Christmas tree" lights (three vertical white lights on a mast) of a tug pulling a barge. Marla hadn't seen the lights and we were headed directly for the tow cable that connected the tug and barge. By jibing hard and running down wind until the barge passed we just barely managed to escape being run down. The rest of the night either Ron or I were out in the cockpit, keeping an eye out for traffic.

We arrived at Manele Bay around four o'clock in the afternoon and went ashore right away. On the beach we met some nice people from another boat in the bay. They had rented a Jeep from the only gas station on the island and asked us if we would take it back for them. We said sure — that meant we wouldn't have to walk or hitchhike the seven miles up to the only town on the island, Lanai City.

When we got to Van and Flower's house, Flower was out working in her garden. She was very glad to see me. I had spent a week ashore with them the last time I had passed through Hawaii, and they had sailed to Maui on *Mahina*. We had a good time talking and finding out how we had changed since we had last seen each other. Flower had been given two milk goats and was still keeping a huge, lush vegetable garden. She said that she had felt her spirit telling her that she should leave Lanai and go live on Kauai, so she was in the process of giving away her goats and packing up to leave.

Van came home from working on a house that he was helping to build, and Flower fixed us all a fantastic dinner of cheese and nuts and salad and fresh homemade bread and thick vegetable soup. After dinner, Marla and Ron and I took turns taking hot showers, and then the five of us sat around playing guitars and flutes and singing.

The next morning, Ron and I had a good time hiking up in the hills of Lanai. We had another fantastic dinner that night and I really enjoyed sleeping ashore for the second night in nearly a year. Most places I don't like to leave *Mahina* anchored by herself at night, but Manele Bay has a good firm sand bottom and is protected from all but southerly winds which are unusual except in the winter. Also, I had down my two heaviest anchors with all the chain I had available.

The next day was Saturday, and since Van didn't

have to work and needed to get some parts for his car, he sailed with Ron and Marla and me to Lahaina, Maui. The air was very light, so we ended up motorsailing the entire way. After we arrived, Ron and I went out to an Italian restaurant for spaghetti and had a lot of fun looking at all the pretty girls. Ron met a beautiful Hawaiian girl at a nightclub later and didn't come back to *Mahina* until four in the morning. He decided that he really liked the Maui maidens, so he stayed at Lahaina the next day when Van and I sailed back to Lanai.

The sail back on Sunday was windless, so once again we had to motor the entire way. It was well after dark when we started walking up the seven mile road to Lanai City; we were very glad to be picked up by a friendly Japanese family that Van knew. Early the next morning I hitchhiked back down to *Mahina* and spent the day scrubbing the bottom and waxing the hull. When I first reached Lanai, there had been a letter waiting for me from Patty, a friend of mine I met a year ago in Hawaii. I had been trying ever since to make connections with her. She said in her letter that she would be arriving on Lanai on Monday, the twenty-first; but I hadn't heard from her after that, so I didn't know whether she would actually be coming to help sail *Mahina* back to the States or not. When I got back to Van and Flower's, the first thing I did was to ask Flower if a letter had come from Patty. Flower motioned to me to whisper and pointed to the extra bedroom where Patty was sleeping after a long day of traveling. I was very glad to see her again. We had a lot of catching up to do since she had been sailing on a charter schooner out of Agana, Guam, for the past year and had explored much of Micronesia. We had a very good night together, sleeping on the floor close to each other and talking until we fell asleep.

The next morning we bought a few groceries at the tiny store and got a ride down to *Mahina*. Patty said that she had planned to meet her brother, whom she hadn't seen for a couple of years, in Tucson in about three weeks. I told her that even if we left immediately, we might not make it in time for her to see him there, and asked if she didn't think she could find a way to visit him later, after he had moved back to the East Coast. Also, I told her that I had just finished a long and tiring passage and I needed at least a week or two's rest and that *Mahina* needed some serious repair work done to the mast support and main bulkhead.

Patty and I left the harbor the next day — Wednesday, July 23 — and had a very rough sail across the Alenuihaha Channel, arriving at Kailua Kona on the west side of the Island of Hawaii early the following morning. Patty was seasick and grumpy the whole time and not really much help at all. This was pretty disappointing as I had been looking forward to having her sail on *Mahina* for nearly a year.

Because the wind was very light in the lee of the island, it was 1300 when we finally anchored at Kailua. Patty and I went out for dinner at a Chinese restaurant that overlooked the bay, and I told her that maybe it would be better if she just flew back to the States to visit her brother since she really wasn't into sailing on *Mahina*. She bought plane tickets that evening and packed her bags and I said a sad goodbye to her as she got into the cab to go to the airport.

Because I was really depressed at her leaving, I called my brother who was home in Seattle between quarters at the University of Munich and ran up a huge phone bill (his) talking to him. I also called a friend of mine, Bruce, who had wanted to come down to Pago to help me sail back and asked him if he would be interested in sailing from Hawaii to Seattle. He said that he thought he would be, but he would have to find out if he could get that much time off work.

I spent Friday morning at a hardware store buying things I needed for *Mahina.* The bill totaled over $60 by the time I was through, and all I had originally planned to buy was some motor oil and some plastic containers for juice and food. I had dinner at the Chinese restaurant again that evening, then went grocery shopping the next morning. I was very glad when a man offered to give me a ride the mile back to the harbor where the dinghy was tied because a staph infection in my knee had begun to get very painful. Rather than go to a doctor which would have been an expensive proposition, I started taking antibiotics that I had on board and putting Neosporin ointment on it.

The annual billfish tournament was about to start at Kailua Kona and the place was absolutely jammed with boats and tourists, so, as soon as I had all the groceries stowed away, I pulled up the anchors and started motoring toward Kealakekua Bay. When I was almost there, I saw a boat coming very fast toward me with its radar going, and as soon as it got close I saw US CUSTOMS painted on the side in huge letters. They came in very close to the stern, then fell back to about fifty yards and followed me for the next ten minutes. They came roaring up close again and said over a loudhailer "Vessel *Mahina,* this is the US Customs. Heave to and prepare to be boarded." With that, they roared up alongside, colliding with *Mahina,* and an armed Customs Agent and Coast Guard officer jumped aboard. I asked them what they were doing, and they said that it was a safety inspection. The Coast Guard officer, who appeared to be just a young boy, checked for safety equipment while the Customs officer pulled everything apart in the cabin. The Coast Guard officer gave me a ticket for not having a bell on board. When I told him that there had never been fog reported in Hawaii and that I didn't see the reason for the ticket, he just kept repeating, "It's the law, and ignorance is no excuse." When he was done writing the ticket, the Customs officer demanded to see the ship's log and then proceeded to fire questions at me about where I had been and how long in each port and when I was leaving Hawaii and where and when I would be arriving next. He then proceeded to go through the boat again, even checking in the bilges and

under the cockpit. I have never had anything illegal on board — I usually don't even have any alcoholic beverages on board — so I wasn't worried about their finding something unless they had planted it on board. They must have known that the boat had already been torn apart and searched very thoroughly three times in the previous two weeks by their fellow officers.

All the time this was going on, *Mahina* was drifting toward the jagged shoreline close by. When I asked the Customs man if he didn't think that we were getting a little close to the rocks, he just told me not to worry about it. When they finally left, an hour and ten minutes after they boarded, I was tired and scared. I could see no reason for anyone being treated the way I had, especially when I wasn't guilty of anything. My leg had grown very painful, so as soon as the anchor was down in beautiful Kealekekua Bay, I went below and tried to go to sleep.

That night was one of the longest in my life. The pain became so intense that the only way I was able to sleep, even for a short time, was by taking pain pills that I had traded Ampicillin for to a Canadian boat in Huahine. The next morning, despite a great amount of pain, I managed to get ashore. I had no idea where the nearest hospital was, and it was Sunday; but I met some very kind people who lived near by and who gave me a ride right to the hospital. The nurse gasped when she took the gauze off and asked me why I hadn't come in sooner. About that time, an ambulance came in with a victim of a car wreck; so I was shuffled back to the waiting room while they tried for an hour to keep her alive. After she died, they gave me a couple of shots and scrubbed the infected part, telling me to soak it three times a day with Phisohex and to keep taking the Ampicillin that I had prescribed for myself. The doctor gave me a ride back down to the bay and I sat for a while on the shore watching the Sunday afternoon picknickers on the beach before rowing back to *Mahina.*

I spent the rest of Sunday and the next three days aboard, barely able to do more than sleep and eat. I did, however, make one trip to the store, six miles up the hill. The pain was so bad that it hurt to get out of bed, and I had trouble sleeping. On my brief trip up to the store, I called my friend Bruce who told me he'd be arriving on Thursday around noon at Kona airport. I called Jack, a ham operator that lived near the south tip of the Big Island, and he said that he'd be glad to take me to the airport to pick him up.

As soon as Bruce arrived, we all went to an excellent seafood restaurant overlooking the dock where they were starting to bring in the big Ahe and Marlin caught in the fishing tournament. When Bruce and I got back to the bay, the surf had picked up until there were actually a couple of guys surfing; so we had quite a time going through the surf with the Avon heavily loaded with all of Bruce's gear.

We spent the afternoon snorkeling around looking at the coral and did a little scrubbing on the bottom of the boat that had begun to look like a small forest. The next morning after breakfast, we really went to work on the hull and got it fairly clean. Each time we scrubbed it, however, we scrubbed more anti-fouling paint off and the stuff grew back faster. That afternoon, we hitched a ride up to the great town of Kealekekua and bought some fresh vegetables and looked in all the little old Chinese stores. We wanted to stay and go to a movie, but the only thing playing that week was a kung fu movie which I didn't quite feel up to.

On Saturday I fibreglassed over the hole that one of the mast support beams had made in the fibreglass cabin sole and glassed the beam back in place. It didn't look very pretty, but I hoped that it would hold together for the remaining 2,400 miles. I took all of our dirty clothes and towels and sheets up to a little laundromat in the town of Captain Cook on Sunday, and Bruce and I went grocery shopping while they were washing. We had quite a load with all the laundry and $50 worth of groceries on the six-mile walk down the hill back to the bay. We again managed to get through the high surf with a heavily-loaded dinghy without tipping over.

That evening I rowed over and met Win and Stoney, two wonderful people that were leaving the next morning for the Marquesas. Monday morning Bruce and I drifted and motored to Kailua where we anchored in the middle of about fifty charter fishing boats. The tournament was going full blast, with a long line of boats waiting to get in to the pier to have their fish weighed.

After another fantastic Chinese dinner, I called home and found out that a replacement hose for my heater that a friend had made up for me had been sent to Hilo. I decided that it would be much easier to take the bus there the next morning than to beat up the north coast of the island into fresh trade winds, so the next morning I caught the daily bus that goes to Hilo. The trip took over three hours, stopping at every little town along the way. The ride along the coastline was spectacular, with the green fields leading down to the beach where the waves were crashing heavily. When I got to Hilo, I found the hose at the post office, but there was no letter from my family although I had expected one. The ride back to Kailua was a sleepy one — I read two of the three new magazines that I had bought to read on the trip back.

8/6 1230 11,692 miles After filling fuel, kerosene, and water tanks, we pulled up anchors and started motoring to the channel. We had to round Upolu Point, the northwesternmost point of the Big Island, before entering the open sea.

1350 Engine off. Light head winds. If the wind holds from the same direction, we'll be able to clear

Maui without tacking.

1620 Just got hit by the blast through the Alenuihaha Channel. Pounding to windward under only the No. 1 jib.

1900 We aren't making enough headway — we're making too much leeway under jib alone. I hoisted the main, which was luffing, and started cranking the roller reefing handle. Bruce yelled and I looked up and watched as the main split from leech to luff. The only thing holding the boom up was the leech line sewn in the sail. I quickly pulled down what was left of the main and lashed it to the boom and went forward to put the storm jib up instead of the No. 1 jib.

1930 Turned around and started running with the seas toward Kawaihae. *Mahina* is surfing along at seven knots under storm jib alone. I wish we could have kept going, but it would have been a two day job to sew the main back together, and I don't think it would hold up for the rest of the trip.

2200 Arrived at Kawaihae. I anchored here in the daytime last year with Diane, but had no idea what it would be like trying to come in at night without a moon. There were excellent range lights, then buoys with reflectors on them once we got in the channel, so we got in safely. We were very tired and glad to be anchored and sitting still. Bruce was pretty frightened by the conditions out there tonight, but I assured him that it is rarely as rough as it was tonight. The currents meeting the tradewinds and seas make a very nasty condition between Maui and Hawaii in the Alenuihaha Channel — it's reputed to be one of the roughest channels in the world.

Early the next morning I went ashore and called the only sailmaker listed on the Island of Hawaii, only to find that he went out of business a year ago. I didn't want to send the sail to a sailmaker in Hono for repairs because I had no idea when I'd get it back, so I called the Vega dealer in Seattle and asked him if he had a spare main I could borrow for a month. He said he didn't, but he called a sailmaker in Seattle while I was on the line and asked what was the absolute soonest they could make a sail for me and have it on a plane to Hawaii. It turned out that that way would have taken about a week and a half, so I thanked them and told them I'd call them back later if I decided to go that route. I was in a hurry to get it fixed because it was already late in the season for going back to the West Coast. Every day we waited meant a greater chance of storms in the North Pacific. Also, Bruce had to be back in Seattle for a board meeting in less than a month. The operator suggested I try calling upholstery shops, so I started at the top of the page and worked my way down. The next to the last number was an interior decorator in Kailua who said he'd be glad to do it even though he had never repaired sails before. I told him that I had spare sailcloth and dacron thread and could even do the sewing myself, but just needed a good strong zig-zag machine.

I took off the main and put it in its bag and started walking toward Kailua, which was thirty miles away. I had walked ten miles on the desert-like unshaded road with the temperature in the nineties when I finally got a ride from a nice Hawaiian man. When I got to the shop, there was no one there, so I went in the greenhouse next door and started talking with the friendly lady who owned it. It was cool and green inside and just like being in a jungle. Through the course of the conversation, she said that she knew a woman who sewed jeep tops and did canvas repair for a living. She called Ginny and asked her if she could mend sails. Ginny said yes, so I was off again.

Ginny, who was very nice, looked at the sail and explained that her machine was for canvas and could only do a straight stitch with a huge needle, so we took the sail next door to Ginny's friend Natasha and tried to sew it up on her machine. We managed to get the two edges sewn together roughly, before Natasha's machine jammed up altogether. We then took it back to Ginny's house so her husband Dave could take a look at it. The seam was uneven, so the three of us pulled out all the stitches and Dave and I glued a patch over the entire area. Dave said that when it dried they would stitch it using the widest stitch on their old machine, and he thought that would hold it. I took them out to dinner that night at the good Chinese restaurant in Kailua to thank them for their help. After dinner we walked along the waterfront looking at all the fishing boats.

I spent the night at a cheap hotel nearby and then went by early the next morning to pick up the sail. It was all finished. They had done a neat job on it and wouldn't accept any money for their work. Dave dropped me off at a corner where he thought I'd be able to get a ride back to Kawaihae without any trouble. I said goodbye to him and thanked him for all their help.

After waiting for a while with no results, I started walking. I ended up getting two short rides out as far as the airport, then suddenly I was in the middle of nowhere with few cars passing and 25 miles left to go. After an hour or so, a Hawaiian man stopped and gave me a lift to Kawaihae Bay where *Mahina* was anchored.

Bruce and I decided that instead of leaving that afternoon, we'd take it easy and get a good night's sleep and start out first thing in the morning. That afternoon Bruce collected shells on the beach and underwater for his aquarium at home, and I went walking along the beach around the bay. A number of Japanese families were picnicking and fishing down at the beach at sunset. Their family ties seem much stronger than those of the average American family; they brought everyone from Grandma and Grandpa to tiny baby sister along when they went to the beach. The adults had a great time fishing and talking by the light of kerosene lanterns, while the teenagers all got together and sang and played guitars down by the shore. Very nice.

The next morning a beautiful island girl named Christie came by and had breakfast with us. She said that if I was going to be sailing in the islands or going south she would really like to join the *Mahina,* but when I told her that we were headed back to the States and asked her if she wanted to go she said that it was too cold.

Chapter 21

Homeward Bound

8/9 1000 11,724 miles Left Kawaihae. Motored along close to the coast for an hour then caught a good strong breeze that sent us on our way out the Alenuihaha Channel again.

1300 Cleared Upolu Point. Goodbye Hawaii! I have mixed feelings about leaving. I would have liked to stay and get a job in Hilo for the winter, but it would have involved problems of where to put the boat. I would have had to move ashore, and that would have probably eaten up any money that I would have earned. Also, I was tired of being hassled by government officials and I wanted to get home to see my family and friends.

1600 Seas very rough. Under triple-reefed main and No. 1 and still pounding hard. The antenna just broke, but fortunately the guy wires to the backstays kept us from losing it. I unscrewed the clamp that held the broken end to the holder and just fitted the antenna back over the base like before, only the antenna is now a foot shorter. I tried the radio and it worked — not as well as before — be we were still being heard clearly.

2000 Still very rough and windy. I'm doing a lot of praying that the main and the boat and we will hold together until we get back.

8/10 0500 Sunrise, grey, cloudy and cool. Seas calmer than last night.

1315 Fix I just got shows that we've covered 113 miles in the first twenty-four hours. Not bad at all considering what we've been driving into. Barometer rising slowly.

2000 Talked with Mom and Dad through a ham named Stu in West Seattle. They were glad to hear that we're on the way and that we're making good time.

8/11 0100 Light variable winds — only doing three and a half knots.

1000 Talked with Charles who is now in Suva, Fiji, and with Gordon. I have never met Gordon, but we left from Samoa the same day, bound for Seattle, but sailing different routes. The *Shaula*'s route was via Suwarrow, Rarotonga, Tahiti, and Huahine, and now she was almost to Hawaii. Gordon said his wife Ruth Ann hadn't gotten used to sailing yet; however, since she never got sea sick as long as she didn't go below, she had taken to sleeping on deck at night. Gordon said that he planned to jump off Mauna Loa with his hang-glider once they arrived in Hawaii. In Samoa, Gordon was known as the "Birdman of Pago" because he often jumped off 2,000 foot Rainmaker Mountain and "flew" the entire way across the bay.

1700 Just completed a two and a half hour job of sewing up more seams on the No. 1 jib where the sun has rotted the original thread. Soon I will have resewn the entire leech and a lot of the seams — and all by hand. What a lot of work!

2330 Beautiful night. Winds Force 3 and seas calm.

There are a million stars out and a tiny sliver of a new moon.

8/12 0400 Just finished reading an Indian book called "Conquering Horse." It was excellent and very exciting, but I've worn out a set of flashlight batteries and my eyes are tired from reading.

0720 Sighted a freighter on the horizon. It passed fairly close in front of us on a course of approximately 275°. I suppose that it is headed for Japan.

1030 Smitty, a ham in Hono, patched us in to Fleet Weather Central at Pearl Harbor. They gave us a forecast from their satellite observations and said that they appreciated our giving them surface information as they had no ships reporting weather observations from our area of the Pacific. Encouraging that **we** can help **them!** I'm having many different thoughts about returning. I'm anxious to sit on the beach at Point Wilson again and watch the tide come in. I hope that I get back in time to see my brother Dave before he leaves for school in Geneva. Maybe he could come out to Neah Bay and meet us there and help sail home.

8/13 Took a cockpit shower and spent the whole day reading Bruce's book "The Zen of Motorcycle Maintenance" all the way through. It made me want to get a bike again and go explore the old US of A.

3/14 0400 I woke up very suddenly in the cockpit after a very clear dream: first I heard a ship—I looked all around the horizon and saw some lights in the distance, but I knew that the ship they were from was too far away to be heard. I became worried and started looking around close. Then I saw a junky looking old steamer right off our bow. It had a rusty white hull and cargo stacked high on the decks, and its engines sounded very rough. Strange dream.

1000 Just talked with Gordon. He said they'd be arriving in Hilo this afternoon. They will have made the

2,100 mile passage from Huahine to Hilo in just fifteen days — really excellent time. I also talked with Mike and Joanie Hitchcock. They are on a forty foot ketch named *Sunday* en route from Samoa to Tonga. Mike said that Tim arrived home safely and had really enjoyed sailing to Hawaii. The barometer is the highest I've ever seen and still rising slowly. I hope that this doesn't mean we are going to get stuck in the middle of the high.

2000 Just had lots of nice thoughts about Janet Rute. It's been four years since we said goodbye to each other down near the Mexican border, and I think I'd like to be with her again. Maybe a bike trip down the coast next spring??? Sure hope *Mahina* holds together until we get back. Really glad Gordon had a good trip. It's cold tonight and I put on my wool Navy surplus pants for the first time in almost a year and a half.

8/15 0840 Last night was clear and beautiful. When we ran over a Japanese glass ball in the middle of the night, it woke me up as it thump - thumped its way down the hull. A Japanese freighter registered in Tokyo just passed. I think it would have run us down if I hadn't started the engine and moved to one side as it passed by. It was modern and very quiet. The men on the bridge waved.

1000 Just got fantastic weather report from Fleet Weather. They said we should be out of the high pressure area that we're in within 24 to 36 hours. Yahoo!!

1425 Even though we've been having a lot of light air, we've covered 105 miles in the last 24 hours. Not bad at all! We picked up six glass fishing floats and one large orange plastic one today. Bruce spent almost the whole day watching for floats, and I spent most of the day being lazy and sleeping. This afternoon I was talking to Homer, the skipper of the *Tumbleweeds,* a 35 foot ketch that is about 1000 miles ahead of us headed for California. When we were through, a ham with an aeronautical mobile call called me and asked where we were. I gave him our position and asked him where he was and what kind of plane he was flying. He came back and said that he was co-pilot on a Northwest Orient 747 enroute from Hono to Seattle-Tacoma. They were flying at 600 knots compared to our four! After talking with him, I was tuning around the dial and picked up another aeronautical mobile station (those were the only two I've ever talked with) calling CQ (asking to talk with anyone). I answered his call and found out that he was pilot of an old DC-6 cargo plane that was just pulling into San Diego from Hawaii. It sure is interesting having the radio on board!

8/16 1600 Another light air day. The barometer is still very high and by the fix I got this afternoon it seems that we are only about fifty miles from the center of the high. We found a lot more glass balls today. I think the total is something like eighteen or nineteen. We have a couple of big ones and lots of little ones. Some aren't any bigger than a light bulb. There is a steady swell from the east; I wish that the wind would come with it. Clear and warm this afternoon.

There is a little black and blue striped fish swimming in front of *Mahina*. I think he is a pilot fish and he must think *Mahina* is a whale that needs leading. I named him Sam — that seems an appropriate name for a fish who only likes corned beef. I fed him part of the last can of corned beef we have on board. He gets mixed up when we tack around in circles trying to pick up balls. Every once in a while he shoots off in pursuit of a fly or bug on the water's surface, then darts back to his position right in front of the bow. He's good company.

I'm often tired these days and not sure why — it will be good to be back.

8/17 2055 A ship with many lights just passed. The wind has been very light and right out of the northwest — the direction we are headed, so I took down the sails and powered all day at four knots.

8/18 0710 Another ship just passed—this is getting to be like the LA freeway on Friday afternoon.

1400 I just finished baking bread in the pressure cooker with a recipe that Homer on the *Tumbleweeds* gave me over the radio. I think the yeast was old or else I didn't put it in a warm enough place because the dough didn't rise very much and tasted yeasty. It was still good — real chewy since I used part seven-grains cereal mixture and part whole wheat flour. I sure wish we'd get some wind because we're getting low on fuel — only about fifteen hours left.

1800 Winds came fast and strong — seas rough and building. Main reefed and No. 1 jib up instead of genoa.

8/19 0700 Main reefed deeper. Seas are crossed and rough and *Mahina* is pounding hard. I just got an interesting forecast that said the wind will switch to NW in a day or so. That would really slow us down if we had to make a long tack north before heading for Cape Flattery.

8/20 0800 Talked with Charles and "the gang" and sewed up the seat of my Navy pants and put some buttons on my blue shirt. One of the hanks on the No. 1 jib cut through its lashing so rather than take the time to sew a new hank on, I screwed on one of the spare plastic ones for the genoa. It looks okay.

1400 Fix N 35° 44', W 147° 44' or 1200 miles west of Monterey, California. Possible ETA at Neah Bay is August 31. Sure hope so! Oh, for a hot shower or a long, hot bath!

8/21 1100 Got lots done this morning. Bruce washed the sheets and pillowcases — they were so filthy that he had to wash them three times. I cleaned all the junk out of the shelf above the port settee berth and straightened up the bookshelf. Also scraped the rust off the CO_2 canister and oiled it. Later, I had a shower and shampoo in the cockpit; now I feel and smell much cleaner. The water is getting much colder and feels like ice when I dump a bucketfull over my head to rinse off.

8/22 Lazy day — aired carpet out — that's about all. Sam is still with us and will come over to the side when we call him. Smart fish!

8/23 0800 Wind NNW at twelve and seas crossed at only four feet. Covering over 115 miles per day! Replaced the burner in the Sea-Swing stove and shut off the leaky galley water pump that has been getting the carpet soggy. We now fill a one-gallon jug every morning from a jerry can in the lazarette. A little more work, but we don't use as much water this way and the carpet stays dry.

8/24 0000 Dense fog — visibility only a couple of boat lengths. I sure hope we don't meet any ships tonight! We can't point high enough to hold a course of 37° that we need to make in order to end up in Neah Bay. Looks like we may end up in Coos Bay instead. I sure hope not!

1000 Just got weather from Fleet Central via the sub base at Pearl Harbor. They said that there are thirty to forty knot winds 300 to 500 miles east of us off the California coast. The pilot chart for this month shows an average wind of Force 5 off the coast, so I don't want to end up having to beat our way north in that stuff. Fleet Weather suggests a northerly course for about 200 miles to avoid that and to pick up the northwesters.

1900 Very discouraging day. I tried to get the Taylor kerosene heater going after a year's inactivity but it ended up belching fire and smoke because some of the hose connections were leaking and refused to stop no matter how hard they were tightened. There is dense fog outside and we are in the middle of the LA shipping lanes.

8/25 0200 Foggy, drizzly, miserable night.

0900 Wind! Yahoo!! And it's changing from NNE to NNW so we are making a course right for Neah Bay instead of for Oregon. A little sun — got carpet and clothes dried out.

8/26 1000 Wind increased last night to forty knots and seas are getting high. We are down to a storm jib and a double-reefed main. The weather forecast on WWV says that there is a gale just to the north of us. Praying very hard that the boat will hold together through this pounding.

2030 Main down and storm trysail hoisted. It reduced our angle of heel considerably and I am afraid of having the main blow out again.

8/27 0400 Massive squall with conditions up to Force 7. Doing six to seven knots under just a storm jib and trysail.

0800 The jam post under the mast has started to split and the main bulkhead is warped heavily at the top — it looks like it will split soon.

1000 I was able to get the radio working again. I think the problem was that the base of the antenna was shorting out because it was constantly taking spray. I cut a one-quart plastic juice container so that it fits over the base and taped it in place. It seems to keep it dry enough. I was able to talk to Charles and George and Mom and Dad. Dad said he'd come out to Port Angeles or to Neah Bay and meet me. That will be great. Mom said that when she called to make reservations for them at Port Townsend she found that my friend Janet is still working at Point Hudson Marina. I'm glad — it will be good to see her. Bruce was able to get a patch from George to his home and talk to his girlfriend Jan.

8/28 0700 Bruce sighted a 25' x 3' log drifting right off our stern. That's the first time I've seen a big log in the middle of the ocean. I'm sure glad we didn't hit it because something that big might sink us in a hurry.

2200 Beautiful night. Some breaks in the overcast and conditions seem to be getting better slowly. We are still averaging almost six knots but aren't pounding as hard. Easier to sleep.

1000 Just got excellent forecast from Fleet Weather. They said that the winds should remain behind the beam for the rest of the trip. That would sure be a lot easier on *Mahina* and would mean we'd arrive sooner.

8/29 1230 Storm jib and trysail finally down — we are sailing under a double-reefed main and the No. 1. Worked hard all morning drying clothes and carpet out and navigating and generally cleaning things up below.

1320 Covered 144 miles in the past 24 hours! That's getting pretty close to a record for *Mahina!* Only 468 miles to go! Bruce is worried about our ETA as he wants to have some time to rest before he goes back to work. I'll be glad to get back, but I can't get very excited about whether we arrive Monday or Tuesday. But I can see Bruce's position since he must go back to work Wednesday night. The days sure have gone by quickly.

8/30 1000 George is switching his patch to his 40 meter band radio since we are too close to talk on 20 meters any more. He's pretty excited about our arrival — says he might come to Port Townsend to meet us.

1410 Our position is N 46° 21', W 131° 56'. We have covered nearly 145 miles in the past 24 hours so we only have 325 miles to go! ETA is for Monday night, September 1.

8/31 0940 Still holding over five and a half knots — only 215 miles to go.

1550 Bruce: New time. We just changed the clocks to Pacific Daylight Savings Time. I sighted a long piece of tubular kelp — land can't be too far off!

1630 Just changed back to Hawaii time because the time change upset our watch schedule. We'll just wait until after we make landfall to change the clocks.

9/1 0400 Moving well at over five knots — only 113 miles to go. ETA tomorrow morning at 0500 local time.

0700 Sighted ship — turned out to be a fishing boat that passed fairly close.

1330 Only 77 miles to go. The fix I just got put us halfway up Vancouver Island and the radio beacon at Estevan Point is stronger than the one at Cape Flattery which would lead me to think that my sextant got jarred when a sudden wave sent me tumbling while I was trying to get a sight this morning. Now the sky is overcast and there is no break in the clouds in sight, so we'll just have to go in on the DR and RDF.

1915 Many fishing boats with strobe lights sighted on the horizon ahead. I just got an RDF fix from the Estevan Point and Cape Flattery beacons that confirm my guess that this afternoon's fix was screwy. Also, there is a very strong Canadian radio beacon at 352 sending YIZ. The radiobeacon chart in my light list doesn't have any station listed with that frequency or call, so I had George call the Coast Guard in Seattle and they didn't know where it was either. I later decided that it must be the beacon at Carmana Point that is supposed to be sending DO at 288 according to the chart.

2000 Cape Flattery beacon is bearing 75° and Estevan Point is at 325° which would put us only 57 miles away from Cape Flattery.

2030 We are doing only one to two knots under sail, so I started powering ahead slowly. We don't have much fuel left.

2300 We must be passing over La Perouse Bank as there are fishing boats all around us. I just counted forty-two strobe lights — it's like we are in the middle of a light show. One of the boats has a **green** strobe!

9/2 0000 Engine off. I don't want to run the tank dry here because we still have 38 miles to go. We are completely becalmed, but not alone because there are still little flashing strobes on the horizon behind us.

0435 14,127 miles. Sun just starting to brighten up the eastern horizon and **I CAN SEE LAND!!!** That must be Cape Flattery dead ahead!

0500 Stopped and asked a fishing boat that was headed out if they could give us a gallon or two of gas. They said that all they had on board was diesel, but that they would ask on their VHF if there were any boats in the area that had gas. They said that it was only about 35 miles to the Cape.

0630 Engine running perfectly. It has run ten and a quarter hours on this tank of gas and it's only supposed to go ten hours on one tank — it should run out any time. I am keeping a gallon extra in another tank so we'll have enough to get from Cape Flattery to Neah Bay, if we can just get that far.

1135 Engine has over fifteen hours running on the tank and is still going. A forty foot sport fishing charter boat named *Wind Song* out of Neah Bay stopped and said that the other boat had told them to watch for us. They said that they didn't have any gas, but would be happy to give us a tow. The boat is run by three blond-haired women whose five passengers look a bit seasick and tired of fishing. We made a bridle using half inch and three-quarter inch nylon lines going to each side of the stern. I told them that six and a half knots was as fast as *Mahina* could safely be towed, but they just smiled and took off at EIGHT KNOTS!! Water started shooting in through the cockpit scuppers, and by the time Bruce had them plugged up, the water was getting close to knee deep. I had to stay on the tiller all the time because *Mahina* would try and dash back and forth from one side of the *Wind Song*'s wake to the other.

1305 *Wind Song* stopped and let go our lines because they said they needed to get their charter passengers back in. They had called the Coast Guard without asking me. Soon, a forty foot launch arrived and an officer asked if we needed assistance. I said no, that we were just a little short on fuel, but I thought we could make it in. They followed behind us to make sure.

1415 14,170 miles The Coast Guard men said that we could tie to their dock to clear Customs and take showers, so we did. They were friendly and helpful. Bruce headed up to call Jan and ask her to come and get him, and I walked into town to buy some food. Neah Bay was still crowded to overflowing with campers and trailers from the Labor Day weekend rush and was a pretty depressing introduction back to the States after nearly a year and a half. The shelves in the grocery store were nearly empty — it had been a busy weekend — but I managed to buy some milk and ice cream and a big bag of cookies which Bruce and I promptly devoured as soon as I got back to the boat. Soon Jan arrived and picked up Bruce.

I had a nice long shower that evening and it felt so good to be clean. I called my parents and told them that we had made it in safely. They were very happy and wanted to know if they could meet me at Port Angeles the next day. I told them that I had to do some work on the engine and fill the gas tanks before I left the next morning and wasn't sure if there would be enough daylight left to make it to Port Angeles since it's about an eleven hour trip. I told them I'd call them the next morning.

I woke up early and walked down to the gas dock and bought ten gallons of gas and stopped and called home. Mom said she had been looking at the charts and that Crescent Bay was closer than Port Angeles; she thought they had docks there, so I told her I'd try and meet them there that evening.

9/3 1010 Left Neah Bay. Straits of Juan de Fuca are glassy calm, not a breath of wind, but now I have enough fuel on board to power the entire way to Seattle if I have to.

1730 Tied up to dock at Crescent Bay Resort. Mom and Dad and Mary greeted me at the dock with hugs. It's sure good to see them. They came aboard for a few minutes and looked at *Mahina,* and I showed them some pictures I had. Then I locked the boat up and went with them up to the room they had rented in the A-frame on the beach for a great dinner. After dinner, Dad and I went for a long walk on the beach and had a good time talking and getting to know each other again.

9/4 0915 After a good breakfast, I said goodbye to everyone and headed for Port Townsend, about forty miles away. It was another calm windless day, so I motored until I got to Point Wilson where I picked up a nice breeze coming around the corner, then I hoisted sail. Just before I got to the entrance to Point Hudson Marina, a red and white float plane buzzed low overhead dipping its wings — it was my good friend Wendy Trosper who had flown by to say hello. Just after Wendy flew over, the sloop *Isle of Wight* sailed out the breakwater and my friends Ann and Dick Wightman came alongside and said, "Welcome back!"

Once I got inside the marina and tied up, I said hello to my brother Dave whom I hadn't seen in almost two and a half years. Soon the bottles of champagne came out and we had a great afternoon. For dinner, we all trouped up to the Surf, a nice little restaurant overlooking Admiralty Inlet. Halfway through dinner, George and his wife Rachel, came in the joined our party, which had swelled to ten people. At dessert time, Lee and Toni and a couple of their kids and Jim and Kathy and their baby daughter came in, nearly filling the back room of the restaurant. They all walked back to *Mahina* with me and came aboard to look at the boat.

The next morning, I sailed in company with the *Isle of Wight* to Port Ludlow. Just as I was entering the inner harbor, Wendy flew low overhead in his plane and landed right behind me. We had a most unusual raft-up in the inner harbor — two sailboats with an airplane tied behind! After lunch, Wendy took off to fly back to work (he was just on his lunch break). We had a much quieter night than the night before.

After breakfast, the *Isle of Wight* sailed back to Shilshole Bay, leaving me at Ludlow. I pumped up the Avon and rowed ashore and went for a walk in the woods. The smells of the trees and the water made me very happy to be home. Some of the leaves had even started to turn color and fall was in the air. I walked back to a waterfall and stood there for a long time, wondering what it would be like to be back in the city.

The End.

Moorea's rugged peaks

Robinson's Cove, Papetoi Bay, Moorea

Apper

The Islands

In this section I will give the prospective visitor information, updated to August 1994, about sailing to some of the islands of the Pacific. This chapter isn't mean to replace detailed cruising references like *Charlie's Charts of Polynesia,* which I have helped revise, or Marcia Davock's excellent *Cruising Guide to Tahiti and the French Society Islands*. For planning ocean passages, I highly recommend *World Cruising Routes* by Jimmy Cornell.

Hawaiian Islands

The best months to sail to Hawaii from the mainland are June and July. Once you arrive, it is necessary to clear U.S. Customs and Agriculture, even if coming from the U.S. mainland. The most logical Port of Entry is Hilo, on the island of Hawaii, since it is closest to the mainland and upwind of the other islands. Customs and Agriculture inspectors are adamant that you first clear in at an official Port of Entry, with only the captain going ashore before any stops are made. All pets (even coming from the U.S.) must go through a mandatory 120 day quarantine whether or not you intend taking the animal ashore.

of Hawaii

s the largest town and the best port to clear into . It is also one of the friendliest cities in Hawaii. is difficult to dangerous to enter in the dark; the city hts are much brighter than the range or breakwater ghts. Radio Bay is a small boat harbor behind the breakwater with Customs, Agriculture, showers, laundromat and a Safeway located nearby.

Because of abundant rainfall and lack of white sand beaches, Hilo has very few tourists and the downtown area looks much the same as it did in the 50's. Several art galleries and museums as well as spectacular waterfalls are within bicycling distance from Radio Bay. Car rentals throughout the state are very competitive, so a trip to Volcanoes National Park, 30 miles away, shouldn't be missed.

The easiest passage from Hilo is to leave just before dawn, sailing up the Hamakua Coast and around Upolu Point, the northwest corner of the island, to Mahukona. Mahukona is the first possible anchorage and the sight of an abandoned sugar mill. If you still have daylight, Kawaihae Harbor - 10 miles to the south, offers better protection with moorings and an anchorage area behind a breakwater. A new small boat marina located just south of the breakwater, has been planned by the state.

Kawaihae is a small, but growing, town with a couple of stores, restaurants and art galleries. Puukohola Heiau is an important Hawaiian religious monument, clearly visible from the anchorage and worth a visit.

Honokohau Harbor didn't exist when I wrote *Log of the Mahina.* It is an excellent small boat harbor blasted out of lava rock with room for a very few visiting yachts amidst the glittering sport-fishing boats. There is a fuel dock and grocery store. A large Travelift, dry storage and work areas are located nearby at Gentry's Kona Marine; the best place in the state to haulout a sail or power boat.

Kailua Kona is the second largest town on the Big Island, but has a rolly, exposed and crowded anchorage, so it's easiest to leave your boat in Honokohau and hitchhike or bicycle the 2 1/4 mile distance to town.

Kealakekua Bay is the most dramatic and historical bay on the island, and is where Captain James Cook was killed and eaten. However, if State anchoring restrictions are being enforced, it may not be possible to anchor there. Be prepared for different stories from each official you talk with. Another option may be to ask permission of one of the day trip charter boats to use their mooring from late afternoon until they arrive in the morning. Spinner dolphins regularly cruise Kealakekua Bay in the mornings, putting on an incredible show. The snorkeling in the area around Cook's Monument is dramatic, with myriads of fish accustomed to daily feeding by the charter boats. In settled weather conditions Honaunau or Kiilae Bay, 3 1/2 miles south, has nice snorkeling and would put you within dinghy distance of Kealakekua Bay.

Milolii, 18 miles south of Kealakekua, is an exposed and rolly anchorage off a small Hawaiian village, where time seems to have stood still since the 1950's. The snorkeling or scuba diving is excellent with good water clarity and interesting caves formed by hot lava hitting the ocean. A more secure anchorage in settled weather is Okoe Bay, 2 1/4 miles south, with a sand and coral bottom at 30'. Look ashore for the restored holua, a ramp made of volcanic stone, which the Hawaiians covered with slippery leaves and used as a sled run for their royalty.

Manuka Bay, 4 1/4 miles south of Okoe Bay, has an anchorage in 22' with lava and coral bottom, great snorkeling, but is sometimes rolly.

The Island of Maui

Maui has a Customs Port of Entry at Kahului on the

windward side, making it less than ideal for sailboats.

Hana, on the eastern tip of the island has a beautiful, uncrowded bay which is unfortunately exposed to the normal northeast trade winds. There is excellent holding, so plan on using two anchors and getting used to the motion at anchor. The town is small, friendly, very picturesque. Don't miss the Seven Sacred Pools, ten miles away by road.

Diane exploring Seven Sacred Pools, Maui

Lahaina has a very small and full harbor; finding moorage inside for more than a few hours is unlikely. The anchorage in the roadstead off the harbor has poor holding, is rolly and totally exposed to Kona or southerly winds. Many yachts have been lost here over the years, after dragging anchor and hitting the coral reef. A slightly better anchorage is 3 1/2 miles north off the hotels at Kaanapali, or six miles further in Honolua Bay.

The Island of Lanai

Lanai used to be heavily cultivated for pineapples by the Dole corporation, which kept the island largely untouched from tourism. However, in the past few years two large and exquisite hotels have been built, the Manele Beach Hotel on Hulopoe Bay and the Inn at Koele, just east of Lanai City. The hotels are running at very low occupancy rates because of high prices.

The island is as friendly as ever, and Lanai City is as picturesque as it was 20 years ago. The State run harbor in **Manele Bay** (east of the hotel) is often full, but it is possible to drop a bow anchor and tie off to rocks astern behind the breakwater, but not quite in the harbor. The harbormistress will let you know if there are any vacant slips available. Showers, barbecue pits and water are all available in the harbor. Excellent surfing, snorkeling and swimming are a five minute walk away at Hulopoe Bay, locally known as White Manele. It is no longer possible to anchor here since the bay was designated an underwater marine park to protect the coral. The Manele Beach Hotel is a short walk up from the beach and is a great place to go for sunset cocktails or dinner.

Lanai has fascinating hikes and beach walks to petroglyphs, archeological sites and shipwrecks, so you may want to rent a car or jeep in Lanai City to go exploring.

The Island of Molokai

Molokai is known for windy anchorages, whether on the north or south side of the island. The main town and commercial harbor is Kaunakakai, where there is a passable, but windy, anchorage in nine feet of water with a sandy bottom. The anchorage is off the northwest corner of Pier Island, near the boat launching ramp. Moorings with stern ties can be found on the opposite side of the wharf, but these are usually filled with permanently moored boats and are exposed to the full force of the tradewinds. The loading dock, also on the northwest side of the wharf, has water. Showers and rest rooms are on the wharf next to the harbormaster's office.

Lono Harbor, near the southwest corner of Molokai, is the site of an abandoned sand quarry and is breakwater-protected in all but southerly winds. There are no houses or people here, but it is a fairly safe anchorage with interesting hiking ashore.

The Island of Oahu

Oahu is by far the most developed of the Hawaiian Islands. Honolulu is a bustling, thriving and vibrant city - truly a crossroads of the Pacific, and a Port of Entry for arriving yachts. The Ala Wai Marina is located 3 1/2 miles northwest of Diamond Head Crater. The entrance is difficult to find at night because the street lights are much brighter than the range markers or channel lights. Don't add your yacht to the list of dozens of boats that have been smashed on the reef while trying to enter in the dark. The channel is relatively narrow and it's common to have surfers on either side of your boat as you head in the entrance. A fuel dock (fuel, propane, water, ice, laundry) is conveniently located just inside the entrance. You may be allowed to tie here while calling for Customs and Agriculture clearance. The harbormaster's office is a five minute walk away. Hopefully, they will find room for you on the new transient wharf, just behind the breakwater. You may also try calling or dinghying over to the accommodating Hawaii Yacht Club, they keep a few slips for visitors. If you need to haul your boat out, Ala Wai Marine (aka Pirate Pete's) is in the same harbor and can take care of hull or engine repairs, welding and metal fabrication or general chandlery needs. Art Nelson's sail loft, on the opposite side of the Ala Wai Shopping Center, does good work at reasonable prices. Since there isn't a West Marine store in Hawaii yet, many cruisers take advantage of West's good prices and fast UPS air service to have large ticket items sent from West's warehouse in California.

Besides the Ala Wai Harbor, there is a noisy mooring at Keehi Lagoon underneath the flight path of Honolulu Airport. Kaneohe Bay has a friendly yacht club and some anchorage areas. At Waianae there is a mostly commercial small boat harbor.

The Island of Kauai

Kaui is aptly nicknamed the Garden Isle and is as lush and green as anyone's idea of a tropical island. Hanalei Bay, in the center of the northern side of Kauai, is one of the loveliest and most popular summertime anchorages in the state. The bay is one mile wide, so it rarely feels crowded. Good holding can be found in 30'-35' of water. The town of Hanalei is a short walk away and has a decent grocery store and interesting shops. Many yachts returning to the West Coast choose Hanalei as their last port in Hawaii. The only difficulty here is that the closest station to purchase diesel fuel is at the Chevron station in Kapaa, 22 miles away by road. It's not unusual for crews of yachts to go together to rent a car from the Princeville Airport, two miles from Hanalei, just to make a fuel run with jerry jugs in the trunk!

You may find space in the small, crowded boat harbor at Port Allen or anchor and tie stern-to in the commercial harbor of Nawiliwili Bay.

Overall, cruising the Hawaiian Islands is interesting, but challenging. The State limits your stay in any one harbor to 30 days per year (with a few exceptions) and there are few all-weather anchorages. Space in the small boat harbors is always at a premium. Hawaii is a good stopping-off place, whether you are sailing from the West Coast or returning from the South Pacific. As for a place to "winter over", while waiting out the South Pacific cyclone season or waiting out the North Pacific winter, it is difficult.

French Polynesia - The Marquesas Islands

Alvaro de Mendana y Castro of Spain discovered the Marquesas in 1595. Captain Cook, the next European visitor, came in 1774. Cook described the Marquesan people and culture quite extensively in his journals. The Marquesans, living in an environment where food was abundant, developed a complex society with many gods and ceremonies. Some of the ancient ceremonial areas described by early visitors are still intact and can be visited today.

The Marquesans were great seafarers. In their golden age they sailed 60' - 80' catamarans north to discover and settle the Hawaiian Islands. To windward they discovered and settled Pitcairn and Easter Islands.

The population of the Marquesas fell from a pre-European contact high of approximately 80,000 to a low of about 1,300 in 1936. The decline was a result of diseases, guns and alcohol introduced by whalers, traders and Peruvian blackbirders (slave raiders). Today the population is 8,000 and growing steadily despite migration to Tahiti by some of the young people.

The culture, land and destiny of the Marquesas is more in the hands of the local population than in many areas of the South Pacific, although the French do provide good medical care and schooling. The Marquesas are so isolated and expensive to reach from Tahiti (approximately. $750 US round trip, 1994) there is still almost no tourism in the group, other than visiting yachts.

Most of the schoolteachers are Marquesans who have gone to Tahiti for university training. The young schoolteachers are very concerned about preserving their culture, recently forming a group which set up the Islands'first museum on Ua Huka Island. They are often interested in outside visitors; inviting cruisers to their homes for volleyball games and pot luck dinners, always ready to explain the local customs and history.

Taiohae, Nuku Hiva and Atuona on Hiva Oa are the only two Ports of Entry. Do not stop anywhere else before clearing customs. The French Gendarmes in Taiohae or Atuona can radio Papeete for permission to grant you a temporary three month visa, renewable in Papeete for an additional three months. At this time it is easier to get the visa upon arrival than through the French Consulates. If you plan to sail on to Papeete within 30 days, you probably will be allowed to wait until Papeete to post a bond equivalent to a one-way open airline ticket back to your country of origin. If you wish to spend longer than 30 days cruising the Marquesas and Tuamotus, you will probably be asked to post the bond in Taiohae or Atuona. The alternatives are to arrive with a valid airline ticket (not a good option, difficult to cash in) or a notarized letter from your travel agent stating that they have an imprint of your credit card and are authorized to issue you an open return ticket on demand. This worked for me and several other cruisers in 1993 &1994 and is certainly worth a try as it costs nothing. The reason for the bond is that in the past several cruisers have run out of money and decided that they were going to "live off the land" and the French government became tired of paying to fly them home. The bond money is returned just before you leave the territory, which for most cruisers is in Papeete or Bora Bora. There is a visa fee of approximately $30 per three month visa, per person, and a service fee of about the same amount from the bank. It is possible to get cash advances on Visa and Mastercards in the Marquesas, but even better is to arrive with enough travelers checks to cover the bond, if needed. This situation changes slightly from year to year.

The French or Tahitian authorities are generally very polite and circumspect if approached in a gentle manner. But, like any government officials, they can make your life very difficult if you are impolite or try to tell them what to do. Any knowledge of the French language is a tremendous asset when working out visa and entry procedures; some Gendarmes do not speak English. Even trying (in my feeble French) to speak their language has always made everything go smoother when I've checked in over the years. A course in French at a community college or even a cassette course on the ocean passage will help, plus you'll be able to communicate with the Marquesan people.

Nuku Hiva Island

Nuku Hiva is the largest island in the Marquesas, in terms of both land and population. Slightly over half of the 2,400 people live in Taiohae, the administrative and commercial center of the Marquesas. Taiohae Bay is one mile wide and nearly two miles deep, is easy to enter under sail, and provides a safe and protected anchorage in 30' - 40' on a sand bottom. Yachts are requested to leave the fairway leading up to the wharf clear for ships. A good place to anchor is in the northwest corner of the bay, near the Keikahanui Inn, owned and run by Rose Courser, an ex-cruiser who serves excellent meals and cold beer and will hold cruisers' mail. Maurice McKittrick's store, which has been a gathering place for yachties over the years, is located right in the middle of town. Maurice is a fascinating old Scottish-Marquesan ex-sailor turned island trader, who has plenty of cold beer and good stories, as well as groceries and fuel. Vegetables are sometimes hard to find in Taiohae, just keep asking. The town water catchment area is occasionally overrun with cattle, resulting in diarrhea for those who forget to boil the water. Other times it is fine. Ask Rose or Maurice or other cruisers if boiling is necessary, otherwise wait to fill up in Hakatea Bay, four miles to the west.

Taiohae has a small hospital, a port office, two banks, five grocery stores. In an emergency you may be able to get parts welded or brazed at Service d'le Equipment near the Gendarmerie.

Excellent hikes or horseback rides from Taiohae to Taipivai, Anaho and Atiheu await adventurous cruisers. Many cruisers only see Taiohae Bay, missing the three bays of Baie de Controleur: Anaho, Atiheu and Aotupa, all interesting anchorages. My favorite bay on Nuku Hiva is Hakatea, also called Daniel's Bay by cruisers. Daniel and Antionette and their extended family are the only inhabitants of this spectacular valley which used to be home to thousands. The two hour hike up the valley to the 1,000' Vaipo waterfall is an unforgettable experience. Part of the way you'll be walking on a stone paved path past stone house foundations and fences over a thousand years old.

The bad aspect of Nuku Hiva are the no-nos, tiny mosquitoes whose bites will continue to itch for one week, if you scratch them, and will quickly become infected if you scratch them hard enough to break the skin. Best to wear lightweight long clothes when going hiking in the woods or going ashore near sunset. Insect repellent does work for no-nos. To make sure that they don't invade your boat, anchor a fair distance from the shore and burn mosquito smoke coils in the companionway.

Ua Pou Island

Ua Pou is a pleasant 25 mile reach directly south of Taiohae and has a number of good anchorages. Hakahau on the northeast coast has a breakwater protecting the anchorage and is situated by the largest town. I have also enjoyed anchoring in Hakatao, Hakamaii, Hakaotu, Vaiehu, Haakuti and most recently in Hakahetau where Etienne, the schoolteacher and mayor, is a wealth of information about Marquesan history. There is a trail completely around Ua Pou, and a Frenchman holds the record for hiking around the island in eleven hours. I have enjoyed hiking between several of the bays and into the dramatic, uninhabited and ruggedly beautiful interior.

Ua Huka Island

Ua Huka is rarely visited because it lies 27 miles directly to windward of Nuku Hiva. In recent visits I've anchored in Haavei, Vaipaee, Hane and Hokatu Bays. The most dramatic is Baie de Vaipaee, also called Invisible Bay, since it is difficult to see the entrance until you are directly in front of it. Anchor in 15' on sandy bottom, 300 yards from the beach in the middle of this very narrow bay. If a swell is coming into the bay, anchor with bow and stern anchor with the bow pointing to sea. The only museum in the Marquesas is located here, started by the mayor and schoolteachers. The island has spectacular hiking, magnificent wild horses and a rugged coastline.

Hiva Oa Island

Hiva Oa is the second largest island in the Marquesas and Atuona, with a population of 1,800, is second in size to Taiohae. The anchorage for Atuona is in Taaku Bay to the east, where the swell is partly blocked by a breakwater. This is not as comfortable or convenient an anchorage as Taiohae.

The stores, bank, post office, clinic and airport are a bit of a walk from the anchorage. Gauguin's grave is located nearby on a peaceful, lush hillside. If you'd like permission to explore a very remote and dramatic bay, ask for Ozanne

Rohi who runs a flashy bonita boat out of Atuona. He owns, but no longer lives in, the spectacular Hana Menu Bay and valley on the northwest corner of Hiva Oa.

Tahuata Island

Tahuata is the smallest of the inhabited islands. It has a population of about 700 and is located just five miles south of Atuona. Take special care when crossing Haava or Bordelais Strait between Hiva Oa and the north end of Tahuata. In this channel and also along the west coast of Tahuata, the wind may suddenly gust to 60 knots. Be prepared to reduce sail quickly, even though this seems like very easy and comfortable day sailing. Plan on anchoring with two anchors when visiting the island, even if conditions seem settled; violent gusts from the mountains have caused several yachts to drag anchors out to sea. Vai Tahu is a small, attractive and friendly village with a fairly good anchorage. Hana Moe Noe, to the north, has a lovely white

Marquesan girls jumping rope

sand beach and is uninhabited. Hapatoni, to the south, has plenty of coral directly in front of the village, but there is a good sandy patch in 95' off Hana Tefau on the north side of the bay. Some of the best snorkeling or scuba diving in the Marquesas is found here.

Fatu Hiva Island

Fatu Hiva, 35 miles south of Tahuata, is the most remote and exotic of the inhabited Marquesas Islands and is the only place in French Polynesia where tapa cloth is still made. The anchorage in Hana Vave, or Bay of Virgins, has spectacular stone pinnacles flanking the shore and is more protected and less rolly than Omoa, three miles to the south. Don't miss hiking up the river to the waterfalls and swimming holes.

Society Islands - Tuamotu Archipelago

The Tuamotus are a group of 76 low-lying coral atolls and two raised coral islands without lagoons (Makatea and Tikei). The Tuamotu cover nearly half a million square miles, but have a total population of less than 15,000. The "land" averages only 6' above sea level, since the tops of the coconut trees are only 70' high, these atolls can only be seen from 5 - 10 miles under ideal conditions. Added to that, the currents around and between the islands varies from nothing to as much as 3 - 4 knots and many of the charts available are not accurate. Before GPS, many yachts and ships were lost on these islands.

The most valuable navigational equipment for cruising through the Tuamotus is radar, which will show you the actual (not mischarted) position of the islands, even in the dark. Even so, it isn't a good idea to approach these islands closer than 30 miles in the dark or in squally weather. The intensity of the squalls in this region often catches cruisers unaware. About half (31 out of 78) of the Tuamotus have passes into the lagoons, the currents in which run from 1 - 12 knots. It can be dangerous to enter or leave the lagoons at anytime other than slack water. Tides can be determined by using the *NOAA Tide Tables for Central and Western Pacific Ocean* or *Admiralty Tide Tables* or using a formula found in the *U.S. Sailing Directions, Admiralty Pacific Islands Pilot Vol. III* or *Charlie's Charts of Polynesia* in conjunction with a *Nautical Almanac.*

When strong trade winds have been blowing or when a large southerly swell is running, additional water comes into the lagoon and may cause continual ebb current in some passes of as much as 12 knots.

Between 1966 and 1992, France conducted over 150 atmospheric and underground nuclear tests on the islands of Moruroa and Fangatufa in the southeast Tuamotus. During that time it was forbidden to enter a zone south of 17 degrees 20 minutes South and east of 145 degrees 45 minutes West. That ban has been modified to now include only a 12 mile radius around the military base island of Hao. Please check with the Gendarmes when leaving the Marquesas to get the latest regulations. The lifting of the ban on sailing means that it is now possible to sail to islands that haven't seen cruising yachts in nearly 30 years! I recently talked with cruisers who anchored at Amanu, 10 miles north of Hao, they said that the islanders had never seen a cruising boat until this year!

The majority of cruisers sailing from the Marquesas to Tahiti stop at Ahe, Manihi or Rangiroa. If you have the time, why not cruise to the less visited islands? You'll need the excellent quality French charts (available from Captain's Nautical Supplies in Seattle, 1-800-448-2278 or 206-448-2278) which are considerably better than the U.S. or British equivalents. I've enjoyed visiting the following Tuamotus over the past 20 years: Raroia, Taenga, Makemo, Katiu, Tahanea, Fakarava, Faite, Toau, Takaroa and Rangiroa.

There are pearl farms in many of the lagoons and you

are financially liable if you drag anchor and damage them, so ask the islanders for anchoring advice. The anchorages in most of the Tuamotus can become dangerous traps when the wind shifts direction (often to strong southerlies) every 5 - 12 days. Try to find sand patches to anchor in so that your chain doesn't destroy the coral or break when the winds change and swell builds across the lagoon.

French Polynesia - Society Islands

Papeete will be your first stop on the island of Tahiti. Even if you are coming from the Marquesas or Tuamotus, you must clear in with Immigration, Customs and the Port Captain, whose offices are conveniently located on the edge of the passenger ship wharf in Papeete. I prefer to anchor off the large and prominent church, go ashore to clear in, then move as soon as possible to the anchorage off Maeva Beach Hotel where it is quieter, cleaner and less crowded. The charge to anchor and use Tahiti Aquatique's dinghy dock is $6 US per day for a 42' boat and the bus ride to town is $1.30. There is also an excellent fuel dock and small (expensive) marina 3/4 mile south of Maeva Beach. Between Maeva Beach and Taina Marina is the giant Continent store, the best place in the Territory to reprovision, in my opinion. Prices are good for French Polynesia (on an average 100% higher than in the U.S or New Zealand) and the "bargains" include frozen chicken from the U.S. for $1 per pound, Swiss cheese, baguettes, New Zealand beef and lamb, canned butter and powdered milk.

Marcia Davock's *Cruising Guide to Tahiti and the French Society Islands* is the best source for details on anchorages throughout Tahiti and the Societies. I'll just outline some highlights of the Societies.

The Island of Moorea

Moorea, only an afternoon sail away from Tahiti, is

much quieter. It is not necessary to clear customs to visit Moorea if you're returning directly to Tahiti. The most popular anchorage is in Cook's Bay where as many as 30 yachts anchor in the peak month of July. A much quieter anchorage is in Opunohu Bay, either just inside the reef to the east or in Robinson's Cove just past the rear range marker. Moorea has excellent hiking and bicycling around the island is not to be missed!

The Island of Huahine

Huahine is an overnight sail (85 miles, so leave just at dusk to arrive in the morning) west of Moorea. The Gendarmerie, where you will need to check in, is located in the town of Fare, on the northwest corner of the island. The anchorage used by the majority of visiting yachts, between the Bali Hai Hotel and the commercial wharf, has poor holding ground, gusty winds and strong currents. Better (but generally 70' - 90' deep) anchorages can be found south in Haavai, Haapu or Avea Bays or in Port Bourayne. Don't miss the interesting archeological sites at Lake Maeva, just past the airport. Pacificar has bikes, scooters or cars for rent at the wharf in Fare. My favorite anchorages on Huahine are on the east side of the island, in the lee of Motu Muri Mahora or in one of Baie Maroe's coves.

Raiatea and Tahaa Islands

Raiatea and Tahaa share a common fringing protective reef and are usually entered through Teavapiti Pass, 1 1/2 miles south of Uturoa, the second largest town in French Polynesia. The Gendarmerie, you'll need to check in here, is located 1/4 mile north of the large commercial wharf. Ships frequently tie to the wharf, so don't leave your boat unattended here. There is a new pleasure boat marina 3/4 of a mile north of the commercial wharf, and if there is space, this is a convenient place to tie while reprovisioning. A new Continent supermarket in downtown Raiatea has the best prices and selection in the Iles Sous le Vent, which Huahine, Raiatea, Tahaa and Bora are referred to as. Marina Apooiti, located just past the airport, and where The Moorings yacht charters are based, is an even better organized marina. Henri Valin, the Moorings manager, is a dynamo and has built a guest dock, club house, restaurant, small store and showers which can be used by cruisers. The charge in 1994 was $12 US per night for a 42' boat. A mile further down the coast he has built Raiatea Careenage, a boat yard with the only two Travelifts in the eastern South Pacific. It is possible to get sails, engine, refrigeration and hulls repaired here, as well as to leave your boat in dry storage without paying duty while returning home. My favorite anchorages at Raiatea and Tahaa are: Faaroa, Hotopuu, Faatemu, Haamene and Hurepiti Bays. There is good snorkeling or scuba diving in several of the passes.

The Island of Bora Bora

Bora Bora is one of the most breathtakingly beautiful islands in the world. Passe Teavanui is wide and well marked. You'll find the Gendarmerie (yes, you have to check in here too), grocery stores, clinic and gas station in Vaitape, the only town. Water is often in short supply, but may be available from the Bora Bora Yacht Club. The club may also has moorings available. Several restaurant/hotels on Raiatea, Tahaa and Bora Bora have moorings for yachties where the anchorages are 70' - 100'. I've never heard of a charge being made for use of the moorings, it is expected that you will at least buy drinks and possibly dinner in return for the mooring.

Bora Bora has its share of very deep anchorages, but spectacular shallow anchorages can be found in the lee of Motu Toopua and Motu Piti Aau. If you're really careful and brave try anchoring between Hotel Bora Bora and Matira. Several outstanding anchorages can be found between the Hotel Bora Bora and the south end of Motu Topua. The snorkeling is exceptional in this area.

The Hotel Bora Bora is one of the classiest in the South Pacific, so don't anchor directly off their over-water bungalows or hang up your laundry in their vicinity. The management at times allows cruisers to use their private dock if you're coming ashore for drinks or dinner.

The Island of Maupiti

Maupiti is 27 miles west of Bora Bora, and has a narrow pass that is best at high slack water (12 noon every day), so plan on departing Bora at first light. A dramatic island, Maupiti viewed from seaward appears to be a miniature version of Bora Bora. I have enjoyed anchorages both at the northwest tip of Motu Pitiahe (which marks the west side of the pass) and Vaiea village. Maupiti sees few tourists or cruisers. The locals are friendly.

The Island of Mopelia

Mopelia (Maupihaa), an atholl, is about130 miles west of Bora Bora and 100 miles west of Maupiti. Plan your arrival for the highest water and weakest ebb current, at noon. Depending on how much water is coming over the reef, the current ebbs continuously from 2 - 3 knots. The population has ranged from 3 to about100 and have always welcomed the few yachts stopping here. I've found anchorages off the village or just north of the southern tip of the island.

French Polynesia - The Austral Islands

The Australs are only 350 miles south of Tahiti, but are rarely visited by cruising yachts. I've spent several months anchored at Tubuai and have stopped at Rurutu and Rimatara. Two of the most isolated islands of French Polynesia are Raivavae and Rapa, both of which have passable anchorages, no airports or tourists and hardly any yachts. French charts provide the best detail and accuracy for the Austral Islands and can be purchased in Papeete.

The Cook Islands

Despite covering over three-quarters of a million square miles, the land area of the Cooks is only 93 square miles. There are 17,000 Cook Islanders living in the country, and another 20,000 living in New Zealand. In 1965 the Cooks received independence and now operate as an independent country in free association with New Zealand. Of the fifteen islands, four (Rarotonga, Aitutaki, Mangaia and Atiu) are volcanic, the rest are low coral islands. The only harbors for yachts are at Rarotonga (exposed), Aitutaki (6' draft maximum.), Suwarrow (exposed) and Penrhyn (good). Rarotonga, Aitutaki, Penrhyn and (provisionally) Puka Puka are Ports of Entry. The government has a caretaker family on Suwarrow who may let yachts who haven't cleared into the Cooks, stop for two days.

Rarotonga Island

Rarotonga is a delightful place to visit. The prices are a fraction of those in French Polynesia, the people speak English as a second language, are friendly and renowned as the best dancers in the Pacific. The only drawback is tiny Avatiu Harbor which is wide open to the north. With winds from NE to NW, the harbor can get rough, uncomfortable and even dangerous. During June to September, the months that cruisers visit Raro, the winds will back to the north each time a weather system tracks by south of the island, roughly every 3 - 10 days. The winds will stay out of the north for 1 - 3 days, then back to the west, then the south, before settling back to the southeast or east. With this in mind, you'll want to do your refueling and reprovisioning soon after arrival so that you can leave if the wind backs to the north. The harbor is very full most of the time with local

Rugby game, Aitutaki

freighters, fishing boats and speedboats. If a large freighter is expected, the harbormaster may have to ask all of the yachts to shift while the ship is turning around. Call Rarotonga Radio on VHF Channel16 when 20 miles out and ask them to relay to the Harbormaster your ETA. If the Harbormaster is monitoring channel 16 he can direct you to the location where you'll be least in the way. There are no plans to enlarge the harbor at this time.

Aitutaki Island

Aitutaki is lovely, its inhabitants friendly and outgoing, but the long, narrow and shallow pass is a problem. The depth varies between 5 1/2' and 6' at high water, with a constant ebb current. The anchorage off the pass is approximately 80' deep with large coral heads.

Penrhyn Island

Penrhyn, in the Northern Cooks, has three passes. The safest is Taruia Pass, just north of Omoka Village, on the eastern extremity of the island. After checking in with the health inspector, clear in with Henry Ford the customs inspector, then head for Tetautua Village on the opposite (windward) side of the lagoon. Make sure you have good light when traversing the lagoon, there is coral which must be avoided. The anchorages off Omoka are in 30' - 50' with large coral heads. This is a lee shore with seven miles of fetch, so you'll appreciate the all sand 20' anchorage 100 yards north of Tetautua Village, by the gap between the motus.

Suwarrow Island

Suwarrow Island has a history of buried treasure, murder, piracy and romance. It was inhabited for many years by Tom Neale, the hermit who wrote *An Island to Oneself.* Presently a family of caretakers look after the island for the government. The anchorage off Anchorage Island (just west of the pass) is deep with many coral heads. Several yachts have drug ashore here in fresh SE to NW winds; the lagoon is large enough to allow the swells to build.

Manihiki and Rakahanga Islands

Manihiki and Rakahanga are rarely visited islands with deep exposed anchorages calling for a Bahamian type mooring with two anchors led to the bow. I have enjoyed visiting both. Manihiki has extensive pearl culturing in the lagoon.

Palmerston Island

Palmerston Island has a fascinating history; one European man settled here siring 63 children with three wives of different nationalities. Shipwrecks have supplied the island with building materials. The anchorage is risky, even during settled conditions. I've felt comfortable using this as a day anchorage only, try to leave someone aboard when ashore.

American Samoa - Tutuila Island

Tutuila Island and Pago Pago Harbor are often a reprovisioning stop for cruisers headed toward New Zealand or Australia. This is not a place to cruise and enjoy, it's a place to get food and fuel and leave as quickly as possible. Because the U.S. pumps $40 million annually into the territory for 35,000 people (10,000 of the population are Eastern Samoans) there is a level of resentment toward Americans by the Samoans. Add the fact that the harbor has poor holding because of plastic bags and garbage, strong winds, plenty of rain and a fairly high level of theft and violence and you'll understand the value of getting what you need and sailing on to more welcoming shores in Tonga and Fiji. There are no haulout facilities for yachts here, but there are good engine, electronic and refrigeration repair services because of the large tuna fleet based here.

The Line Islands - Christmas Island

Christmas Island is the largest and most populous of the Line Islands and was discovered by Captain Cook on December 24, 1777.

The currents around Christmas Island and the other Line Islands are very strong and unpredictable. In the days before GPS, I met several skippers who tried for days to locate the Line Islands, but eventually gave up.

In settled easterly conditions it is possible to anchor off London village and go ashore. The channel into the lagoon is shallow and subject to strong currents. But, it may be possible to carry as much as 5 1/2' of draft into the lagoon, if the harbormaster is aboard to guide you into the more protected inner harbor.

Kiribati has been settling its people on Christmas Island to relieve land pressure on overcrowded Tarawa Atoll, the capitol. Although Christmas Island does have air service and more supplies than its neighbor Fanning Island, water, food and fuel can be scarce. Don't count on Christmas as a supply stop.

Fanning Island

Fanning Island has a wide pass and a fairly good anchorage inside the lagoon. It is also being settled with the overflow from Tarawa. The Cable and Wireless Station and copra plantation are no longer operating but are interesting to explore. At times the island runs very low on food and water, so don't plan on purchasing anything here.

Weather Information for the South Pacific

The most detailed voice weather information and interpretation is available from Arnold Giddons, Nikau Radio, Rarotonga at 0400 UTC and 1800 UTC on 14.818 (ham) and 8814 (marine SSB). While in the Societies, listen at 2100 and 2200 UTC on VHF channel 26 or 27 for local weather bulletins in French. Weatherfax charts from New Zealand and Honolulu provide fairly detailed information. If in doubt about the weather, call or visit the nearest airport meteorological office.

Appendix II

Selecting and Outfitting a Small Boat for Offshore Cruising

I bought *Mahina* in December, 1973, planning to sail her to Hawaii and back the following summer, so I spent the next six months converting a weekend sailor into a modestly-equipped ocean cruising boat. I removed and rebuilt the engine and transmission, replaced the rigging, added storm sails, a windvane self-steering device and dodger and spray canvas. I was working with a *very* modest budget and was only planning to be gone for a summer, so the equipment list was short.

Mahina is a Vega 27 built by Albin Marine in Sweden in 1969. Although Per Brohall, her designer, told me that he never designed the Vega as a long distance cruising boat, several owners have made extensive cruises including at least six world circumnavigations. The strong, one-piece hull with internal lead ballast and attached and protected rudder is amazingly fast. My best 24 hour run was a blistering 181 miles (on a 27'- boat) and I had many days runs of between 150 and 165 miles. The lightweight (5,000 lb.) boat meant a pretty quick motion at sea and hard pounding when going to windward into any kind of a sea.

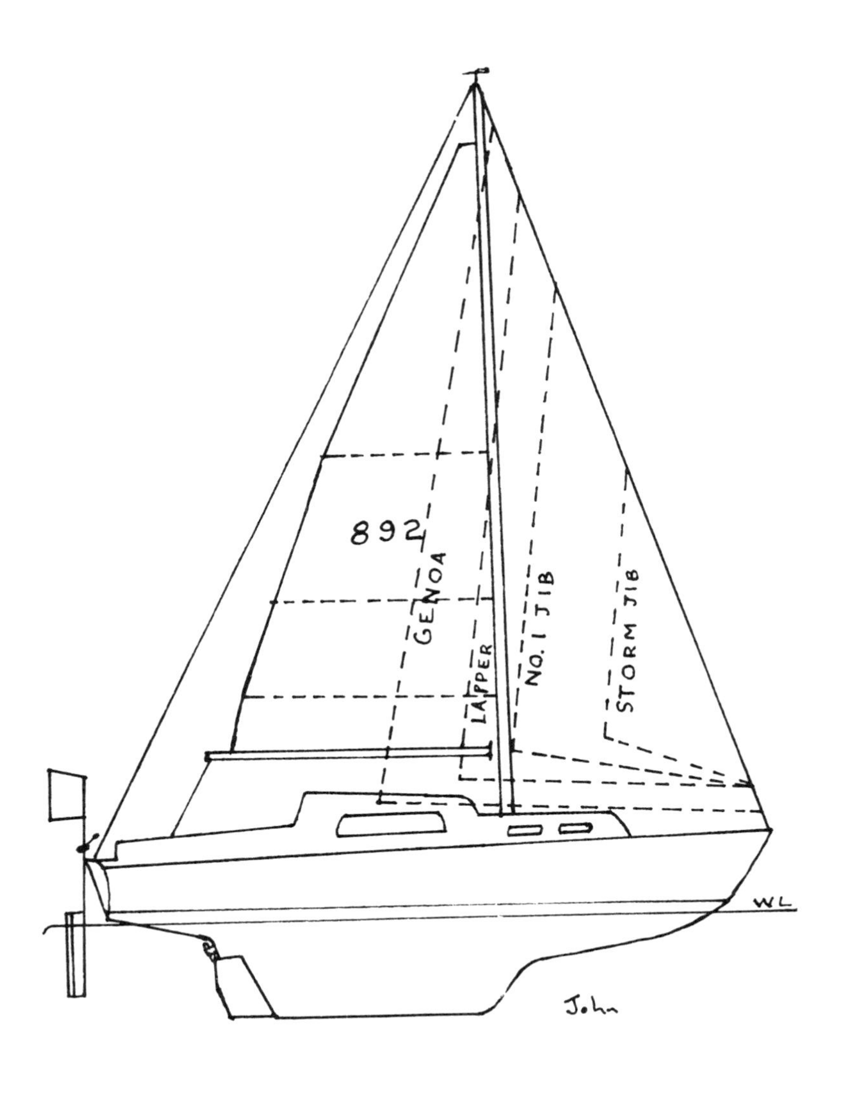
892
GENOA
LAPPER
NO. 1 JIB
STORM JIB
WL
John

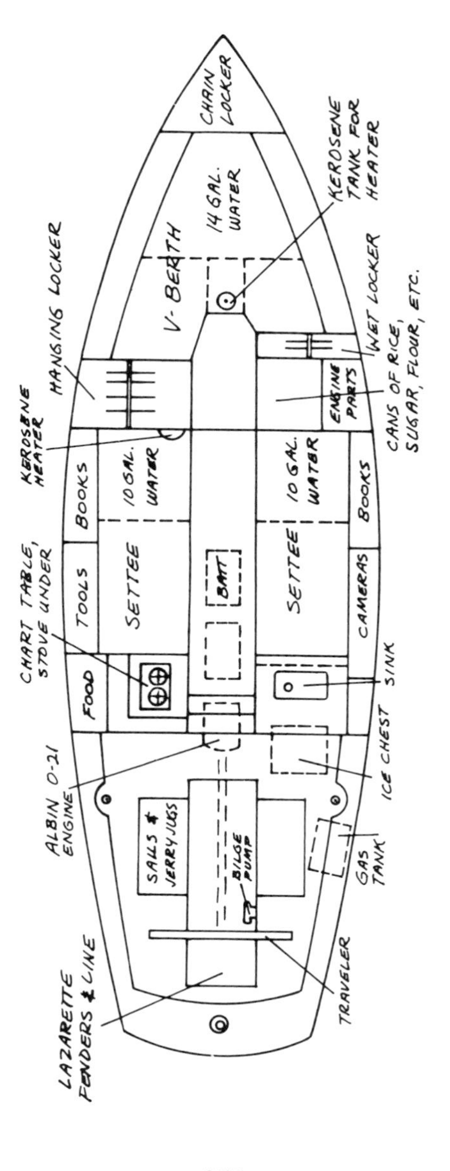
CHAIN LOCKER
14 GAL. WATER
KEROSENE TANK FOR HEATER
V-BERTH
HANGING LOCKER
WET LOCKER
ENGINE PARTS
CANS OF RICE, SUGAR, FLOUR, ETC.
KEROSENE HEATER
BOOKS
10 GAL. WATER
10 GAL. WATER
BOOKS
CHART TABLE, STOVE UNDER
TOOLS
SETTEE
BATT
SETTEE
CAMERAS
FOOD
SINK
ICE CHEST
ALBIN O-21 ENGINE
SAILS & JERRY JUGS
BILGE PUMP
GAS TANK
TRAVELER
LAZARETTE FENDERS & LINE

SELECTING A BOAT

Selecting a cruising boat is one of the most important decisions in preparing for an offshore voyage. The boat you choose should be safe, comfortable, well-built and prove to be a good investment. The process of selecting and purchasing an offshore boat usually takes six to 12 months. Be patient, ask questions and consult a good surveyor, specializing in offshore boats.

Make a good choice, and you'll have a safe, comfortable boat capable of fast passages - a boat which will hold its value well. Make a poor choice, and you'll be plagued with structural problems, leaks, slow passages, endless repairs and a low resale price. Purchasing a cruising boat uses a substantial part of many people's savings; you'll want to recoup as much of your investment as possible when it comes time to sell.

Size and Cost

Few people realize that outfitting for a long distance cruise can easily take 30% to 50% more than the initial purchase price of the boat. This can mean an additional $10,000 to $25,000 for a small or mid-sized cruiser, for essential equipment including: additional sails, ground tackle, liferaft, safety gear and dinghy. This excludes optional equipment such as: refrigeration, autopilots, electronics, outboard motors.

The common scenario is, you overspend on the initial purchase of the boat, spend more money on unessential equipment, then run short of funds once you've completed your initial provisioning and have actually started cruising. I speak from experience, having done this several times during the past 20 years.

A more realistic approach is to spend less on the initial purchase price by either purchasing a well-built used boat or a smaller boat. Purchase the priority equipment first, provision (or set aside $2,000 for it), set aside an average of $700 - $1,800 (for a couple) per month for the period of time you want to cruise then see if there is enough for nonessential equipment.

In selecting a boat, if you can find one that has already been outfitted and cruised recently, you'll save thousands of dollars and months of time on installations. Used boat prices vary geographically and tend to be lowest in areas experiencing economic downturns and weak real estate markets.

If you are interested in cruising specific areas in Europe, and aren't interested in long passages, purchasing a boat on location may be a good choice. If you are considering purchasing a boat overseas and plan to sail it back to the U.S., try to select a well-known builder who has dealers in the States. You'll find it much easier to sell a well-known boat for a reasonable price.

Boat Selection Checklist

1. Design: Was the boat truly designed for ocean sailing? Did the boatbuilder follow the designer's construction criteria? If possible contact the designer *before* purchasing.

2. Builder: If selecting a used boat, is the builder still in business? Ask them about the boat you are considering; have the serial number and date of manufacture ready.

3. Performance: How easily can the boat be sailed and how well will it perform? Does it have a long bowsprit which might prove difficult or dangerous when changing headsails? Low freeboard may indicate a design which may ship a lot of spray and water on ocean passages. Excessive freeboard may cause poor windward performance and a tendency to "sail" back and forth at anchor. A small amount of weather helm as the wind increases is desirable, but an excessive amount which cannot be decreased by sail trim or rig tuning may mean that a boat will be difficult to steer by hand, windvane or autopilot. If the design is excessively tender, you'll have to get used to living, cooking, navigating and sleeping at 30 degrees angle of heel every time you are sailing to windward, something you may find fatiguing. Will your boat have a comfortable motion at sea, or will it tend to hobbyhorse to windward because of a short waterline and uneven weight distribution? Will the design roll excessively when sailing downwind?

Few potential cruisers think of passage-making speed as an important criteria in the boat selection process; after 120,000 miles and 20 years of ocean cruising, it is quite high on my list of priorities. The shorter your passages, the less chance of encountering heavy weather conditions. Also, a boat with light-air sailing performance will require less motoring and fuel and will be more responsive and fun to sail.

How well can the boat sail to windward? Will upwind passages back home be impossible or extremely difficult? Will you be able to sail off a lee shore in an emergency?

4. Self-steering: How easily can the boat be made to self-steer? Is it unduly squirrelly when sailing downwind in a good breeze? Is it easily balanced? Is the transom free of overhanging stern pulpits which can make mounting a windvane steering device difficult?

5. Comfort Below: Will the boat make a comfortable home? This factor is just as important as each of the above factors, because a boat may have the best sailing characteristics in the world, but if your partner thinks of it only as a deep, damp dungeon, you'll either be singlehanding or giving up your liveaboard cruising dreams. Remember, most cruisers are underway less than a quarter of the time, so comfort at anchor is very important.

6. Stowage: What is the stowage capacity of the boat? Will there be room for additional sails, tanks, food, bosun locker supplies, lines, spare parts, medical and safety supplies, or has the space under the settees and berths already been filled with tankage that could have been designed into the keel?

7. Weight capacity: What is the weight carrying capacity of the boat, compared to your needs? Can the boat carry the additional weight of three anchors, a windlass and several hundred pounds of chain, as well as additional water (8 lbs. per gallon) and fuel (6 lbs. per gallon), a liferaft, dinghy and outboard? You'll be adding several thousand pounds of additional equipment. If the boat you're considering is already on her waterline before you start loading cruising equipment, you may end up several inches below the designed waterline. On some designs this may be a dangerous problem; it drastically effects sailing performance.

8. Hull: If you choose a fiberglass boat, do the builder's boats have a history of severe osmotic blister problems? If the hull is balsa-cored, there may be problems with water being absorbed into the wood, if thru-hulls weren't installed properly, or if the boat has gone on the beach. Foam-cored hulls have good insulation properties and impact resistance. Is the hull thick and brittle from too high a resin to glass ratio? I highly recommend *Surveying Fiberglass Sailboats,* by Henry C. Mustin, International Marine, 1994, for a clear and concise view of hull and deck design, structure and condition.

9. Hull to deck joint: Is the hull to deck joint fastened properly? Are there screws or nuts protruding through on the inside? In my experience, this type of mechanical clamp joint which is relying on the bond of a sealant/adhesive (3M 5200 is often used), often starts leaking in 10 to 12 years. The sealant/adhesive loses some if its elasticity, and since the toerail and hull are expanding, contracting and flexing at different rates, the bond eventually weakens. Water follows the bolt or screw threads down, becoming drips on the inside.

10. Bulkhead attachment: Are the bulkheads adequately attached to the hull? On a fiberglass boat, they should be glassed to the hull on both sides and to the deck with multiple layers of tape. When builders skimp on this, their boats' bulkheads and interior cabinetry becomes unbonded from the hull, allowing the hull to flex more than it should.

Are there internal stiffening systems (grid floor systems, and / or full length glass over foam stringers) or is the interior woodwork just lightly attached to the hull, only to break loose after a few thousand miles of ocean sailing? Is there proper access to hull and deck areas, or do fiberglass liners make leak-stopping very difficult?

11. Chain plates: Are the chain plates going to lift the deck or distort the hull, or is the load evenly spread out by properly transmitting the load to bulkheads and structural members?

12. Mast Support: Is the mast supported adequately? Deck stepped masts work well, only if proper structural members transmit the load to the keel; otherwise deflection and possibly delamination under the mast will occur. On keel stepped masts, check for corrosion at the base of the mast. Check the mast for trueness - even if it is an aluminum mast.

13. Keel Design: Is the keel designed to withstand a hard grounding? In my experience (having run aground in varying conditions and areas) the best type of keel for serious cruising is relatively long, where the keel is either part of the hull, with the ballast added internally and the top heavily fiberglassed over, or else attached to a substantial stub which is an integral part of the hull. Crealock 37 and Valiant 40/42 are examples.

Wing keels have a shape similar to a Bruce anchor and can be very difficult to refloat if you've run aground in sand or mud.

High aspect deep and short fin keels (in a fore and aft measurement) are best suited for racing boats because running hard aground can result in damage to the area where the trailing edge of the keel meets the hull and can cause leaks around the keel bolts. In many cruising areas there aren't Travelifts available to lift the hull off the keel for repairs.

If external ballast is used, keel loading must be spread out through the floor system. Internal lead ballast eliminates some potential problems with keels, but check closely during survey for any voids or water penetration in the keel area between the ballast and fiberglass. Read *Surveying Fiberglass Sailboats* for more details.

14. Rudder: How well is the rudder protected from logs and flotsam? Can the rudder take impact and grounding without jamming or being damaged? How easily can it be removed with the boat in the water for repair? Unprotected spade rudders are much more likely to be a problem than skeg-hung rudders. I know of three Swans which lost their spade rudders between Panama and Tahiti in one year alone.

15. Engine: Is the engine a common make which will be easy to find parts and service for? Is it a purpose-built marine diesel, or is it an automotive truck engine that has been "marinized". How good is everyday access for checking and changing oil and filters? Can the engine be removed without having to destroy the cockpit or companionway? Is there an engine hour meter and logbook showing maintenance history? What is the fuel consumption? Range under power? Six to 800 miles minimum under power for long distance cruising, where fuel may not be readily available, is ideal. Being able to maintain six knots under power will get you in most passes and channels at the time of least current. A rule of thumb is two horsepower per thousand pounds of displacement, for a sufficiently powered cruising sailboat. Purists may say that this is excessive, but it is an advantage to have sufficient power to deal with currents and the ability to motorsail to windward for short distances into steep chop when necessary.

16. Steering System: Is the steering system reliable? If the boat has wheel steering, is the system built by a reputable company like Edson? Will you be able to get spare parts quickly if necessary?

Is the steering position located where the helmsperson can be easily sheltered without having to resort to a huge dodger? What is the visibility from the helm like? I prefer tillers on most designs under 38'; there is less to go wrong and installing most windvane steering systems is less complicated than with wheel steering.

17. Rig: Will the rig you choose allow for easy sail handling in all conditions? The majority of long distance cruisers are choosing cutter rigs, which are most logical on boats over 32' because handling hanked on sails on sloops over 38' or 40' can get unwieldy. Ketches allow a lot of flexibility for different sail combinations and give you the ability to drop half the total sail area (the mainsail) in less than a minute, without having to resort to mechanical devices.

Many cruisers are adding a solent stay, or removable inner forestay, on which they can fly a storm staysail once they have furled or dropped their working headsail.

Over the years, I've met many people who have bought or are saving to buy a cruising boat in the 40'-50' range, so they can cruise with "all the comforts of home". These folks might ultimately be happier if they were to settle for a smaller boat (under 40') which would be paid off sooner and have lower operating costs once cruising. The advantages of a smaller boat include: lower purchase and operating costs, shallower draft allowing access to places larger boats can't enter. Advantages of a larger cruising boat include: more comfortable and faster passages, more water, fuel and food storage.

SAILS AND RIGGING

The main and No. 1 jib on *Mahina* were Ratsey sails, original equipment on the Vega. The lapper, storm jib, and storm trysail were made by Franz Schattauer in Seattle. They held up extremely well with almost no signs of wear in 15,000 miles. The storm trysail and storm jib had hand-sewn bolt rope going almost all the way around them and the lapper had bolt rope on part of the leech and foot; this greatly reduces wear on sails. When I returned, Schattauer sails made me a new mainsail. It had a flat leech with no roach and no battens and three sets of hand-sewn reef points. Most of the previous two years I had sailed with a reefed main because *Mahina* is light and I don't like reefing, so the new main had the same area as a single reefed main. Schattauer sails are slightly more expensive than most, but have certainly turned out to be worth it in the long run. I have met cruisers who have purchased inexpensive Hong Kong sails which have turned out be more expensive per mile than sails produced by a domestic loft specializing in ocean cruising sails (lofts like Schattauer or Hasse and Petrich Sails in Port Townsend, WA). The Hong Kong sails required restitching, recutting and replacement much sooner. If you have more time than money while outfitting your boat, Sailrite Kits, Columbus, IN, 800-348-2769, will sell you a computer designed and cut kit and even the machine to sew your own sails.

The storm trysail is a sail that isn't talked about very much, but I certainly think it is worth its weight in gold when conditions call for it. I originally tried lacing mine on the mast, but found the friction caused when trying to hoist it was too great and made it a slow process. I then riveted stainless steel track on the mast alongside the regular sail track. This way I was able to have the trysail bent on and lashed to the mast in its bag; all I had to do was drop the main, connect the halyard and sheets, and hoist it on its own track. Other advantages the trysail has over a deeply reefed main, are that the main isn't being worn out and there is no boom to zonk you on the head if you accidentally gybe. Instead, the trysail just flops back and forth harmlessly. I usually sheet the boom down so that it is just above the dodger, putting equal tension on it between the mainsheet, topping lift, and boom vang. This makes it an immovable support in the center of the cockpit, to put an arm over to hold on to, or to clip a safety harness to.

Just before I left, I unstepped the mast and had a new forestay and upper shrouds made out of heavier stainless steel wire. I also replaced the split backstay with double backstays to balance the load on the mast better in downwind conditions. I kept the old rigging on board with plenty of extra cable clamps to repair any possible rigging failure. The wire and rope halyards were replaced with all prestretched dacron, which has held up very well and is much easier on the hands.

Before leaving on an offshore passage, I always hoist myself to the top of the mast and check for problems. Twice I have found cracks in the cast aluminum spreader fittings which could have resulted in a broken mast if I hadn't repaired them. It's an excellent idea to unstep the mast before departure then check it completely every five years.

ENGINES AND TANKAGE

I had wanted to replace *Mahina's* 12 hp., two cylinder, Albin gas engine with a small diesel, but since it worked and I didn't have a spare $2,000 at the time, I left it in. The fuel filter and water separator I put in just before leaving restricted the gravity flow too much. I didn't know what the problem was, so when I left, the engine wasn't working. I considered taking the engine out and using the space for stowage and additional water tanks, but it was still working well when I sold *Mahina*. It burned about 1/3 gallon per hour at 4 1/2 knots. I think the most common problem with diesel engines in boats is water in the fuel system, which stops the engine and damages the injectors. A diesel engine on a cruising boat should have at least two large water separators with replacement filters.

Mahina had one permanent five-gallon copper gas tank and I carried two five-gallon jerry cans, giving Mahina a range of about 180 miles under power. At the time this was sufficient for me. I felt that if I ran out of wind I could wait. Now, I carry as much extra fuel as I can. I view it as a safety precaution, allowing me to shorten my passages and avoid storms by motoring when winds are light.

I've never had any problems finding gasoline. There are outboard motors in some of the most isolated places. Diesel is at least as easy to find and many trading ships have pumps rigged which measure the fuel as they pump it directly from their tanks to yours.

Mahina carried a single 14-gallon plastic tank in the forepeak under the bunk. I added two ten- gallon flexible plastic tanks under the settees, just aft of the main bulkhead. I rarely used the water in them - they were mostly for ballast, making *Mahina* considerably stiffer and a smoother sailer in open water. I also carried three five-gallon plastic water jugs under the cockpit seats as well as a number of collapsible plastic water jugs. These made going to get water only a one or two trip affair in places where I had to row ashore and ferry water out in the dinghy. I didn't have pressure water on the boat because it wastes water and is one more gadget to break down. I've found a half gallon of water per person, per day, to be a *minimum,* but I always carry at least twice this amount.

DODGERS

Dodgers and weather canvas along cockpit sides are very essential to comfort while cruising on a small boat. I thought I would be folding *Mahina's* dodger down as soon as I arrived in the tropics, but I never did. In cool weather it provided a warm spot out of the wind and spray, and in the tropics it afforded protection from the sun. Unfortunately, the dodger had an aluminum frame which collapsed when I fell against it while going forward for a sail change. A stainless frame would have been a little more expensive, but far stronger. The stronger frame would have been something to hold onto while steering or going forward to reef.

Cockpit weather cloths are not necessary on larger, drier boats, but on *Mahina* they really helped to block some of the spray when the wind was forward of the beam. Snaps along the bottom, which I would unsnap in rough weather, prevented the stanchions from being broken or the canvas ripped by the force of breaking waves.

LIGHTS

Mahina came with running lights in the pulpits and a steaming light on the front of the mast which lit up the sails and foredeck during sail changes. After returning, I added a masthead tricolor navigation lamp, which was much more visible and required less electricity. I haven't relied on ships sighting me, instead, I've tried to maintain a watch 24 hours a day, even when singlehanding. Often the person on watch is below, reading at the chart table, coming on deck to check the horizon every 12 minutes. Careful watchkeeping is also a good way to prevent being overtaken by a tropical squall with light-air sails up.

RADIOS AND ELECTRONICS

Until I reached Pago Pago, the only radio I had on board *Mahina* was a Zenith Trans-Oceanic receiver. This versatile (but bulky) radio is no longer available, but smaller and lighter radios from Radio Shack, Sony and Grundig will provide time and weather information for today's cruiser. On many contemporary cruising boats, a single amateur transceiver provides all band reception as well as communication. I had no transmitter aboard *Mahina*, not even a

VHF marine radio. If outfitting *Mahina* today, budget permitting, I would install a quality VHF radio (the Icom M-57, for example) and would permanently mount a small, waterproof handheld GPS (Magellan or Garmin). The GPS is an incredible navigation tool for the long-distance sailor and takes much of the concern out of landfalls in overcast conditions where celestial navigation is impossible.

For longer range communication on a limited budget, amateur or ham radio or a marine single sideband is an option. The Atlas transceiver which I installed in Samoa is no longer available, but equally small, even more versatile units from Icom and Kenwood are now on the market. For sailors not wanting to bother with the amateur radio licenses, new marine single sideband radios are compact, powerful and simple to operate. Icom M-600 or M-700 with AT-120 tuners are a good choice. Every morning at 1800 UTC there is a weather net run by Arnold Gibbons on 8814 and in the evening the Pacific Maritime Mobile Ham Net on 14.315 provides a check-in service during passage making for licensed ham operators.

The instrumentation on *Mahina* consisted of a 100' sounder, a knotmeter and log. A good choice today would be a combination unit that displays boat speed, distance log to 99,999 miles, and depth to 600', such as the Autohelm Tridata.

ANCHORS

Mahina carried four anchors: a 25 lb. CQR with 60' of 5/16" chain (the working anchor), a 22lb. Danforth with 15' of 5/16" chain, a 13 lb. Danforth stern anchor (mounted on the stern pulpit) with 65' of 1/4" chain and a 2 1/2 lb. Danforth dinghy anchor. There were several times, especially in relatively exposed Marquesan anchorages, when I had the CQR and larger Danforth off the bow and the small Danforth off the stern. The CQR is a very versatile anchor which doesn't get bent up by coral as Danforths do, but the

Danforth's holding power in sand is unbeatable.

I didn't feel *Mahina* could handle the weight of an all-chain anchor set up and the windlass that would be needed to retrieve it. There were a few times when the nylon anchor rode following the chain did chafe on coral. I found early on this voyage, that snorkeling over the anchor to check its position, whenever water clarity permitted, was important to assure there wasn't any nylon anchor line chafing on coral heads.

I carried a scuba tank and regulator; on several occasions I wouldn't have been able to untangle the anchor and chain from coral heads in 40'+ depths without this gear. The scuba gear was also essential for removing the broken rudder at Aitutaki. Finding air refills was never a problem, either ashore at a resort or dive shop or from a large yacht.

LIFERAFTS

I had wanted to purchase a canister self-inflating liferaft before departing, but couldn't afford one. Instead, I purchased an optional $C0_2$ inflation bottle for the Avon Redcrest, and kept the Redcrest lashed just aft of the mast with a "grab bag" of emergency gear in the cockpit. It would have taken several minutes to launch this rig. Ballasted sailboats often sink quickly; budget permitting, a regular liferaft is by far preferable.

In my emergency bag I carried a 121 type EPIRB (emergency radio). Since that time, a new 406 EPIRB has hit the market. It provides a much better chance of rescue with fewer false alarms. The drawback is the $900 price tag.

The emergency bag also contained: fishing supplies, space blanket, compass, cans of water, survival food, fruit juice, sunscreen, paper and pencil, signalling mirror, flares, hard rock candy, first aid cream, zinc oxide and a knife. I always kept three to five five-gallon jerry jugs full of water where I could easily toss them in the dinghy. Recently, a palm-sized manual watermaker (Survivor 06) came on the market. I wouldn't go cruising today without one of these units!

DINGHIES

The Avon Redcrest was a good tender for *Mahina* and would have been even better if I had purchased the optional floor boards. It held up well; the only possible improvement on it in recent years would be the Avon Roll Away 2.85, which costs double the Redcrest.

STOVES, FUELS, REFRIGERATION

While in port or under way in normal conditions, I used a two burner Optimus stove fitted with an internal kerosene tank. There wasn't enough clearance to gimbal it and still have the counter top which doubled as a chart table fit over it, so it was bolted down and not gimballed. During rough weather I used a one-burner Sea-Swing kerosene stove. It was very simple to cook on, but the burner required more attention than the Optimus. I've found that kerosene burners need to be rebuilt or replaced about once a year, and the parts are often easier to find outside the U.S.

Mahina also had two gimballed kerosene cabin lamps, a reflector lamp, anchor lamp and hurricane lantern, which all burned kerosene. I averaged about one gallon of kerosene per month for 2 1/2 years for the stoves, lamps and heater. Alcohol is difficult to find and expensive outside the U.S., so is not a practical stove fuel. Larger boats usually choose propane for a cooking fuel these days. It is cleaner, easier to use and has become available in most major ports.

I don't feel it's worth listening to the engine run for two or three hours per day in the tropics to run a freezer. Refrigeration also adds another complex system to maintain and repair. Ice for an icebox is often available in major ports. The simplest thing, if you're planning on cruising on a small boat and modest budget, is to get used to provisioning and planning meals without the use of a freezer or refrigerator. This means shopping every few days for fresh produce, where available, and relying on local foods as much as possible.

HEATERS AND FIREPLACES

Mahina came with a small sheet metal fireplace which I replaced with a Taylor's kerosene heater. The pressure kerosene heater ran off a two-gallon tank under the v-berth and produced dry heat, even when the boat was under way. Aside from time spent in the Northwest, I only used the heater going down to San Francisco and on the trip home from Hawaii. The Force 10 and Dickinson bulkhead mounted heater are much easier to find than Taylor's today. Later versions of the Vega 27 had an optional Espar diesel forced air furnace, a very welcome, easy-to-regulate heat source for cold water cruising.

PROVISIONING

There are many books and articles written about provisioning; I won't try to duplicate them. Your monthly food costs while cruising are dependent on your tastes and flexibility. On a small boat without refrigeration, and on a limited budget, it's a challenge to make food interesting and nutritious. While cruising on *Mahina*, I had a diet that included rice, soups, pasta, eggs, cheese, fish, grains, bread, and either canned or fresh vegetables and fruit. Breakfast options included oatmeal, omelets, pancakes, french toast and fruit, if available. Lunches often involved a can of tuna, in one form or another. When bread was available, tuna or cheese sandwiches were quick and easy; when it wasn't, I'd often make a tuna-vegetable salad from a can of vegetables, tuna, mayonnaise, chopped onions and fresh bean sprouts I had grown.

Rice, flour, sugar, and some form of pasta are available most places; peanut butter, nuts, raisins, dried fruit, oats and granola may be much harder to find and very expensive. The more food you store aboard before departing on your cruise, the lower your costs of cruising will be for your first 1 to 1 1/2 years of cruising.

To gain more storage space for food, I removed the head and sink on *Mahina* and built a large storage bin for cans of food instead. Using a bucket for a head is OK when you're 21, but the novelty wears thin after a few years!

FIRST AID

A well-planned first aid kit and some knowledge of what to do in emergencies is very important on a cruising boat, since you may often be outside the range of professional medical help. I strongly encourage anyone planning a long distance cruise to take an advanced first aid course oriented to isolated situations. *Advanced First Aid Afloat* or *The Ship's Medicine Chest* plus the *Merck Manual* are excellent references to have aboard. Whenever possible, go to the local clinic for treatment.

The most common medical problems are: dehydration, heat stroke, coral cuts and staph infections. Small scrapes and abrasions that would never get infected in temperate climates can quickly turn into painful infected sores in the tropics. The best treatment is a vigorous scrub with Betadine or hydrogen peroxide followed by a topical antibacterial ointment such as Neosporin. Minor brushes or puncture wounds from coral will also quickly become infected, if not scrubbed vigorously with hydrogen peroxide on a sterile gauze pad and kept dry for several days. Staph infections can occur quickly, are painful and difficult to clear up without antibiotics. If left untreated, staph infections can spread to the bone, resulting in amputation. Once a skin staph infection has started, the affected skin will swell up, turn red and hot to touch, with a hard lump under the skin.

At this point oral antibiotics (cephalosporin, tetracycline, amipicillin, amoxocillin, erythromycin) and soaking four times a day in hot water are in order. If you are anchored in a place that has a hospital or clinic, by all means go there for treatment instead of trying to treat yourself. In the Marquesas, the local nurses have been trained in Tahiti and are accustomed to treating skin infections. They usually give a strong shot followed by oral antibiotics for treatment.

Saltwater sores and boils can also be a painful problem on small, wet boats. The best prevention I've found is to: avoid sitting around in wet shorts, take vitamins, eat plenty of fresh fruits and vegetables on passages; when possible, sun those buns.

NAVIGATION

Satellite navigation and GPS were not available in 1974, so celestial navigation was essential to ocean cruising. I had been so busy working and outfitting *Mahina* for cruising that I didn't pay close enough attention during my celestial navigation course. Halfway to Hawaii, after meeting another sailboat whose captain gave us our position, I finally figured out how to reduce sun lines of positions (LOP's) successfully. Although I've never been a whiz at math, I can add, subtract and look up numbers in tables, and that is all that is required for celestial navigation. With nearly every cruising boat today carrying at least one GPS unit on board, some sailors have decided that celestial navigation is no longer important. Every year many cruising boats loose their charging or electrical system or the GPS dies. Often the captains of these vessels use their radios to ask for assistance finding the next port.

The plastic Ebco sextant that I started out with warped in mid-arc and became useless by the time I arrived in the Marquesas. I had a Tamaya metal sextant shipped to me in Tahiti. The Chinese Astra IIIB is a reasonably priced (around $450) sextant on today's market. If you are planning to carry a handheld backup GPS unit that doesn't rely on ship's power, you might instead choose a less expensive Davis plastic sextant. Remember, however, that it may read differently in different temperatures. Keep it out of the sunlight as much as possible to avoid warping. A couple of quartz wrist watches for timing sights and a receiver which allows you to accurately set the watches, a *Nautical Almanac* and either *H.O. 229 or 249 Sight Reduction Tables*, plotting sheets, dividers and parallel rules, and you're ready to navigate. Keep in mind that you still need manual back-ups for any of these items you replace with a handheld navigational computer or navigational software and a laptop computer.

A useful and interesting aspect of navigation, often overlooked in our electronic era, is the natural signs or Polynesian navigation techniques so well described by David Lewis in *We the Navigators*. Lewis details the traditional navigation techniques still practiced in Micronesia. Micronesian voyagers know their exact position by observing the clouds, swells, birds, stars and wave patterns; without the use of charts or instruments.

I've used these traditional techniques on many occasions. For example, the last three days before landfall in the Marquesas, I watched the direction the birds were coming from at sunrise and the direction they flew just before sunset. The direction was always to the closest island.

A half hour before I made landfall at Rangiroa in the Tuamotus, a heavy, sloppy swell was running. I was experiencing swell and wave refraction from the long ocean swell patterns being altered when they hit the atoll, causing them to bounce back to windward. The change in motion woke me up and saved me from running into the island at night.

I've been able to smell islands as far as thirty miles off; long before they were in sight. This type of navigation is worth studying. There may be times when your electronics are out, the sky is overcast or sextant damaged, and you need to find land.

SELF-STEERING AND AUTOPILOTS

Self-steering really makes cruising less tiring and more enjoyable, especially for short-handed sailing. The RVG windvane on *Mahina* was made of dissimilar types of aluminum and the rudder eventually fell off due to corrosion. If I were outfitting *Mahina* again today, I would choose a Navik or Monitor windvane with an Autohelm or Navico autopilot as a backup. I wouldn't recommend depending solely on an autopilot for a small boat crossing oceans because it is reliant on your electrical system. Windvane self-steering doesn't require electricity or replacing of motors. Navik and Monitor windvanes are very reliable.

STORMS

The two questions I've been asked most since returning are "Well, don't you get scared?" and "Have you hit any big storms?" The answer to both questions is, "yes"; but I feel that experiencing rough conditions has added to my appreciation of the people and places I encounter when I make landfall. I have often been afraid, but through that fear I've come to learn more about myself and how much I can handle.

My only heavy-weather experience at the time I left was crossing the Straits of Juan de Fuca in a near-gale, in my 20' Vivacity sloop. But serious heavy weather was just around the corner. Two days after leaving Neah Bay I was slammed with winds in excess of 75 knots and 25'-35' seas, 80 miles west of the Oregon coast. *Mahina* was threatening to pitchpole while running at 8 knots under only a storm trysail with 500' of warp towed astern, so I decided to try heaving to. *Mahina* laid well under storm trysail or under bare poles with the helm lashed lightly to keep the stern quarter to the seas. Unfortunately, that's how the rudder was broken in the Cook Islands. I had lashed the tiller too hard and an extra large sea picked up *Mahina* and smashed her down on her beam; the force broke the rudder. Now I lash the tiller so that it has some give to it. Each boat handles heavy seas differently, trial and error is the best way to discover the most comfortable and efficient way to manage heavy weather in your boat.

CREW AND EXPENSES

Finding crew who are compatible in the confines of a small boat, for weeks at a time, is one of the greatest challenges of the cruising lifestyle. People who know each other well and are in a committed relationship seem to fare the best. Lacking a relationship (my girlfriend changed her mind and decided not to sail with me a week before we were planning to leave), I picked up crew along the way and then spent six months singlehanding through the South Pacific. I value the singlehanding experience, but found it exhausting and lonely and have no desire to do it again.

In most countries, the captain of a vessel is responsible for his crew; if a crew member is unhappy, he can demand that the captain pay his airfare back to the point where he joined up. Over the years, I've met several skippers who were stuck with large airfares from disgruntled crew. So, it pays to make sure a prospective crew member is someone who you really want on board. It's a good idea to sail a short distance on a trial basis before committing to crew on a long term basis.

In the past, many boats had crew who chipped in money for food and general expenses. In 1994 in Tahiti, the average contribution for food and fuel is $10 a day, but paying crew are few and far between these days.

Costs of cruising have steadily increased over the past twenty years, and most of the boats cruising in the 90's are on budgets of at least $700 to $1,800 per month, per couple. My budget on *Mahina* in the mid-seventies was $100 a month for everything. There are very few boats like *Mahina* cruising long distances today. Most cruisers are older (50 seems like an average age now) and their boats and budgets are larger.

Expenses are generally less in areas like the Marquesas where there aren't many places to spend money, and higher in places like Tahiti and Hawaii where people reprovision, buy luxury items and enjoy eating out. It is generally much cheaper to live outside our society than in it. When I left, I sold my car and no longer had to pay gas, oil and insurance bills; I didn't have moorage, electricity and phone bills coming in either. I did have to pay port fees, but they were always reasonable and generally less than guest moorage fees in the States. In the last decade many South Pacific countries have instituted an entry or exit fee averaging $10 - $25 per person, so if visiting several countries in a season it's wise to budget money for fees.

The time I've spent in Polynesia has been a highlight of my life. After living and learning from Polynesians, I feel they lead a simple, good life. I seriously wonder whether we have developed positively from their stage of existence to our society of polluted cities and unhappy people. I'm glad however, that the French, Cook Islands, Tongan and Fijian governments rarely let foreigners stay more than six months. Hawaii is a sad example of what Americans can turn beautiful islands into.

I received a wonderful reception when coming into an isolated village in the Marquesas, Tuamotus, or Cooks by myself. The people realized that since I was alone, I needed and wanted to be with them. I wasn't just coming to take pictures then leave.

I hope you have enjoyed reading this adventure. If you

have the urge to go cruising, now is the time to go. However, before selling your house and possessions, take a little trip and stick your nose out in the ocean for a few days to see if it really is for you. There are too many sad cases of people leaving to go on the cruise they've dreamed and saved all their lives for, only to come back a week or two later and put their boats up for sale. They weren't ready to handle the conditions of self-reliance where there is no Coast Guard to call and where one realizes that the sea is so vast and powerful that she can sink any vessel, no matter what size or how well built.

I have come to a state of mind where I feel that the Pacific is an all-powerful being, when she smiles, I go as fast as I can; when she is angry all I can do is wait. I've learned a lot from her - about me, about her, and about life.

The End

Postscript - Tahiti 1994

Many people have written or asked over the years, "Whatever happened to Nana on Aitutaki?" At the time it was too close and too private, so I didn't write the whole story. On my arrival in Samoa I sent a telegram to Nana, asking her if she wanted to come to Samoa and fly back with me to the States after I sold *Mahina*. She cabled back a simple answer, "Yes, I'm willing to come, send tickets," but the Post Office lost the reply. On the final day, after not hearing from her in a couple weeks, and having decided to sail back to the States instead of selling *Mahina*, the Post Office gave me her response.

I often wonder if I'd be living on the beach on Aitutaki, surrounded by brown-skinned children if I had received that telegram earlier. Nana and I corresponded a couple of times, and I later returned to Aitutaki on my next boat, *Mahina Tiare*. Nana's brother told me that she had moved to Auckland, married, and now has four children.

As for me, I'm still hooked on this vagabond lifestyle. *Mahina Tiare: Pacific Passages,* is a book about a later voyage on my next boat, *Mahina Tiare*, a 31' Hallberg-Rassy sloop. It's a story of sailing through a hurricane to the Galapagos, Easter Island, Pitcairn Island, Marquesas, Cooks, Tonga, Wallis, Fiji, New Zealand, Vanuatu, New Caledonia to Australia.

As I write this update, I'm anchored off an uninhabited islet north of Tahaa island in French Polynesia aboard my second *Mahina Tiare*, this one is a Hallberg-Rassy 42' ketch on which I have conducted sail and navigation training expeditions for the past five years. In a month I'll be sailing from Tahiti for the coast of Chile, then down past Cape Horn to Antarctica. . . the next adventure.

About the Author

John Neal was born in Sudan, Africa and grew up in Seattle, Washington. After two years studying for a psychology degree and working as a supervisor in a rehabilitation workshop, John became enamored with boats and the sea. He has been sailing ever since. John has logged over 120,000 sea miles, sailing as far north as Alaska and as far south as Chile.

He conducts sail training expeditions on the ocean on his 42' Hallberg-Rassy ketch, *Mahina Tiare* and teaches offshore cruising seminars in the classroom.

John's articles have appeared in *Cruising World, Latitude 38, Sail, Yachting, Santana, Bay and Delta Yachtsman, Northwest Yachting and 48 North.* He is co-author of *Mahina Tiare: Pacific Passages.*

If you would like information on sail training expeditions aboard *Mahina Tiare* or on weekend offshore cruising seminars, conducted by John contact: Armchair Sailor, 2110 Westlake Ave. N., Seattle, WA 98109 USA, (800) 875-0852, (206) 283-0858 or Fax, (206) 285-1935, or write Mahina Productions, Box 1596 Friday Harbor, WA 98250

Thank you for your interest in our books. To order additional copies, please send check or money order to:

Pacific International Publishing
P. O. Box 101, Friday Harbor, WA 98250
(206) 378-5242 Fax: (206) 378-4392

Log of the Mahina $16.95
John Neal

Mahina Tiare: Pacific Passages $19.95
Barbara Marrett & John Neal

North to Alaska $19.95
(45 min. video/slides of sailing the Inside Passage)

Washington Residents add 7.5% sales tax ______

Shipping and Handling (per item) .... $ 2.00

Total $ _____

Shipping Information:

Name ______________________________________

Postal Mailing Address______________________________

City ____________________ State ____Zip________